THE EUROPEAN UNION AND DEPRIVATION OF LIBERTY

The European Union and Deprivation of Liberty examines the EU legislative and judicial approach to deprivation of liberty from the perspective of the following fundamental rights and principles: the principle of legality and proportionality of penalties; the right to liberty; and the principle that criminal penalties must aim for the social reintegration of the offenders. The book measures the relevant EU law against those rights; this constitutes the very core of the relationship between public powers and individual liberty. The analysis shows that the ultimate goal of the Union is the creation and preservation of the EU as a borderless area. The holistic approach adopted in the book explains how different legal phenomena connected to deprivation of liberty have come into being in EU law. It also shows that those phenomena call for solutions suitable for the peculiarities of the EU legal order.

Volume 9 in the series Hart Studies in European Criminal Law

Hart Studies in European Criminal Law

Series Editors: Professor Katalin Ligeti, University of Luxembourg;
Professor Valsamis Mitsilegas, Queen Mary University of London;
Professor Anne Weyembergh, Brussels Free University

Since the Lisbon Treaty, European criminal law has become an increasingly important field of research and debate. Working with the European Criminal Law Academic Network (ECLAN), the series will publish works of the highest intellectual rigour and cutting edge scholarship which will be required reading for all European criminal lawyers.

The series is happy to consider both edited and single authored titles. The series defines 'European' and 'criminal law' in the broadest sense, so books on European criminal law, justice and policy will be considered. The series also welcomes books which offer different methodological approaches.

Volume 1: *EU Criminal Law after Lisbon: Rights, Trust and the Transformation of Justice in Europe* by Valsamis Mitsilegas

Volume 2: *Challenges in the Field of Economic and Financial Crime in Europe and the US*
Edited by Vanessa Franssen and Katalin Ligeti

Volume 3: *Chasing Criminal Money: Challenges and Perspectives On Asset Recovery in the EU*
Edited by Katalin Ligeti and Michele Simonato

Volume 4: *Limits to EU Powers: A Case Study of EU Regulatory Criminal Law*
by Jacob Öberg

Volume 5: *The Needed Balances in EU Criminal Law: Past, Present and Future*
Edited by Chloé Brière and Anne Weyembergh

Volume 6: *Redefining Organised Crime: A Challenge for the European Union?*
Edited by Stefania Carnevale, Serena Forlati and Orsetta Giolo

Volume 7: *White Collar Crime: A Comparative Perspective*
Edited by Katalin Ligeti and Stanislaw Tosza

Volume 8: *Criminal Liability of Managers in Europe: Punishing Excessive Risk*
Stanisław Tosza

The European Union and Deprivation of Liberty

A Legislative and Judicial Analysis from the Perspective of the Individual

Leandro Mancano

•HART•

OXFORD • LONDON • NEW YORK • NEW DELHI • SYDNEY

HART PUBLISHING

Bloomsbury Publishing Plc

Kemp House, Chawley Park, Cumnor Hill, Oxford, OX2 9PH, UK

HART PUBLISHING, the Hart/Stag logo, BLOOMSBURY and the Diana logo are trademarks of Bloomsbury Publishing Plc

First published in Great Britain 2019

A catalogue record for this book is available from the British Library.

Library of Congress Cataloging-in-Publication data

Names: Mancano, Leandro, 1989- author.

Title: The European Union and deprivation of liberty : a legislative and judicial analysis from the perspective of the individual / Leandro Mancano.

Description: Oxford, UK ; Portland, Oregon : Hart Publishing, 2019. | Series: Hart studies in European criminal law ; volume 9 | Includes bibliographical references and index.

Identifiers: LCCN 2018052893 (print) | LCCN 2018055177 (ebook) | ISBN 9781509908097 (EPub) | ISBN 9781509908080 (hardback)

Subjects: LCSH: Detention of persons—European Union countries. | BISAC: LAW / Civil Rights. | LAW / International. | LAW / Criminal Law / Sentencing.

Classification: LCC KJE9405 (ebook) | LCC KJE9405 .M36 2019 (print) | DDC 345.24/0527—dc23

LC record available at https://lccn.loc.gov/2018052893

ISBN: HB: 978-1-50990-808-0
ePDF: 978-1-50990-807-3
ePub: 978-1-50990-809-7

Typeset by Compuscript Ltd, Shannon

To find out more about our authors and books visit www.hartpublishing.co.uk. Here you will find extracts, author information, details of forthcoming events and the option to sign up for our newsletters.

To liberty.

FOREWORD

One of the most far-reaching developments in European integration in the past twenty years has been the evolution of the European Union into an Area of Freedom, Security and Justice (AFSJ). This evolution has been underpinned by a series of key constitutional and policy developments, resulting into the adoption of a plethora of EU measures focusing on enforcement, both in the field of immigration law and in the field of criminal law. Notwithstanding the symbiosis between freedom and security in the articulation of the EU AFSJ objective, the vast majority of EU secondary law underpinning the latter have focused on enhancing effectiveness in law enforcement, with the position of the individual and the protection of fundamental rights coming as an afterthought, even after the constitutionalisation of the EU Charter of Fundamental Rights by the entry into force of the Lisbon Treaty. While there has been a growing attention in the academic literature on the fundamental rights implications of specific EU AFSJ measures and policies, single-authored attempts to evaluate critically and holistically the impact of AFSJ law on fundamental rights spanning both immigration and criminal law remain rare. This book by Leandro Mancano constitutes a welcome and impressive piece of scholarship managing to provide a holistic overview of a key fundamental rights challenge running through EU immigration and EU criminal law: the impact of EU law on the right to liberty. The book is remarkably all-encompassing, by analysing forensically the impact of EU law on the right to liberty in a number of separate sub-fields of EU criminal law (substantive criminal law and various aspects of mutual recognition) and EU immigration law (including both asylum and immigration law). Moreover, in what is one of the volume's key strengths, Leandro examines the intersection between both EU constitutional law and EU citizenship law with the right to liberty viewed from the specific enforcement aims of the AFSJ. The analysis is rigorous and grounded on a first-class knowledge and understanding of the intricacies of this rather complex legal field and the book is bursting with fresh and innovative ideas. This is a highly original monograph which, in producing a new analytical framework of the legal implications of deprivation of liberty in EU law, makes a substantial contribution to the scholarly debate on the development of EU immigration law, EU criminal law, EU citizenship law and EU law more broadly. In my capacity as member of Leandro's supervisory team and as co-editor of the Hart Studies in European Criminal Law, I am proud to see this book published in our series. It is an exemplary piece of scholarship by an outstanding early career scholar with remarkable potential and its publication meets the key aim of our series to advance ground-breaking scholarship in the growing and important field of European Criminal Law.

Valsamis Mitsilegas
January 2019

ACKNOWLEDGEMENTS

This book is a revised and updated version of the PhD thesis I defended in December 2015 at the Scuola Superiore Sant'Anna (Pisa). I would like to thank my supervisors, Alberto di Martino and Valsamis Mitsilegas. A special mention goes to Tullio Padovani, who has stimulated my interest in issues of deprivation of liberty. My thanks are also due to Giuseppe Martinico, whose mentorship and support were key throughout the PhD and afterwards.

During the PhD and shortly after, I was a visiting researcher at Queen Mary University of London, Université Libre de Bruxelles and the University of Copenhagen. I thank Anne Weyembergh and Jørn Vestergaard for their guidance.

These research periods abroad have also given me the opportunity to meet people and make friends. In this regard, I owe ECLAN a considerable debt. Their PhD seminars (among other things) have enriched me to a great extent, both personally and academically. For all the laughs, discussions and pleasant moments enjoyed together I want to thank in particular Chloé Briere, Fabio Giuffrida, Adriano Martufi, Niovi Vavoula, Irene Wieczorek and Auke Willems.

Since I started as a lecturer in EU Law at Edinburgh Law School, I have met and interacted with excellent colleagues. I wish to thank Giacomo Delledonne, Tobias Lock, Tony Marguery, Frank Meyer, Jannemieke Ouwerkerk, Niamh Nic Shuibhne and Dirk van Zyl Smit for their insightful comments on my drafts.

Thanks to Tom Adams, Joanne Choulerton, Richard Cox, Sinead Moloney and all the people at Hart for their hard work on the manuscript and the whole publication process.

A special and wholehearted thanks to my parents Maria Assunta and Rodolfo, my sisters Giorgia and Giulia, and all the amazing friends that made this book possible.

CONTENTS

TABLE OF CASES

CJEU Cases

ECtHR Cases

European Commission of Human Rights

Prologue

I. The European Union and Deprivation of Liberty. The Importance of the Origins

The origin of something is the source of its nature.[1] While the general validity of such a statement can be debated, it certainly proves true in the case of the present story. The significance of the *origins* to the nature of this study is manifold.

Firstly, there is the origin of the research question and the hypothesis: is the European Union (EU)[2] law approach to deprivation of liberty compliant with EU Fundamental Rights Law? EU law on deprivation of liberty complies with fundamental rights, but only because the current content of the rights mainly involved has not yet been adjusted to the peculiarities of the Union legal order. In other words, there is compliance since the standard at present is not as high as it should be. As a third-year law student at Scuola Superiore Sant'Anna (Pisa), I attended a course entitled *Intersezioni di legalita fra diritto penale ed amministrativo* (*Intersections of Legality between Criminal Law and Administrative Law*), delivered by Professor Alberto di Martino. A key part of the course was the *Engel* test,[3] elaborated by the European Court of Human Rights (ECtHR) when interpreting the meaning of *criminal charge* pursuant to Article 6 of the European Convention on Human Rights (ECHR).[4] The *Engel* case laid the basis for a seminal case-law, whereby the ECtHR claimed the autonomy of the concept of *criminal charge* under the ECHR from domestic classifications. The following judgments allowed the detection of a plethora of 'labelling frauds' perpetrated by states against individuals; the classification of a measure as *non-criminal* (but rather as administrative, civil, disciplinary and the like) being used to deprive the persons affected of the guarantees better offered by criminal law.[5] That was for me the start of a journey: the engagement with the broader universe of legal concepts historically belonging to the realm of states, and developed beyond the boundaries of national sovereignty.

[1] M Heidegger, *Off the Beaten Track* (Cambridge, Cambridge University Press, 2002) 1.

[2] For the purposes of this book, the EU refers to the legal framework both post and pre Maastricht.

[3] ECtHR, *Engel and others v The Netherlands*, 8 June 1976, Application no 5100/71; 5101/71; 5102/71; 5354/72; 5370/72.

[4] Art 6 ECHR states that 'In the determination of his civil rights and obligations or of any criminal charge against him, everyone is entitled to a fair and public hearing within a reasonable time by an independent and impartial tribunal established by law'.

[5] An example concerns the burden of proof. Criminal penalties require a much higher standard to be reached, in order for them to be imposed against individuals.

Secondly, the origins of the EU law involvement in deprivation of liberty explain the holistic approach adopted in this book. Why analyse a phenomenon so inextricably tied to national sovereignty with an – almost – exclusive focus on EU law? Why do so through a comprehensive assessment of Union law, rather than focusing on a specific area? The decision stems from the nature of deprivation of liberty as a legal phenomenon, and of the Union as a polity, on the one hand; and on the other, the fact that it is underpinned by an existing gap in the debate on deprivation of liberty in EU law.

Standard works such as *Surveiller et Punir* and *Asylums* cast light on the dynamics governing internment in 'total institutions', and prisons in particular.[6] Philosophers have debated on liberty from public authorities,[7] while other authors focused on the use of detention as a punishment,[8] as well as on detention facilities.[9] Far from being a measure in decline,[10] deprivation of liberty continues to draw attention, as shown by the great deal of studies published over recent decades.[11]

Such a wide interest proves to exist within the area of legal research as well. Deprivation of liberty can be labelled – mainly – as administrative or criminal; the former being controversially[12] regarded as a form of preventive deprivation of liberty, which is not directly linked to a criminal conviction and, as such, pursues no retributive function per se.[13] Furthermore, the distinction between deprivation

[6] M Foucault, *Surveilleur et punir: naissance de la prison* (Paris, Gallimard, 1975); E Goffmann, *Essays on the Social Situation of Mental Patients and Other Inmates* (New York, Doubleday, 1961).

[7] I Berlin, *Four essays on liberty* (Oxford, Oxford University Press, 1982); JS Mill, *On liberty* (Sioux Falls SD, Nu Vision Publications, LLC, 2008).

[8] Also in this case the literature is endless. Among the cornerstones on the topic, one may recall C Beccaria, *Dei delitti e delle pene* (Milano, Mondadori, 2003); G Filangeri, *La scienza della legislazione* (Napoli, Grimaldi & Co, 2003).

[9] J Bentham, *Panopticon. Ovvero, la casa d'ispezione* (Venezia, Marsilio, 2002); J Howard, *The State of the prisons in England and Wales* (Warrington, T Cadell et al, 1784); G de Beaumont and A de Tocqueville, *Origin and outline of the penitentiary system in the United States of North America* (London, J & A Arch, 1833).

[10] The evidence would suggest the contrary, as shown by the deplorable and countless episodes of prison overcrowding in our beloved and civilised Europe.

[11] See, among a plethora of publications, D Garland, *The culture of control. Crime and social order in contemporary society* (New York, Oxford University Press, 2001); M Tonry, 'Symbol, substance, and severity in western penal policies' (2001) 3 *Punishment and Society* 517–36; D Scott (ed), *Why Prison?* (Cambridge, Cambridge University Press, 2013); RL Lipke, *Rethinking Imprisonment* (Oxford, Oxford University Press, 2007); A Liebling and H Arnold, *Prisons and their Moral Performance. A Study of Values, Quality, and Prison Life* (Oxford, Oxford University Press, 2004); T Padovani, *L'utopia punitiva. Il problema delle alternative alla detenzione nella sua dimensione storica* (Milano, Giuffrè, 1981).

[12] D Husak, *Preventive Detention as Punishment?* in A Ashworth, L Zedner and P Tomlin (eds), *Prevention and the Limits of the Criminal Law* (Oxford, Oxford University Press, 2013) 178–93.

[13] See among a plethora of publications P Keyzer (ed), *Preventive Detention: Asking the Fundamental Questions* (Cambridge, Intersentia, 2013); J Pejic, 'Procedural principles and safeguards for internment/administrative detention in armed conflict and other situations of violence' (2005) 87(858) *International Review of the Red Cross* 375–91; MC Waxman, *Administrative Detention: The Integration of Strategy and Legal Process*, Working Paper of the Georgetown University Law Center; ID, 'Administrative Detention of Terrorists: Why Detain, and Detain Whom?' (2009) 3(1) *Journal of National Security Law and Policy* 1–37; A Aldea, 'The Legal Nature of Administrative Detention' (2012) 5(54):2 *Bulletin of the Transilvania University of Brașov*, Series VII: Social Sciences, Law 27–32.

of liberty, detention and imprisonment is far from clear. In line with the holistic approach adopted in this book, the broader focus of this research is on deprivation of liberty understood as a 'measure taken by public authority by which a person is kept against his or her will for a certain amount of time within a limited space and hindered by force, or a threat of the use of force, from leaving that space'.[14] The following chapters will then tell the story of EU law engaging – in different forms – with deprivation of liberty and with those situations having deprivation of liberty as one of their constituting elements: specifically 'detention', 'imprisonment' and 'custodial penalty'.

Detention is therefore studied here as a penalty in criminal law, but also as a form of migration control and limitation to the exercise of free movement and citizenship rights. Be it the consequence of a criminal conviction, or of an administrative measure pending removal, deprivation of liberty is one of the harshest expressions of what is (or used to be) the state monopoly over the use of violence. Representing one of the toughest faces of sovereignty, deprivation of liberty brings with it broad considerations with regards to the use and organisation of public powers. Attention to such questions has only increased following the Second World War, with the establishment and consolidation of liberal democracies being flanked by the development of international and human rights law. Furthermore, deprivation of liberty requires that all public powers take an active part in it (legislative, judicial, administrative), which increases the possible perspectives from which to assess deprivation of liberty in a polity. Hence, the adoption of a broad perspective accords with the nature of detention.

The *origins* of the EU law of deprivation of liberty are intimately connected to its nature as a polity. One of the strands of the story of the Union as a 'new legal order' of international law[15] relies on the ambiguous nature of its constitutionalisation.[16] There is no agreement in the scholarship on the definition of the EU constitutionalisation process. On the one hand, there are authors who see constitutionalisation mainly as federalisation through legal integration.[17] Resting on the foundational doctrines of – above all – primacy and direct effect, legal integration has been

[14] See on this S Trenchsel and S Summers, *Human Rights in Criminal Proceedings* (Oxford, Oxford University Press, 2006) 412.

[15] Case 26/62, *Van Gend en Loos v Nederlandse Administratie der Belastingen*, EU:C:1963:1, at 12.

[16] On such ambiguity, see F Snyder, 'The unfinished constitution of the European Union: principles, processes and culture' in JHH Weiler and M Wind (eds), *European Constitutionalisation beyond the State* (Cambridge, Cambridge University Press, 2003) 55–73.

[17] E Stein, 'Lawyers, Judges, and the Making of a Transnational Constitution' (1981) 75(1) *The American Journal of International Law* 1–27. In the essay legal integration and constitutional development seem to go hand and hand, with a focus on: primacy and direct effect, and the scope of community treaty-making powers. See also 'Integration through law', where integration and federalism are seen as twin concepts. G Itzcovich, points to the ambiguous nature of 'integration', meant to represent both a process and a result. Integration would be purportedly chosen as a more neutral concept in opposition to unification, with the latter having a more explicit political *telos* (G Itzcovich, 'Integrazione giuridica. Un'analisi concettuale' (2005) 3 *Diritto pubblico* 749–86.

pursued through the internal market paradigm, mainly embodied by the principle of free movement or mutual recognition. On the other hand, scholars read constitutionalisation as 'humanisation' of EU law beyond the logic of the internal market through the development of a system of fundamental rights protection.[18] That was achieved thanks to the use of general principles by the EU Court of Justice (CJEU or Court) first,[19] and then via the adoption of the EU Charter of Fundamental Rights ('CFREU' or the Charter) with legally binding value in 2009.

Over the years, market freedoms (goods, persons and capital) have *given way to*,[20] or *prevailed over*,[21] fundamental rights protection, with the latter emerging as a (positive) driver distorting the coherence of free movement case-law.[22] From the core construction of the internal market, the Union project has expanded into a plethora of other sensitive areas: the European Monetary Union (EMU), citizenship, and the creation of an Area of Freedom Security and Justice (AFSJ).

The AFSJ, which includes migration and asylum law, and judicial cooperation in civil and criminal matters, is a striking example of the threefold role of the internal market and free movement as *paradigm*, *genesis* and *laboratory*. Paradigm, as integration in those new areas of competence was pursued through the same method, such as 'free movement' of judgments and asylum claims. Genesis, since the AFSJ was considered essential *because of* the completion of the internal market. The abolition of internal borders within the EU required stronger external frontiers, and enhanced cooperation to *fight the exploitation* and *secure the safe exercise* of free movement. Laboratory, as the importance of EU law to the deprivation of liberty primarily emerged from the interaction between the use of custodial penalties by Member States in areas covered by free movement law.[23] The changes brought about by Lisbon Treaties embody the evolutionary nature of the EU as revolving around the two souls of constitutionalisation: legal integration and fundamental rights protection. On the one hand, the Treaties

[18] K Lenaerts, 'Fundamental Rights in the European Union' (2000) 25 *European Law Review* 575; JHH Weiler, 'The Transformation of Europe' (1991) 100(8) *The Yale Law Journal, Symposium: International Law* 2403–83, who includes human rights and the implied powers.

[19] Case 11/70, *Internationale Handelsgesellschaft mbH v Einfuhr- und Vorratsstelle für Getreide und Futtermittel*, EU:C:1970:114, para 4.

[20] Case C-112/00, *Eugen Schmidberger, Internationale Transporte und Planzüge v Republik Österreich*, EU:C:2003:333.

[21] Case C-438/05, *International Transport Workers' Federation and Finnish Seamen's Union v Viking Line ABP and OÜ Viking Line Eesti*, EU:C:2007:772; Case C-341/05, *Laval un Partneri Ltd v Svenska Byggnadsarbetareförbundet, Svenska Byggnadsarbetareförbundets avdelning 1, Byggettan and Svenska Elektrikerförbundet*, EU:C:2007:809.

[22] N Nic Shuibhne, *The Coherence of EU Free Movement Law: Constitutional Responsibility and the Court of Justice* (Oxford, OUP, 2013) 7.

[23] The CJEU set aside as disproportionate Member States' rules punishing too severely – ie with custodial penalties – formal infringement of EC law. See, among many, Case 203/80, *Criminal proceedings against Casati*, [1981] ECR 2595; Case C-193/94, *Criminal proceedings against Skanavi and Chryssanthakopoulos*, [1996] ECR I-929; Case C-274/96, *Criminal proceedings against Bickel and Franz*, [1998] ECR I-7637; Joint cases C-338/04, C-359/04 and C-360/04, *Criminal proceedings against Placanica, Palazzese and Sorricchio*, [2007] ECR I-1891.

have – nearly – fully communitarised areas highly relevant to deprivation of liberty, such as criminal and immigration law.[24] On the other, Article 6 TEU now gives the EU Charter of Fundamental Rights (the Charter or CFREU) the rank of primary law.[25]

While the Union as a polity has been growing, as have EU competences, the pole star guiding this expansion has remained untouched: the Union as an area of free movement must be constructed and maintained. What was at first free movement of persons, capital and goods, then extended to judgments, personal data, and asylum- and migration-related decisions.[26] This has resulted in the emergence of a broad body of EU law on deprivation of liberty (consisting of legislative instruments and case-law), ranging from free movement to immigration detention and citizenship, passing by substantive and procedural criminal law.

The EU and its Member States have been particularly concerned with offsetting the detrimental consequences of such a borderless area; hence the creation of the AFSJ. They have, however, disregarded the need for balances in terms of individual rights protection ensuing from the expansion of the integration horizons of the Union. The increasing tension between these two poles of constitutionalisation is not surprising then.

Such legal and institutional ferment has not been entirely reflected in the scholarship hitherto. Following the adoption of the Treaty of Lisbon in 2007 – which is the main chronological reference of this book – many stories have been told on deprivation of liberty beyond the perspective of national law. However, the broader approach of EU law to deprivation of liberty has been underexplored so far. Research conducted within the framework of the Council of Europe (CoE)[27] captures the potential role of the Union in the development of a European prison law and policy, but touches upon the role of the EU marginally. Studies that engage to a greater extent with EU law either see the latter mainly as the background to comparative analysis,[28] or focus on specific topics such as immigration detention.[29] The former thread brings to the fore the challenges posed by free

[24] This includes, inter alia, the introduction of one legislative procedure for all areas of EU law, and the full jurisdiction of the CJEU over those ambits. For limits of communitarisation of criminal law, see V Mitsilegas, 'European Criminal Law and Resistance to Communitarisation after Lisbon' (2010) 1(4) *New Journal of European Criminal Law* 458–80.

[25] Or, as the provision stipulates, 'the same legal value as the Treaties'.

[26] Such a category spans from asylum claims to expulsion measures and border control.

[27] D van Zyl Smit and S Snacken, *Principles of European Prison Law and Policy. Penology and Human Rights* (Oxford, Oxford University Press, 2009).

[28] E Cape, J Hodgson, T Prakken and T Spronken (eds), *Suspects in Europe. Procedural Rights at the Investigative Stage of the Criminal Process in the European Union* (Antwerpen, Intersentia, 2007); AM van Kalmthout, MM Knapen and C Morgenstern (eds), *Pre-trial Detention in the European Union. An Analysis of Minimum Standards in Pre-trial Detention and the Grounds for Regular Review in the Member States of the EU* (Oisterwijk, Wolf Legal Publishers, 2009). PH van Kempen (ed), *Pre-trial detention. Human rights, criminal procedural law and penitentiary law, comparative law* (Cambridge, Intersentia, 2012).

[29] G Cornelisse, *Immigration Detention and Human Rights: Rethinking Territorial Sovereignty* (Leiden, Martinus Nijhoff, 2010); D Wilsher, *Immigration Detention: Law, History, Politics* (Cambridge, Cambridge University Press, 2012).

movement to the right to liberty. A person investigated/convicted in a country different to that of his/her residence or living is less likely to be granted measures alternative to detention (eg release on bail). The latter highlights the perversion of fundamental rights for the purposes of migration control. These different stories offer enriching contributions to the understanding of the phenomenon of deprivation of liberty above national law. None of them, however, adopt the holistic approach espoused in the present book, where detention in EU law unfolds from a Union-wide perspective.

The two souls of constitutionalisation constitute the horizon of the present story.[30] This research traces the origins of deprivation of liberty in EU law, so revealing the essence of its nature. The *diachronic* analysis of such a phenomenon through the lens of integration–fundamental rights protection offers a privileged insight into the evolution and current state of the Union DNA.

Analysing deprivation of liberty in light of the peculiarities of the EU legal order has its raison d'être in the origins of the narrative in this book. This story features many characters, the main ones being the internal market and the principle of free movement as *laboratory*, *paradigm of integration* and *genesis* of the expansion/integration of the Union project.

II. A Holistic Approach

The holism of the story is twofold, and involves the nature of both the EU and deprivation of liberty. The approach builds on the following methodological assumptions. Firstly, a study on deprivation of liberty is inextricably linked to the structure and content of the polity in which detention is provided for, ordered and carried out. Secondly, a better understanding of the approach of the EU to deprivation of liberty can be achieved through a comprehensive approach, without limiting the analysis to a specific aspect such as substantive or procedural criminal law.

A study concerning personal liberty comes with a reflection on public powers impinging upon individual personality:[31] problems related to personal liberty are to be discussed against the broader legal and historical contexts in which they occur. Studying personal liberty from the perspective of its deprivation,[32]

[30] The present author is far from claiming the integration and constitutionalisation as a priori mutually exclusive. It is undeniable indeed that fundamental rights and general principles as well have fulfilled a pivotal role in (legal) integration.

[31] G Amato, *Individuo e autorità nella disciplina della libertà personale* (Milano, Giuffrè, 1967) 2 onwards.

[32] Detention is used in a general sense, by equating it to deprivation of liberty. The issue of a difference between detention strictly understood and arrest is analysed later. See on this topic S Trenchsel and S Summers, *Human Rights in Criminal Proceedings* (Oxford, Oxford University Press, 2006) 407.

in particular, means examining a situation (liberty) that is a precondition for the potential expression of any other aspects of individual personality. In this sense, personal liberty is indeed *special*: unlike other forms of liberty recognised over the centuries, it has been upheld continuously.[33] Its uniqueness shines when we look at the apparent similarity of legal formulas that have protected it throughout history: namely, the claim not to be arrested *sine legale iudicio* (or *per vim, contra legem terrae* and the like).[34] Another key feature of deprivation of liberty is its connection to security concerns. Personal liberty is regularly interfered with by public authorities for the purposes of crime control and, more broadly, in relation to the exercise of a polity's sovereign powers. However, deprivation of liberty can be carried out lawfully (ie not arbitrarily) as long as this happens in the *cases* and according to the *procedures* strictly defined by the law. Any individual is entitled not to be subject to – and to challenge – arbitrary forms of deprivation of liberty: this is the right to liberty, the cornerstone of any liberal democracy under the rule of law.

Therefore, a study on personal liberty involves a reflection on the relationship between public powers and the individual: in other words, the constitutional framework of a legal order in a given historical moment. Detention has had major implications concerning 'public law' over the centuries.[35] It represents the most 'classical' expression of state sovereignty over the individual, which in turn reveals its very nature in the use of the monopoly of force. As Max Weber put it, a state is a community that successfully claims the monopoly of the legitimate use of physical force, the sole source of the 'right' to use violence.[36] Such a state, according to the well-known formula introduced by Bodin, concretises its *sovereignty* over an established *territory* and *people* within it.[37] Furthermore, the same theory of separation of powers was related by Montesquieu to the protection of the life and liberty of the citizen,[38] which highlights how the very structure of sovereign powers is also relevant in studying deprivation of liberty.

[33] See for instance Article 8 of the *Magna Carta*, stipulating that 'No widow shall be compelled to marry, so long as she prefers to live without a husband; provided always that she gives security not to marry without our consent, if she holds of us, or without the consent of the lord of whom she holds, if she holds of another'.

[34] See Article 39 of the 1215 *Magna Carta*, which stated that 'No freeman shall be taken or imprisoned or disseised or exiled or in any way destroyed, nor will we go upon him nor will we send upon him except upon the lawful judgement of his peers or the law of the land'. An important step in the crystallisation as a source of law is the Habeas Corpus Act 1679.

[35] For a comprehensive examination in this respect, see Amato, *Individuo e autorità*, n 31 above.

[36] M Weber, 'Politics as a vocation' in D Whyte (ed), *Crimes of the powerful: A reader* (New York, Open University Press, 2009).

[37] J Bodin, *On sovereignty*, edited by JH Franklin (Cambridge, Cambridge University Press, 1992).

[38] C Montesquieu, *The spirit of the law* (Cambridge, Cambridge University Press, 1989). On the role played by criminal law in the context of sovereignty, and the seminal changes brought about by EU law, see among many, also B Davies, 'EU Criminal Law in National Courts: Breaking the Monopoly?' (2013) 34 *Liverpool Law Review* 241–59; M Delmas-Marty, 'The European Union and Penal Law' (1998) 4(1) *European Law Journal* 87–115; E Guild, 'Crime and the EU's Constitutional Future in an Area of Freedom, Security, and Justice' (2004) 10(2) *European Law Journal* 218–34.

The broad importance of deprivation of liberty also has a historically influenced dimension. The democratic constitutional states that have arisen after the Second World War[39] have placed the protection of personal liberty against the arbitrariness of public powers at the very core of their systems. The Universal Declaration of Human Rights (UDHR), the International Covenant on Civil and Political Rights (ICCPR), the ECHR and the CFREU all state the right to liberty,[40] which has been then fleshed out by the competent implementing and interpretative bodies.[41]

The right to liberty is not the only fundamental right to be considered in a work on detention. Indeed, deprivation of liberty may take place for different reasons, and be enforced in several ways. In particular, four 'levels' must be taken into account: procedural, substantial, imposition and enforcement. The first level focuses on rules governing the position of the individual in proceedings where decisions over deprivation of liberty are stake; here, detention can be a tool for the correct completion of those proceedings,[42] or an outcome thereof.[43] Such a level involves strongholds of the rule of law such as the right to a fair trial, and the presumption of innocence.

The second level concerns the substantive provisions forming the basis for the exercise of the use of force, and its extent. In the context of criminal law, this is the definition of the offence and the levels of penalty provided by the legislature. The third level relates to the extent of deprivation of liberty to which the competent authority decides to subject the person concerned. The fourth level has to do with the enforcement of deprivation of liberty: the intramural treatment, consisting of detainees' rights and duties in prison; the provisions 'accompanying' the

[39] Other nations such as England and the United States, had already developed a constitutional system akin to those affirmed in the second part of the last century.

[40] In detail, the Universal Declaration of Human Rights, adopted by the General Assembly of United Nations on 10 December 1948, stated that 'Everyone has the right to life, liberty and security of person' (Art 3) and that 'No one shall be subjected to arbitrary arrest, detention or exile' (Art 9). The International Covenant on Civil and Political Rights, adopted by the General Assembly of the United Nations on 19 December 1966, stipulates as follows: 'Everyone has the right to liberty and security of person. No one shall be subjected to arbitrary arrest or detention. No one shall be deprived of his liberty except on such grounds and in accordance with such procedure as are established by the law' (Art 9). The European Convention on Human Rights, 1950, prescribes that 'Everyone has the right to liberty and security of person. No one shall be deprived of his liberty save in the following cases and in accordance with a procedure established by the law' (Art 5).

[41] For the ECHR, see R White and C Ovey, *Jacobs and White: The European Convention on Human Rights*, 4th edn (Oxford, Oxford University Press, 2006) 122 onwards; C Grabenwarter, *The European Convention for the Protection of Human Rights. A commentary* (Oxford, Hart Publishing, 2014) 60 onwards; AR Mowbray, *Cases, Material and Commentary on the European Convention of Human Rights*, 3rd edn (Oxford, Oxford University Press, 2012) 245 onwards.

[42] For example, detention pending removal or asylum claim, pre-trial measures. Indeed, such forms of detention are legitimated by the risk that the person concerned tampers with evidence, absconds or obstructs. Some countries, such as Italy, also foresee the controversial possibility of custody on remand to prevent the individual from committing another offence.

[43] Custodial penalties or post-conviction measures alternative to detention.

person outside the prison walls, such as early release, probation and alternative sanctions granted while serving the custodial penalty.

All institutional actors in a polity are involved in detention, and all of them must comply with fundamental rights. The legislature must respect the principle of legal certainty and frame criminal law norms in a foreseeable and accessible way.[44] Police, other enforcement authorities and prosecutors are tasked with investigating crime and apprehending suspects. In doing so, they are to respect the prohibition of torture and inhuman or degrading treatment or punishment, as well as the right to a fair trial. The same may hold true for judges in charge of deciding on pre-trial custody, the length of imprisonment and alternative measures. The administration is to ensure the correct enforcement of deprivation of liberty.

How is this holistic and state-centric picture relevant to the EU, a supranational organisation that (1) presents a 'constitutional' structure that many scholars would not associate with that of a state, and (2) has neither real and direct entitlement to the use of source, nor its own police force, prison system and the like? The relevance is twofold: legislative and judicial.[45] The discussion of those sources follows the outline of the relevant policy background. That aspect is key to the legal analysis. It contributes to a more rounded assessment and deeper understanding of the hard law. On a broader level, it is true that Member States are those ultimately in charge of implementing EU law.[46] It is equally true that, in doing so, they are to comply with what EU law prescribes: namely, the specific rules they implement *and* the Charter. Union norms are therefore both input and standards that states are required to abide by. This is an important source of the responsibility of the EU legislature for enacting appropriate norms governing deprivation of liberty. Are they in compliance with the principles of proportionality and subsidiarity?[47] Are they drafted clearly and coherently? Do they safeguard individual rights adequately? All these questions should be considered carefully.

The legislative level goes hand in hand with the judicial one. The CJEU handles a triangular relationship between three sources: the inputs, EU rules involving deprivation of liberty; the Charter, acting as standard of review; and national laws involving deprivation of liberty, either because they implement the input

[44] As I underline above, especially in light of the ECtHR's case-law the duty to respect the principle of legality concerns not only the legislature, but also judicial law-making.

[45] Here, the legislative and judicial dimensions refer to the sources analysed, namely EU legislation and case-law of the CJEU. This administrative dimension (police, law enforcement) is not mentioned because it is not present at EU level with direct relevance for deprivation of liberty – as it could be, for example, if there were an EU penitentiary system.

[46] Here the term is used in a broader way, in the sense that Member States are practically responsible for the application of Union rules. Furthermore, most of the EU law on deprivation is not endowed with direct effect.

[47] Proportionality and subsidiarity must be understood here as the principles governing the exercise of EU competences under Article 5(3) TEU.

EU rules, or because they are in an area covered by EU law.[48] The CJEU not only reviews input rules against the Charter, but also pronounces on the compatibility of national laws and practices with the input rules and the CFREU. Such a complex framework is very prone to causing conflicts, and it does indeed. The fact that the Charter is the barycentre of the EU system of fundamental rights protection, but co-exists with the ECHR and national constitutional traditions, further complicates the plot of our story. Those being the perimeter and methodological assumptions of the story, the next section explains the structure and main argument of the book.

III. Plot and Main Characters

This book examines the EU legislative and judicial approach to deprivation of liberty from the perspective of fundamental rights and principles that are inextricably linked to that use of force over the individual. These are: the principle of legality and proportionality of penalties; the right to liberty; and the rehabilitative function of penalties. It aims to measure Union law involving deprivation of liberty against those rights, constituting the very core of the relationship between public powers and individual liberty. The setting of the story is the EU legal order, which has implications on three related levels. Firstly, the overarching framework is the dynamic *integration–fundamental rights protection*: the two souls of EU constitutionalisation. The argument is that the balance between expansion of the horizons of the Union project, on the one hand, and level of individual protection, on the other, constitutes the very DNA of EU law. Deprivation of liberty suits the study of that dynamic: it expresses the exercise of sovereign powers par excellence, while requiring for that reason high standards of safeguarding.

Secondly, the objective of the research is not limited to a specific topic. To achieve the overall objective, the EU law involvement in deprivation of liberty is grouped into four main areas, each of them forming a constitutive episode of the story: substantive EU criminal law; mutual recognition and procedural EU criminal law; EU immigration and asylum law; free movement and citizenship. The sources (almost exclusively from EU law, though references to national law or the ECHR are made when needed)[49] are tested against a set of fundamental rights and general principles.[50]

[48] For example, a national rule restricting free movement of goods, and sanctioning the violation of that restriction with custodial penalties.

[49] This is the case, for example, when the CJEU is asked to rule on the compatibility of a national provision with EU law. Here the law of the Member State in question must be touched upon. Furthermore, the standard of analysis of this book is mainly the provisions of the CFREU. As a rule, these must be read jointly with the corresponding provisions of the ECHR, as interpreted by the Strasbourg Court.

[50] As to the theoretical foundations of methodology of research in social science and, more particularly, in (EU) law, I benefited from a number of texts. Just by way of example, see A Bhattacherjee, *Social*

In each area, the discussion is carried out by the joint use of a default-benchmark and a 'flanking' benchmark, selected in light of the specificity of the area analysed in turn. The default-benchmark is the principle(s) of proportionality, understood as proportionality under Articles 5(4)[51] TEU and 52 CFREU.[52] The former measures the proportionality of the exercise of EU competence in adopting an instrument involving deprivation of liberty. The latter looks at the limitations of Charter rights and freedoms imposed by the Union institutions and Member States when implementing EU law. A specific understanding of proportionality is relied on, depending on the characteristics of the area analysed.

The story follows a chronological – and circular – structure. Consistently with the overarching framework of the research, the first Part tells how EU law started giving importance to deprivation of liberty. The situations addressed here concern the use of custodial penalties in areas covered by the law of free movement, and how the CJEU has handled this interaction. Chapter one prepares for the subsequent Parts. Firstly, it shows the spill-over effect that led the EU – and the Court in this specific circumstance – to have a say on the Member States' use of deprivation of the liberty through the channel of the internal market. It 'introduces' the importance of the specificity of EU law in the process of shaping its own approach to deprivation of liberty. This can be seen in the use of the principles of effectiveness and proportionality, non-discrimination, and the need to build and preserve the Union as a borderless area. Secondly, it highlights how that trend has interacted with the development of a system of fundamental rights, started with the creation of general principles and strengthened by the recourse to the CFREU. Thirdly, this Part presents principles and arguments that, while first stated in the context of the internal market, might be successfully used to solve legal dilemmas in other areas of EU law. Lastly, the discussion highlights the possible drawbacks of connecting protection of personal liberty to free movement. The conclusion on the 'dark side' of the internal market and deprivation of liberty paves the way to the following Parts, where free movement is used as an argument to justify the adoption of measures involving deprivation of liberty.

Science Research: Principles, Methods, and Practices (Global Text Project, 2012) Textbooks Collection, Book 3, available at: http://scholarcommons.usf.edu/oa_textbooks/3/?utm_source=scholarcommons.usf.edu%2Foa_textbooks%2F3&utm_medium=PDF&utm_campaign=PDFCoverPages; R van Gestel, H-W Micklitz and M Poiares Maduro, 'Methodology in the New Legal World', EUI Working Papers LAW No 2012/13; M Van Hoecke (ed), *Methodologies of Legal Research. Which Kind of Method for What Kind of Discipline?* (Oxford, Hart Publishing, 2011); T Hervey and others, *Research Methodologies in EU and International Law* (Oxford, Hart Publishing, 2011); R Banakar and M Travers (eds), *Theory and Method in Social-Legal Research* (Oxford, Hart Publishing, 2005).

[51] 'Under the principle of proportionality, the content and form of Union action shall not exceed what is necessary to achieve the objectives of the Treaties'.

[52] 'Any limitation on the exercise of the rights and freedoms recognised by this Charter must be provided for by law and respect the essence of those rights and freedoms. Subject to the principle of proportionality, limitations may be made only if they are necessary and genuinely meet objectives of general interest recognised by the Union or the need to protect the rights and freedoms of others'.

Part II deals with substantive EU criminal law. The Union's use of imprisonment as punishment is assessed against the default-benchmark (proportionality under Article 5 TEU) and Article 49 CFREU, stating the principles of legality and proportionality of penalties. The emergence of this body of law follows and builds on the seminal *Greek Maize* case: starting with the requirement that Member States sanction violations of EU law with *effective*, *proportionate* and *dissuasive* penalties, the Union legislature has moved onto the enactment of instruments of approximation of the definition of offences and of penalties. Here, an overview of the recourse to deprivation of liberty sets the basis for three case studies (the Anti-Drug Trafficking Directive, the Market Abuse Directive, and the Directive on the Protection of the EU Financial Interests) revealing how the peculiarities of the Union legal order shape its approach.

Likewise, Part III revolves around two main areas: enforcement and protection. The former addresses mutual recognition as the cornerstone of judicial cooperation in criminal matters in the EU. It focuses on four mutual recognition instruments involving deprivation of liberty, namely, the Framework Decisions on the European Arrest Warrant (EAW FD); transfer of prisoners; probation measures; and the European Supervision Order (ESO). The latter section homes in on the measures that aim to enhance procedural rights protection. In particular, the Directives on the rights to (1) translation and interpretation, (2) information, and (3) legal aid in criminal proceedings, and EAW procedures are discussed. While the main setting remains the souls of constitutionalisation, proportionality under Article 52 CFREU is flanked by Article 6 (the right to liberty). This Part confirms the presence of patterns characterising the EU approach to deprivation of liberty and shows great continuity across different areas of Union law.

Part IV discusses administrative detention of asylum seekers and irregular migrants. Chapter ten evaluates provisions on detention featured in the Common European Asylum System (CEAS), while the Chapter eleven is concerned with the barycentre of EU law on return procedures: Directive 2008/115/EC ('the Return Directive'). As in Part III, the law is tested against the principle of Article 52 CFREU proportionality and the right to liberty.

Part V then discusses the relationship between deprivation of liberty and EU citizenship. The story finishes with an analysis of what role the EU envisages for detention and detainees. This Part describes a paradigmatic example of the across-the-board involvement of Union in deprivation of liberty. Here, the triangular relationship between EU citizenship, EU criminal law and Member States' use of custodial penalties is assessed in the light of Article 52 CFREU proportionality and the rehabilitative function of custodial penalties. The epilogue retraces the steps taken by the EU in the construction of its overall approach to deprivation of liberty. It stresses once again the continuity of that approach throughout Union law as a whole, and raises questions and opens up possible future avenues of development.

The story reveals that free movement is the backbone of the EU law of deprivation of liberty. At first, that principle was used to limit states' use of custodial penalties as they would jeopardise the exercise of free movement. The abolition of internal frontiers has sparked the creation of a wide body of compensatory measures involving deprivation of liberty in different areas: substantive criminal law, procedural criminal law and judicial cooperation, asylum and migration law. In all these cases, the analysis shows that the ultimate horizon and target of the Union's action is the creation and preservation of the EU as a borderless area – or, as alternatively referred to, the safe exercise of free movement. Such a depersonalisation of free movement goes hand in hand with the elevation of the borderless area to the role of raison d'état.

Against that background, the EU law of deprivation of liberty serves to protect free movement through forced movement. Here, static rules (eg approximation of the definition of offences and levels of penalties) works together with dynamic instruments (measures governing intra or extra EU transfer, such as the EAW or expulsion of irregular migrants). This system – and, more broadly, the peculiarities of the Union as a legal order – poses new challenges to traditional strongholds of personal liberty. However, the current understanding of these strongholds (the right to liberty, the principle of legality) in EU law offers an unsuitable and inadequate standard of protection. This is so because the present conceptualisation of those rights pays no heed to the characteristics of the EU as a polity. The level of under-protection is even more paradoxical when considering that the physiognomy of the EU law on deprivation of liberty is strikingly influenced by those peculiarities.

The sense of continuity is reinforced by the regular emergence of few characters, playing different *roles* depending on the specific areas. Free movement acts as laboratory, trigger and objective of EU law on deprivation of liberty. Besides this, security and effectiveness are two further – interacting – protagonists of the story, providing oft-used arguments for the adoption of coercive measures at EU law level. In opposition to that, we find the strongholds used to assess the Union approach: the principle of legality, the principle(s) of proportionality, the right to liberty, and the rehabilitative function of custodial penalties. Last but not least, the actors involved in shaping the Union's understanding of deprivation of liberty: the constitutive parts of the EU legislature and their different stances (Commission, the Council and the Parliament), the CJEU, Member States, and the person concerned – the true centre of gravity of the story.

The holistic, Union-specific approach adopted here serves not only to explain how different legal phenomena connected to deprivation of liberty have come into being in EU law. It also shows that those phenomena create a conundrum that calls for tailored solutions. The discussion carried out in each chapter highlights that the rights involved in the EU law on deprivation of liberty need to be reconceptualised and adjusted to the challenges brought about by the intersection between different areas of EU law, as well as between the latter and states' rules. The present book aims to cast new light on unprecedented legal phenomena from an unexplored perspective.

PART I

Free Movement and Deprivation of Liberty in EU Law

1

Free Movement and Deprivation of Liberty. Paradigm, Genesis, Laboratory

I. Free Movement and the Origins of Deprivation of Liberty in EU Law

EU law is not just a framework of coexisting watertight areas. Quite the opposite, it is a 'whole' whose constituent parts are highly connected and influence each other. As time has gone by, the connection has been strengthened, with the CJEU playing a major role in this respect. While criminal law and immigration detention are now part and parcel of the Union's approach to detention, EU law and deprivation of liberty is a story that started in the context of free movement. The plot of the book is placed in the context of the EU as a polity mainly developing around the dynamic *integration-fundamental rights protection*. This chapter presents free movement (and the construction of the Union as an area without internal frontiers) in its threefold role of paradigm, genesis and laboratory of EU law involvement in the deprivation of liberty.

This follows from the holistic approach adopted in this book. Interdependence is an inherent feature in the EU, where interaction takes place not only among the different areas of Union law, but also between the latter and national systems. Deprivation of liberty is a case in point. Rulings on the Member States' use of custodial penalties in the context of the internal market have led the CJEU to state and develop principles which then become the bread and butter of EU criminal law.

Three different expressions of interaction can be seen here.[1] Firstly, the impact of EU law on Member States' law has concerned the infringement of EU law provisions punished with imprisonment at national level, where the CJEU has set aside those rules that limited the rights established by EU law in a disproportionate manner.[2]

[1] V Mitsilegas, *EU Criminal Law* (Oxford, Hart Publishing, 2009) 60.

[2] ECJ, Case 203/80, *Criminal proceedings against Casati*, [1981] ECR 2595; ECJ, Case C-274/96, *Criminal proceedings against Bickel and Franz*, [1998] ECR I-7637; ECJ, Joint cases C-338/04, C-359/04 and C-360/04, *Criminal proceedings against Placanica, Palazzese and Sorricchio*, [2007] ECR I-1891.

Secondly, the use of criminal penalties has been upheld by the EU as a tool in maintaining the effectiveness of EU law. The *Greek Maize* case is the landmark judgment in this respect.[3] The ruling concerned an episode of fraud against the Community's financial interests. Maize had been exported to Belgium from Greece. Although the maize had previously been imported from the former Yugoslavia, it was sold as having Greek origin. The fraud was facilitated by Greek civil servants, and perpetrated to avoid paying levies due to the Community because of the initial import from a third country into a Community Member State.

The Court, by founding its reasoning on the principle of loyal cooperation,[4] established the *principle of assimilation*. Here the obligations are for Member States to treat comparable violations of Community and national law with analogous means, for Member State reactions to amount to *effective, proportionate and dissuasive* penalties, and for these to be enforced with the *same diligence* as those applied to national situations. The Court did not mention a specific type of sanction – although it referred to the Greek authorities' failures to 'institute criminal or disciplinary proceedings' against the persons involved in the fraud.[5]

Over the years, the obligations ensuing from the *Greek Maize* case have developed considerably. At first, the Court referred to the Member States' obligation to punish an infringement of EU law through criminal penalties in subsequent judgments.[6] Secondly, the *Greek Maize* 'formula' – requiring effective, proportionate and dissuasive sanctions – was used in instruments of substantive EU criminal law, and progressively accompanied by an explicit obligation for states to impose penalties involving deprivation of liberty.

In the third type of interaction, national law principles (especially in the area of criminal law) have been regarded as general principles of EU law, particularly in order to ensure the application of Union law in compliance with the principles of legal certainty and non-retroactivity in criminal proceedings.[7] In all these cases, interaction has arisen between states' (mis)use or (non)use of custodial penalties in areas covered by the law of free movement.

The expansion of the Union's competence in the area of criminal law and migration and asylum has only increased the likelihood of interaction between free movement and deprivation of liberty. This is even more the case since the Treaty of Lisbon has demolished the pillar-based structure of the EU and 'communitarised' areas of EU law such as the former third pillar.

[3] ECJ, Case C-68/88, *Commission v Greece*, [1989] ECR 2965. See also the forerunner Court decision, Case 50/76, *Amsterdam Bulb BV v Produktschap voor Siergewassen*, [1977] ECR 137.

[4] Art 4(3) TEU, former Art 5 EC Treaty.

[5] *Commission v Greece*, n 3 above, para 26.

[6] See on this F Giuffrida, 'Effectiveness, Dissuasiveness, Proportionality of Sanctions and Assimilation Principle: The Long-Lasting Legacy of the Greek Maize Case' in V Mitsilegas, A Di Martino and L Mancano (eds), *The Court of Justice and European Criminal Law. Leading Cases in a Contextual Analysis* (Oxford, Hart Publishing 2019, forthcoming).

[7] ECJ, Case C-168/95, *Criminal proceedings against Arcaro*, [1996] ECR I-6065, paras 36–37; ECJ, Case C-384/02 *Criminal proceedings against Grøngaard and Bang*, [2005] ECR I-9939, paras 29–30.

Broadly speaking, the interplay between deprivation of liberty and free movement has increased at the EU level over the years, with two broad fronts of interaction emerging in particular. On the one hand, we have seen the use of the legal rules, and their interpretation by the CJEU, where deprivation of liberty is overtly resorted to. In the Area of Freedom, Security and Justice (AFSJ), detention is explicitly used in EU instruments since the Union has specific competences in this respect. On the other hand, until recently the use of deprivation of liberty was not part of the Union's project, which was mainly concerned with construction of the internal market and exercise of the fundamental freedoms. In this way rules involving detention have been put under the spotlight by the interaction between EU and national laws, with the Court (mainly) deliberating on the role attached to Member States' custodial penalties.

The high relevance of the interaction between fundamental freedoms (or, more broadly, Union law) and deprivation of liberty has been extensively analysed.[8] Indeed, free movement has been, and is, the core of EU law since the Community was born, though many other areas have been gaining ground over the years. Right from the establishment of the EU, national provisions involving deprivation of liberty have been increasingly covered by the law of the four freedoms (consisting of the Treaty and secondary law). Thereby, the chance for both kinds of rules (national and EU) to interact has significantly heightened. Such dynamics have triggered many interpretative dilemmas, the resolution of which has been referred to the CJEU by national judges. In these contexts, the CJEU has been asked to find an equilibrium between economic freedoms and state sovereignty. Two fundamental questions arise in this respect: is deprivation of liberty (mainly in the form of custodial penalties) restricting, or capable of restricting, a fundamental freedom; and if so, may such a restriction be allowed?

Many studies have focused on the use of general principles by the CJEU to increase protection of individual rights,[9] also with regard to the use of deprivation of liberty by Member States. This first chapter illustrates the relevance of free movement to EU law and deprivation of liberty: genesis, paradigm and laboratory, and objective. Firstly, the following pages show that the story told in this book has originated primarily in the context of the internal market. They also highlight that such an interaction has resulted in the elaboration of principles that have then found application in other areas. The twofold function of the internal market as origin and laboratory features a bright side – use of EU law to limit states' coercive powers – and a dark side, with the connection between deprivation of liberty and free movement relied on to adopt measures involving detention at EU level. Secondly, the chapter discusses how the creation of an area without

[8] Mitsilegas, n 1 above; A Klip, *European Criminal Law: An Integrative Approach* (Cambridge, Intersentia, 2012).

[9] On general principles, see above all T Tridimas, *The General Principles of EU Law* (Oxford, Oxford University Press, 2006).

internal frontiers has facilitated the spread of cooperation against criminals, so requiring a joint effort by the Member States through further integration and cooperation in the fight against transnational crime. Thirdly, and relatedly, it points to the (safe) exercise of free movement – again, creation and preservation of a borderless area – as the main horizon of the incremental use of deprivation of liberty in EU law.

The chapter is structured into two main sections. Firstly (in section II), the case-law where the interaction has materialised is presented in two main scenarios. Here, the discussion focuses on the role of free movement as genesis and laboratory of the Union's involvement in deprivation of liberty. The first scenario concerns the use of the principle of proportionality, and its application to the cases of *Skanavi*[10] and *Awoyemi.*[11] They examine exactly the same situation (driving in a host Member State with a non-recognised licence) and the same penalty (criminal sanctions, in particular imprisonment and a fine). The only difference lies in that Mrs Skanavi was an EU national, while Mr Awoyemi was not. Therefore, these two decisions are jointly read to contrast the differences between the proportionality test applied by the Court to an EU citizen, and that applied to a third-country national (TCN). They are paradigmatic examples of the double-edged nature of the EU's uniqueness when it comes to deprivation of liberty. On the one hand, the connection to free movement and the use of proportionality proved a valid tool to enhance individual rights. On the other, it is shown how that same link to the Union's very DNA may create a vacuum of legal protection, and confusion as to the content and meaning of principles in different contexts (eg proportionality in EU, and criminal, laws).

The second scenario deals with the *Berlusconi*[12] and *Caronna*[13] rulings. These cases confirm the role of the internal market as a laboratory for principles then applied elsewhere and currently translated into the Charter. The cases form part of a consistent case-law of the CJEU, according to which criminal liability cannot be directly determined or aggravated by EU law, without a national law of implementation. Therefore, the Court seems to allow the possible non-compliance of national law with EU secondary law.[14] It does so by arguing that the implementation of the latter might cause the infringement of a general principle or a fundamental right. At stake in particular was the principle of legality now enshrined in Article 49 CFREU. The first reason for choosing these cases is that the CJEU backed up its

[10] ECJ, Case C-193/94, *Criminal proceedings against Skanavi and Chryssanthakopoulos*, [1996] ECR I-929.

[11] ECJ, Case C-230/97, *Criminal proceedings against Awoyemi*, [1998] ECR I-6781.

[12] ECJ, Joined cases C-387/02, C-391/02 and C-403/02, *Criminal proceedings against Berlusconi and Others*, [2005] ECR I-3565.

[13] ECJ, Case C-7/11, *Criminal proceedings against Caronna*, judgment of 28 June 2012, [2012] OJ C258/5, 25.08.12.

[14] However, and depending on the circumstances of the case, Member States would not be able to run away easily from EU law obligations. For example, the Commission might initiate infringement proceedings under Art 258 TFEU.

argument by explicitly referring to a general principle (as in the case of *Berlusconi*) or a fundamental right of criminal law (Article 49 Charter in *Caronna*). It is argued that the rationale behind the decisions in the second scenario provides EU criminal law with an important tool to better protect fundamental rights in the context of mutual recognition.

Section III discusses free movement as a *trigger* and *objective* of the increased engagement of EU law in deprivation of liberty. The abolition of internal frontiers has led to increased cooperation amongst Member States, which in most cases took the shape of measures involving deprivation of liberty. The main objective of those measures remained the secure exercise of free movement of Union citizens and business, and higher effectiveness of Union law. The conclusions retrace the first steps of EU law in deprivation of liberty told in this chapter, and prepare for the next Parts of the story.

II. EU Law and Deprivation of Liberty. The Internal Market as a Laboratory

A. Custodial Penalties and Exercise of Free Movement. The Case of Driving Licences

The two main scenarios show how the internal market is the area where the Union not only started engaging with the use of deprivation of liberty, but has also stated principles that might find application somewhere else. The first scenario concerns the connection between the use of custodial penalties and exercise of free movement, and is discussed through two cases on driving licences: *Skanavi* and *Awoyemi*.

The question in the *Skanavi* arose in the context of criminal proceedings against Mrs Skanavi and her husband, Mr Chryssanthakopoulos, who were charged with driving without a licence. According to German law, the conduct was an offence punishable by imprisonment or a fine. As far as EU law is concerned, driving licences were first harmonised by the First Council Directive 80/1263/EEC of 4 December 1980 upon the introduction of a Community driving licence.[15] That instrument in particular set a system for the mutual recognition and the exchange of driving licences, when the holder had her/his residence or workplace in another Member State. By virtue of that Directive, when the holder of a valid driving licence took up residence in another Member State, the licence would remain valid for up to a maximum of a year after the establishment of residency. At the

[15] First Council Directive 80/1263/EEC on the introduction of a Community driving licence, [1980] OJ L375/1, 31.12.80.

request of the holder within that period, and against the surrender of the licence, the host Member State was to issue the driver with a Community model driving licence for the corresponding category or categories without requiring the holder, inter alia, to pass a practical and theoretical test or to meet medical standards. According to the subsequent Directive 91/439/EEC,[16] the holder of a valid driving licence residing in another Member State was not obliged to exchange it for a Community one.

The Court was firstly asked whether, as EU law stood prior to the implementation of the latter Directive, a Member State could require the holder of a driving licence issued by another Member State to exchange that licence within one year from the establishment of the residence in the host state, in order to retain the entitlement to drive in the state. The Court recognised that the rules concerning a driving licence can have a significant impact on the freedom of movement for workers, as well as on the freedom of establishment and provision of services.[17] The Court also found that the gradual harmonisation carried out at EU law level allowed the Member State to retain some powers in this respect. Such latitude included requiring the holder of a valid licence to exchange it in the Member State to which s/he had moved.

The Court was further asked whether the Treaty precluded the act of driving a motor vehicle by a person who had not exchanged licences from being treated as driving without a licence, and thus rendered punishable by imprisonment or a fine. The Court acknowledged that the obligation to exchange the licence was compatible with EC law, but also that it constituted a mere administrative requirement.

Though the Member State remains competent regarding the use of criminal law, the latter must be used in such a way so as not to obstruct free movement. This is especially the case when it comes to imprisonment,[18] where on that ground the CJEU ruled that EU law prohibited the Member State from treating driving without the exchange of the licence as a criminal offence, since it would jeopardise the enjoyment of free movement.[19]

Awoyemi concerned exactly the same situation as that which occurred in *Skanavi*, but the difference lay in the fact that the person concerned was a third-country national. Mr Awoyemi had lived in the United Kingdom for years, where he was the holder of a Community model driving licence. He was stopped by the police in Belgium, and found to be driving a motor vehicle without being in possession of a Belgian driving licence.

The Court was asked whether EU law precluded the Member State from treating driving without exchanging a licence as a criminal offence. The Court found

[16] Council Directive of 29 July 1991 on driving licences, [1991] OJ L237/1, 24.8.1991.
[17] ECJ, Case 16/78, *Criminal proceedings against Choquet*, [1978] ECR 2293, para 4.
[18] Case C-265/88 *Criminal proceedings against Messner*, [1989] ECR 4209, para 14.
[19] *Skanavi*, n 10 above, Court's judgment, para 39.

that the former Directive applied irrespective of nationality, and also recalled *Skanavi*, when stating that the Member State must use criminal law in compliance with EC law and the principle of free movement.[20] However, the Court found that a person such as Mr Awoyemi, as a third-country national, may not rely on the principle of free movement of persons, which applies only to a national of a Member State.[21] As the law stood at that moment, the position of the person concerned was not governed by provisions of EU law, as he was not entitled to free movement.

The Court mitigated this statement by means of the principle of retroactivity of a more favourable norm. The Court relied on the applicability of Directive 91/439/EEC on driving licences, which in the interim had substituted Directive 80/1263/EEC. The newest Directive imposed on a Member State the prohibition (effectively the removal) of the requirement to exchange driving licences issued by another Member State, regardless of the nationality of the holder. The Court recognised that the situation of Mr Awoyemi fell under the principle that an individual may rely – against the Member State – on provisions of a Directive which are unconditional and sufficiently precise, where that Member State failed to: transpose the Directive within the prescribed period, or implement the Directive correctly.[22] On that ground, the Court found that EU law allowed a national judge – by reason of the principle that forms part of national law in certain Member States of the retroactive effect of more favourable provisions of criminal law – to apply such a provision even where the offence took place before the date set for compliance with that Directive. The Court recalled the principle of the retroactive effect of more favourable provisions of criminal law.

B. The Impact on Proportionality

The cases offered a paradigmatic example of how the uniqueness of the EU – a polity built and developed around free movement – has influenced its approach to deprivation of liberty. One must bear in mind that the judgments were given when the Charter did not have legally-binding value. Therefore, it is appropriate to raise the question as to how the principle stated therein can be upheld in the EU legal framework as developed by the Treaty of Lisbon. At stake there, in particular, is the connection between deprivation of liberty on the one hand, and the interaction between different understandings of the principle of proportionality, on the other. Scholars have debated on the principle of proportionality in general terms,[23]

[20] *Skanavi*, n 10 above, paras 36 and 38.

[21] ECJ, Case C-147/91, *Criminal proceedings against Laderer*, [1992] ECR I-4097, para 7.

[22] *Awoyemi*, n 11 above, Court's judgment, paras 39–45.

[23] See in particular A Robert, 'The Construction of Constitutional Rights' (2010) 4(1) *Law and Ethics of Human Rights* 21–32; B Aharon, 'Proportionality and Principled Balancing' (2010) 4(1) *Law and*

as well as with reference to EU law.[24] In the latter area, it has been highlighted that the multiform application of proportionality depends on the peculiarities of the area of law at stake, and the nature of the interests involved.[25] For the purposes of this story, we can distinguish between three main understandings of proportionality: the principle governing the exercise of the Union's competences under Article 5 TEU; proportionality as a limit to restrictions of rights and freedoms laid down in the Charter, as stated in Article 52 CFREU; and the proportionality of penalties in relation to seriousness of offences under Article 49 CFREU.

Proportionality is a pole star (jointly with the principle of subsidiarity) for the Union in the exercise of its competences, and requires that 'the content and form of Union action shall not exceed what is necessary to achieve the objectives of the Treaties'.[26] As we know, the CJEU usually reviews Union actions with a rather loose application of proportionality. The action would be struck down only if manifestly in violation of proportionality. This could be the case if the party claiming the infringement shows that the real objective of the measure was not one the EU could pursue in compliance with the Treaty, or if it emerges clearly that other less intrusive means might have led to the achievement of that goal.[27] In this sense, evaluating criminal law on the basis of *this* principle of proportionality is to examine how the Member State justifies its use of criminal law, and more specifically, how criminal law is related to a given objective, and which function the former is supposed to fulfil.

Article 52 CFREU crystallises in the Charter the proportionality principle as a test to review restrictions of Charter rights by the EU or the Member States.

Ethics of Human Rights 1–16; DM Beatty, *The Ultimate Rule of Law* (Oxford, Oxford University Press, 2004); T Endicott 'Proportionality and Incommensurability' (2012) *University of Oxford Legal Research Paper Series*, 40, available at: http://ssrn.com/abstract=2086622; JH Gerards, 'Proportionality Revire in EU Law' (2009) *IVR Encyclopedia of Jurisprudence, Legal Theory and Philosophy of Law*, available at: http://ivr-enc.info/index.php?title=Proportionality_review_in_European_law.

[24] Among many, see G De Búrca, 'The Principle of Proportionality and its Application in EC Law' (1993) 13(1) *Yearbook of European Law* 105–50; P Craig, 'Proportionality, Rationality and Review' (2010) 35(2) *New Zealand Law Review* 265–302; F Fontanelli and G Martinico, 'Browsing The XX Files – The necessity test in the GATT, and why it is not like proportionality in the EU' (2013) *SWUPL International Law Review* 32–58; FG Jacobs, 'Recent Developments in the Principle of Proportionality in European Community Law' in E Ellis Evelyn (ed), *The Principle of Proportionality in the Laws of Europe* (Oxford, Hart Publishing, 1999) 1–22; N Reich Norbert, 'How proportionate is the proportionality principle? Some critical remarks on the use and methodology of the proportionality principle in the internal market case law of the CJEU' (2011) available at: http://www.jus.uio.no/ifp/forskning/prosjekter/markedsstaten/arrangementer/2011/free-movement-oslo/speakers-papers/norbert-reich.pdf; Tridimas, n 29 below.

[25] T-I Harbo, 'The Function of the Proportionality Principle in EU Law' (2010) 16(2) *European Law Journal* 158–85.

[26] Art 5(4) TEU.

[27] See for example Case C-310/04, *Kingdom of Spain v Council of the European Union*, [2006] ECR I-7285.

It requires that the restriction be suitable and necessary to achieve a legitimate aim – an objective of general interest, to use the wording of Article 52 CFREU.[28] The proportionality test is a threefold one, and implies an assessment of the measure in terms of its suitability, necessity and proportionality *stricto sensu*.[29] The suitability test evaluates appropriateness of the means (the restriction) in relation to the achievement of the objective pursued. The necessity test implies that the measure chosen is the least intrusive measure available for the right or freedom restricted, on condition of being equally effective to meet that objective. Proportionality *stricto sensu* will be complied with if the means adopted does not impose an excessive burden on the right. This last part of the test is considered to be the least clear. According to Alexy, proportionality *stricto sensu* comes with a threefold sub-test:

> the first stage involves establishing the degree of non-satisfaction or of detriment to the first principle. This is followed by a second stage in which the importance of satisfying the competing principle is established. Finally, in the third stage it is established whether the importance of satisfying the latter principle justifies the detriment to or non-satisfaction of the former.[30]

Proportionality has also a criminal law understanding.[31] Scholars have written extensively on the reach of proportionality[32] at EU criminal law level, and on its

[28] Art 52(1) CFREU stipulates that 'Any limitation on the exercise of the rights and freedoms recognised by this Charter must be provided for by law and respect the essence of those rights and freedoms. Subject to the principle of proportionality, limitations may be made only if they are necessary and genuinely meet objectives of general interest recognised by the Union or the need to protect the rights and freedoms of others'.

[29] Authors see proportionality mainly as a twofold test, the last two components usually being assessed together by the Court: see Tridimas, above n 9.

[30] R Alexy, 'On Balancing and Subsumption. A Structural Comparison' (2003) 16(4) *Ratio Juris* 433, 436, 437.

[31] On the subject, see A Ashworth, *Sentencing and Criminal Justice* (Cambridge, Cambridge University Press, 2010) 104–55; PH Robinson and JM Darley, 'Does Criminal Law Deter? A Behavioural Science Investigation' (2004) 24(2) *Oxford Journal of Legal Studies* 173–205; A von Hirsch, 'Proportionality in the Philosophy of Punishment' (1992) 16(1) *Crime and Justice* 55–98; A von Hirsch and A Ashworth, *Proportionate Sentencing: Exploring the Principles* (Oxford, Oxford University Press, 2010) 131–63.

[32] See P Asp, 'Two Notions of Proportionality' in K Nuotio (ed), *Festschrift in honour of Raimo Lahti* (Helsinki, Faculty of Law, University of Helsinki, 2007) 207–19; A Bernardi, 'I principi di sussidiarietà e di legalità nel diritto penale europeo' (2012) 25(1)–(2) *Rivista Trimestrale di Diritto Penale dell'Economia* 15–65; M Böse, 'The Principle of Proportionality and the Protection of Legal Interests (Verhältnismäßigkeit und Rechtsgüterschutz)' (2011) 1(1) *European Criminal Law Review* 34–42; M Fichera and E Herlin-Karnell, 'The Margin of Appreciation Test and Balancing in the Area of Freedom Security and Justice: A Proportionate Answer for a Europe of Rights?' (2013) 19(4) *European Public Law* 759–88; AH Gibbs, 'Reasoned "Balance" in Europe's Area of Freedom, Security and Justice' (2011) 17(1) *European Law Journal* 121–37; C Sotis Carlo, 'I principi di necessità e proporzionalità della pena nel diritto dell'Unione europea dopo Lisbona' (2012) 2(1) *Diritto Penale Contemporaneo* 111–22.

interaction with the principle of subsidiarity in criminal law.[33] The interaction between the meanings of proportionality and subsidiarity in EU law and (EU) criminal law is highly relevant. As they can overlap and be understood in more than one way, their interaction can significantly impact on the individuals concerned.

Subsidiarity in criminal law (also known as *ultima ratio* or last resort principle) means that penal sanctions should be resorted to only where other instruments would be insufficient to protect the interests at stake. This is the *outer dimension* of *ultima ratio*,[34] which looks at criminal law in relation to other less intrusive means. As Husak states, it focuses on the *alternatives to* punishment, rather than on what *kind of* punishment to prefer and alternative *means of* punishment.[35]

In this sense, Giudicelli-Delage argued that *necessity* under the EU law proportionality test is imbued not only with a utilitarian logic (relation between means and end), but also with the principle of criminal law as *ultima ratio*. Therefore, such a *necessity* would cover two fundamental guarantees: punishing

> as long as it is useful and as long as it is fair. The legitimacy of the punishment rests on its fairness and utility. The combination of these two principles is key to establishing conditions and limits of the punishment … since considering both of them in isolation would lead to dangerous consequences.[36]

Such a picture is made even more complicated by the advent of the Charter with legally-binding value, where Article 49[37] established the proportionality test between the level of punishment and the seriousness of the offence. Furthermore, the evaluation of proportionality under criminal law involves both the legislative and the sentencing levels; that is to say the penalties as provided by the law and applied to concrete cases by judges.[38]

[33] See on this P Asp, 'The Importance of the Principles of Subsidiarity and Coherence in the Development of EU Criminal Law' (2011) 1(1) *European Criminal Law Review* 44–55; M Donini, 'Sussidiarietà penale e sussidiarietà comunitaria' (2003) 46(1)–(2) *Rivista italiana di diritto e procedura penale* 141–83; E Herlin-Karnell, 'Subsidiarity in the Area of EU Justice and Home Affairs Law – A Lost Cause?' (2009) 15(3) *European Law Journal* 351–61; M Kaiafa-Gbandi, 'The Importance of Core Principles of Substantive Criminal Law for a European Criminal Policy Respecting Fundamental Rights and the Rule of Law' (2011) 1(1) *European Criminal Law Review* 6–33; S Melander, 'Ultima Ratio in European Criminal Law' (2013) 3(1) *European Criminal Law Review* 45–64.

[34] Melander, ibid.

[35] D Husak, 'The Criminal Law as Last Resort' (2004) 24(2) *Oxford Journal of Legal Studies* 207–35.

[36] G Giudicelli-Delage, 'Droit pénal de la dangerosité – Droit pénal de l'ennemi' (2010) 71(1) *Revue de sciences criminelles et de droit pénal comparé* 69–80. According to the original version, the EU law of *necessity* would imply punishing 'pas plus qu'il n'est juste, pas plus qu'il n'est utile. Les principes du juste et de l'utile constituant les deux éléments sur lesquels repose la légitimité de la peine en se combinant pour en tracer les conditions et limites – combinaison indispensable … car, isolés l'un de l'autre, le juste et l'utile conduiraient à des conséquences également dangereuses'.

[37] For a commentary on Art 49 Charter, see V Mitsilegas, 'Article 49' in S Peers and others (eds), *The EU Charter of Fundamental Rights. A Commentary* (Oxford, Hart Publishing, 2014) 1351–72.

[38] On the importance of proportionality in sentencing, see D van Zyl Smit and A Ashworth, 'Disproportionate Sentences as Human Rights Violations' (2004) 67(4) *The Modern Law Review* 541–60.

The Court's judgments in *Skanavi* and *Awoyemi* show exactly the importance of these different understandings. In these cases, the application of the principle of proportionality has been linked to the entitlement to free movement, which applies to persons satisfying the following conditions: being an EU citizen or a TCN spouse of theirs; having moved to another Member State; having been or being engaged in some economic activity in the Member State where s/he has moved to. The reach of the Treaty freedoms is expanded to cover the driving licence system. As such, the protection offered by free movement law is significantly enhanced, so that the compatibility of criminal sanctions with EU law is tested in light of this enlarged dimension. The consequence is evident: the broader the area within which criminal law is required to be consistent, the higher the chances that it will be found not in compliance with EU law. Personal liberty might have been treated as an instrument for the purposes of exercising an economic freedom. More than one question arises in this respect: are there penalties which are disproportionate while not hindering free movement, and if so, how could they be justified? However, one should not overlook that in cases such as those discussed, the Court ruled on the compliance of a national measure with Treaty freedoms, so that the latter are assumed to be a benchmark of lawfulness. Furthermore, in a way the CJEU was deciding on the fairness of a national criminal law system, at a moment where a (weak) Union competence in criminal matters had just come into being.

Nonetheless, such an approach may have its drawbacks, as seen in *Awoyemi*; in that case, the Court was true to the general principle according to which the free movement law applies only to EU citizens, so that a non-EU individual may be subject to a penalty which the Court has explicitly recognised as disproportionate. One may uphold the CJEU coherence as follows: a criminal penalty is disproportionate where related to the exercise of free movement; that sanction ceases to be disproportionate when applied to a person not entitled to free movement.

Admittedly, there are at least two elements that must be considered in the analysis of the case. Firstly, at that time the Charter had not yet been adopted. Secondly, the Court might have opted for that interpretation because there were no elements capable of triggering the application of EU law. Indeed, at stake there was the protection of the exercise of free movement. The principle of free movement could not apply, because in that case Mr Awoyemi fell outside the scope of EU law; neither the Treaty, nor secondary law, governed that situation.

That said, it must be pointed out that there was relevant EU law in the area, namely Directive 91/439/EEC, confirmed by the fact that the Court resorted to it when applying the principle of retroactivity of more favourable provisions of criminal law. However, it was not considered a matter of EU law because the person concerned did not enjoy free movement.

The main problem in upholding such a hands-off approach is that it takes for granted the link between the application of the principle of proportionality and the entitlement to free movement. Indeed, the Court found that the penalty was lawful, and proportionality did not apply, because that principle was subject to the exercise of free movement. This caveat notwithstanding, it is submitted that *Awoyemi* should be regarded as a case on the proportionality of penalties, rather than a case on the application of free movement.

The advent of the legally-binding force of the CFREU seems to corroborate such an interpretation. If the Court were to be asked the same question today, the following circumstances would be taken into account. Firstly, Article 51 CFREU states that the Charter applies when a Member State *implements* EU law. In a case such as *Awoyemi*, it would be difficult to affirm the non-application of the CFREU, since the national law would be implementing EU law.[39]

Secondly, Article 49(3) lays down the universal principle that the severity of penalties must be proportionate to the seriousness of the offences. Arguing for the application of such a principle to EU citizens only would seem rather unsound. In light of these arguments, there appears to be the possibility that the Charter challenges the well-established link between the entitlement to free movement and the principle of proportionality of penalties.[40] Otherwise, the right to free movement would become a prerequisite of the enjoyment of fundamental rights, which appears in sharp contrast to the framework provided for in the Treaties. Now the story moves on to the second scenario, where *Berlusconi* and *Caronna* are discussed.

C. Custodial Penalties and Hierarchy of Compliance with EU Law

The *Berlusconi* case concerned the interaction between EU company law and the implementing Italian law. At stake there, was compliance between the latter and a number of Directives adopted according to Article 54(3)(g), stating the obligation for the Commission and the Council to remove obstacles to freedom of establishment through coordination of the safeguards required of companies by Member States. A key part of that system is the system of appropriate penalties for infringement of rules laid down in the Directives. In compliance with EU company law, Italian law initially provided for effective (custodial) penalties. However, the law was amended by a subsequent law, which decriminalised the specified conduct to some extent. The referral for a preliminary ruling arose in the context of criminal proceedings that concerned facts dating back to the earlier version of

[39] For a thorough assessment of the academic debate on the CFREU's scope of application, see F Fontanelli, 'The implementation of European Union law by member states under article 51(1) of the Charter of Fundamental Rights' (2014) 20(3) *Columbia Journal of European Law* 193–247.

[40] As noted, the Charter 'puts into the limelight two issues that have been discretely managed in the past by the CJEU, but now demand a clear and direct answer: the division of competences between the Union and its Member States, and the status of the individual as a Union citizen'. See D Sarmiento, 'Who's Afraid of the Charter? The Court of Justice, National Courts and the New Framework of Fundamental Rights Protection in Europe' (2013) 50(5) *Common Market Law Review* 1267–304.

the Italian law. As a consequence, the alleged behaviour could have been subject (in theory) to imprisonment. On the other hand, the subsequent legal framework introduced by the newer law set a regime more favourable to the accused, but potentially less effective than the former one. Therefore, at stake here was a contrast between the need for effective penalties at national law level for infringements of EU law (embodied by the earlier Italian law), and the respect of the principle of retroactivity of more lenient penalties in criminal law.

The Court firstly stated that the principle of the retroactive application of the more lenient penalty is a general principle of EU law, which '*national courts must respect when applying the national legislation adopted for the purpose of implementing EU law*' (emphasis added), and is now expressly laid down in Article 49 CFREU.[41] Following this principle would have led to the application of the subsequent Italian law, potentially contrary to EU law.

The Court further found that, in case of non-compliance of the national law with EU law, 'the national courts would be required to set aside, under their own authority, those new articles without having to request or await the prior repeal of those articles by way of legislation or any other constitutional procedure.'[42] However, the Court also recalled the principle that a Directive cannot determine or aggravate criminal liability, in the absence of a national law of implementation.[43] As the application of EU law, and the consequent disapplication of the newer Italian law, could have set aside those two principles (retroactivity and requirement of national law for criminal liability), the Court concluded that the provisions of EU secondary law in question 'cannot be relied on as such against accused persons by the authorities of a Member State within the context of criminal proceedings.'[44]

Caronna concerned the interpretation of Directive 2001/83/EC on medicinal products for human use,[45] and the Italian law implementing it. The Directive imposed on the Member State a general obligation to make the wholesale distribution of medicinal products subject to the possession of a special authorisation. Such an obligation should also apply to 'persons authorised or entitled to supply medicinal products to the public if they may also engage in wholesale business.'[46] This also concerned pharmacists, who according to Italian law are authorised to operate as wholesalers in medicinal products. The Italian law correctly implemented the Directive through Decree 219/2006. Following amendments introduced over

[41] *Berlusconi*, n 12 above, Court's judgment, paras 67–69.

[42] ECJ, Case 106/77, *Amministrazione delle Finanze dello Stato v Simmenthal*, [1978] ECR 629, paras 21 and 24; ECJ, Joined Cases C-13/91 and C-113/91, *Criminal proceedings against Debus*, [1992] ECR I-3617, para 32; ECJ, Joined Cases C-10/97 to C-22/97, *Ministero delle Finanze v IN.CO.GE.'90 and Others*, [1998] ECR I-6307, para 20.

[43] ECJ, Case C-80/86, *Criminal proceedings against Kolpinghuis Nijmegen BV*, [1987] ECR 3969, para 13.

[44] *Berlusconi*, n 12 above, Court's judgment, para 78.

[45] Directive 2001/83/EC of the European Parliament and of the Council of 6 November 2001 on the Community code relating to medicinal products for human use, [2001] OJ L311/67, 28.11.2001.

[46] Ibid, Article 77, paras (1)–(2).

the years, that law also treated wholesale distribution without authorisation as a criminal offence.

The criminal liability of Mr Caronna was based specifically on the Italian law implementing the Directive. Doubts arose as to whether the law applicable at the material time in the main proceedings made pharmacists subject to *the requirement of a special authorisation* and, in case of infringement, to *criminal liability*. If not, criminal liability could be established only by means of an interpretation consistent with EU law, as it was not explicitly stated by a national provision. In this regard, the Court firstly reaffirmed the principle that a Directive cannot, of itself and independently of a national law adopted by a Member State for its implementation, have the effect of determining or aggravating the liability in criminal law of persons who act in contravention of the provisions of that Directive.[47] More interestingly, the Court concluded that:

> the principle that criminal penalties must have a proper legal basis, enshrined in Article 49(1) of the Charter of Fundamental Rights of the European Union, would prohibit the imposition of criminal penalties for such a conduct, *even if the national rule were contrary to European Union law* (emphasis added).[48]

What emerges from these judgments is that the CJEU establishes a hierarchy of different levels of compliance with Union law. The Court states that fundamental rights and general principles prevail over the full implementation of EU secondary law by Member States. In both cases the Court confirmed the adage that EU law can never result in aggravating or determining criminal liability without a national legal basis. More broadly, respect for the principle of legality and the Charter outweighs compliance with EU secondary law.

The case-law discussed above shows the pivotal role of free movement in the emergence and development of an EU law approach to deprivation of liberty. Furthermore, it introduces two topics – use of proportionality principle(s), and the relationship between secondary EU law and fundamental rights protection – that will remerge regularly over the next Parts of the book. In the following, the other two dimensions of the internal market relation to deprivation of liberty in EU law (trigger and objective) are presented.

III. Beyond the Internal Market. Free Movement as Trigger and Objective of Deprivation of Liberty in EU Law

In section II, we have discussed the role of the internal market as laboratory of the EU and deprivation of liberty. In that sense, the internal market has been

[47] ECJ, Case C-60/02, *Criminal proceedings against X*, [2004] ECR I-651, para 61.
[48] *Caronna*, n 13 above, Court's judgment, para 55.

the first and natural context for the beginning of the present story. By approaching personal liberty as functional to the exercise of free movement, custodial penalties used by Member States were struck down as disproportionate. Furthermore, the use of imprisonment in areas covered by EU law has led the CJEU to state important principles then applied (or applicable) to other areas of EU law where deprivation of liberty is at stake.

The present section deals with the two – related – functions of *trigger* and *objective*. The exercise of free movement is to be understood as being at the same time the cause of the adoption of EU rules involving deprivation of liberty, and their ultimate horizon.

Historically, deprivation of liberty has been inevitably linked to national sovereignty, as the most visible expression of the state monopoly over the use of force. Over recent decades the EU's 'new legal order of international law',[49] has challenged this pattern.

Firstly, we have seen deprivation of liberty at Union level *coming into being from*, and *being adjusted to*, the peculiarities of the EU: by way of example, one could mention the application of mutual recognition to judicial cooperation in criminal matters and the adoption of criminal norms through intergovernmental procedures.[50] Secondly, and subsequently, national rules on deprivation of liberty have been redefined owing to the former trend.[51]

The gradual abolition of frontiers within the EU was deemed to contribute to the spreading of pre-existing criminality threats, such as terrorism and drug trafficking.[52] An even closer connection between free movement and an increase in crime rate was pointed out with regard to those forms of criminality strictly related to the major migratory flows that started before the adoption of the 1992

[49] Case 26/62, *NV Algemene Transport- en Expeditie-Onderneming van Gend en Loos v Nederlandse Administratie der Belastingen* [1963] ECR 1, 3. For a masterpiece on the originality of the EU and its evolution, see JHH Weiler, 'The Transformation of Europe' (1991) 100(8) *Yale Law Journal* 2403–83.

[50] This was especially the case before the entry into force of the Lisbon Treaty, when criminal rules were enacted under the law of the so-called 'third pillar' and the European Parliament had little involvement in the law-making process. See among the plethora of contributions on the subject, also with regard to the aspects of judicial review, A Hinarejos, *Judicial Control in the European Union* (Oxford, Oxford University Press, 2009); N Walker (ed), *Europe's Area of Freedom, Security, and Justice* (Oxford, Oxford University Press, 2004); E Baker and C Harding, 'From Past Imperfect to Future Perfect? A Longitudinal Study of the Third Pillar' (2009) 34(1) *European Law Review* 25–54; E Denza, *The Intergovernmental Pillars of the European Union* (Oxford, Oxford University Press, 2002).

[51] To maintain the example of mutual recognition, see G Vernimmen-Van Tiggelen, L Surano and A Weyembergh (eds), *The Future of Mutual Recognition in Criminal Matters in the European Union* (Bruxelles, Editions de l'Université de Bruxelles, 2009).

[52] On some occasions, as in the case of abolition of controls on persons, the national concerns produced a significant slowdown in a process that had been much quicker as far as free movement of goods and capital was concerned. See on this E Guild, 'The Single Market, Movement of Persons and Borders' in C Barnard and J Scott (eds), *The Law of the Single European Market: Unpacking the Premises* (Oxford; Portland, Oregon, Hart Publishing, 2002) 295–310.

Maastricht Treaty. Unsurprisingly, scholars have advocated the adoption of an integrative approach to EU criminal law, which involves placing the latter in the context of free movement.[53]

The creation of an area without border checks resulted in Member States' calls for 'compensative' measures.[54] Since the collapse of border controls had been (and would be) conducive to cooperation *amongst* criminals, a joint endeavour *against* criminality was required. The connections between free movement and deprivation of liberty in specific areas of EU law will be analysed in turn in each of the following sections. The following pages introduce the two main dimensions of this connection, embodying the uniqueness of deprivation of liberty in the Union legal order: security and effectiveness. This part of the discussion – approached mainly from the legal perspective – will first be placed in the broader context of the debate on the development of the Union agenda on Justice and Home Affairs (JHA) coercive measures.

Security and effectiveness here are not standards for reviewing the materials analysed in this book. The benchmark is the set of fundamental rights and principles presented in the prologue. They are, instead, the two main argumentative patterns transversally used by the EU in legislation, case-law and policy documents to support its choices where deprivation of liberty is involved. In this sense, the core analysis tests the impact of these patterns on the rights and principles adopted as benchmarks.

A. The Broader Debate on Security

Over the years, a number of factors have influenced the EU agenda in JHA. Scholars point in particular to the following aspects: the decrease of the threat of military attack, the blurring of boundaries between internal and external security and, correspondingly, the close link between these two dimensions of security.[55] These trends are seen as mainly stemming from the collapse of Soviet communism,[56] the increasing global integration (in terms of economic transactions, transport and technology) and the attack on the World Trade Center on 11 September 2001. On the one hand, 'The mass mobility [underlying globalisation] prompts concerns about the threat of transnational organized crime,

[53] A Klip, *European Criminal Law: An Integrative Approach*, 3rd edn (Antwerp/Portland OR, Intersentia, 2016).

[54] See among many V Mitsilegas, J Monar and W Rees, *The European Union and Internal Security* (Basingstoke, Palgrave Macmillan, 2003); V Mitsilegas, *EU Criminal Law* (Oxford/Portland OR, Hart Publishing, 2009) 5 onwards.

[55] M Anderson and J Apap, 'Striking a Balance between Freedom, Security and Justice in an Enlarged European Union' (2002) Centre for European Policy Studies Paperback, 4 onwards.

[56] This is confirmed by the circumstance that, during the Cold War, security studies were composed mostly of scholars interested in military statecraft. See DA Baldwin, 'The Concept of Security' (1997) 23(1) *Review of International Studies* 9.

trafficking of people, drugs, and other goods, and terrorism'.[57] On the other, 'As the EU expands, mobility has increased as a result of globalization, the free movement of persons, and more sophisticated opportunities of communication and transport. Criminals take advantage of these opportunities as well'.[58]

In this regard, scholars have highlighted the difficulty of detecting fugitives or preventing them from continuing criminal activities in another country.[59] This triggered two parallel processes involving internal (understood as Member State) security: Europeanisation, as the abolition of internal frontiers (allegedly) facilitated crime and criminals, so requiring a common response at EU level; and externalisation, namely the designation of security threats by looking at sources outside the EU (migration, terrorism, organised crime). Historically, security *at state level* has received significant attention. Possible perspectives of analysis proliferated, particularly starting from the latter half of the last century,[60] with a classic approach referring to security as 'the absence of threats to acquired values'.[61] In this sense, national security has traditionally included political independence and territorial integrity as values to be protected.

Furthermore, the issue of the balance between such a concept and other values arises.[62] Though attempts had already been made to elaborate on an understanding of security beyond the national level,[63] there have also been discussions on the Union's approach to security due to the trends mentioned above and growing European integration.

As far as the EU is concerned, a major issue in this respect concerns the relationship between security and freedom: not only because they are two centrepieces of the AFSJ,[64] but also in light of the apparent prevalence of the former in the name

[57] M Bosworth, 'Border Control and the Limits of the Sovereign State' (2008) 17(2) *Social & Legal Studies* 199–215.

[58] C Rijken, 'Re-Balancing Security and Justice: Protection of Fundamental Rights in Police and Judicial Cooperation in Criminal Matters' (2010) 47(5) *Common Market Law Review* 1457.

[59] See JHAM Grijpink, 'Criminal Records in the European Union, The Challenge of Large-Scale Information Exchange' (2006) 14(1) *European Journal of Crime, Criminal Law and Criminal Justice* 1–19.

[60] K Knorr, 'National Security Studies: Scope and Structure of the Field' in FN Trager and PS Kronenberg (eds), *National Security and American Society: Theory, Process and Policy* (Lawrence KS, University of Kansas Press, 1973) 5; B Buzan, *People, States & Fear: An Agenda for International Security Studies in the Post-cold War Era*, 2nd edn (Colchester, ECPR Press, 2007).

[61] A Wolfers, '"National Security" as an Ambiguous Symbol' (1952) 67(4) *Political Science Quarterly* 485; Baldwin, 'The Concept of Security', n 56 above, 13, rather refers to 'a low probability of damage to acquired values'.

[62] Baldwin, 'The Concept of Security', n 56 above, 18 onwards, identifies three main approaches in this respect: (1) the prime value approach, which looks at security as a prerequisite for the enjoyment of other values; (2) the core value approach, which regards security as one amongst other important values; (3) and the marginal value approach, according to which the value of security varies, depending on the country, the historical context, as well as the level of security needed and already acquired in a specific context.

[63] RA Dahl and CE Lindblom, *Politics, Economics and Welfare* (New York, Harper & Brothers, 1953).

[64] Walker, 'In Search of the Area of Freedom Security and Justice. A Constitutional Odyssey' in Walker (ed), n 50 above.

of the latter.[65] To this end, Bigo noticed a process of *unfreedomisation to strengthen freedom* in the EU action:[66] security is a liberty and the first liberty. Such criticisms have been made by scholars who have seen 'liberty (in all its guises) … being eroded, and security … morphing into an assumption for the affluent and a distant dream for everybody else'.[67]

B. Securing Freedom of Movement

From a legal perspective, the 1992 Maastricht Treaty empowered the Union to adopt norms in the area of police and judicial cooperation in criminal matters, as well as border control.[68] However, Member States started cooperating in this area in the 1970s, when the major threats of terrorism, drug trafficking and organised crime came to the fore. The growth of international trade, financial transactions and economic interpenetration significantly contributed to the spread of transnational criminality in Europe, such as economic crime, sexual exploitation of women and illegal traffic in works of art.[69] The joint action of Member States took place at the United Nations (UN),[70] the Council of Europe (CoE)[71] and at

[65] S Douglas-Scott, 'The Rule of Law in the European Union – Putting the Security into the Area of Freedom, Security and Justice' (2004) 29(2) *European Law Review* 219–42; AH Parga, 'Law and Order and Internal Security Provisions in the Area of Freedom, Security and Justice: Before and after Lisbon' in C Eckes and T Konstadinides (eds), *Crime within the Area of Freedom, Security and Justice: A European Public Order* (Cambridge, Cambridge University Press, 2011) 249–71; Anderson and Apap, 'Striking a Balance between Freedom, Security and Justice in an Enlarged European Union', n 55 above; See, with particular regard to terrorism, C Eckes, 'EU Restrictive Measures against Natural and Legal Persons: From Counterterrorist to Third Country Sanctions' (2014) 51(3) *Common Market Law Review* 869–905.

[66] See D Bigo, 'Liberty, whose Liberty? The Hague Programme and the Conception of Freedom' in S Carrera and T Balzacq (eds), *Security Versus Freedom?: A Challenge for Europe's Future* (Aldershot, Ashgate Publishing Limited, 2013) 35–44. The author refers to six possible relations between freedom and security: the anarchist approach (freedom is the only principle with no limits); the libertarian view (freedom as a rule and security as the exception, the limits between freedoms in interaction); the constitutionalist view (freedom encompasses security – it is the freedom of the individual under the name of safety); the exceptionalist view (freedom exists only after security is ensured); the permanent emergency view (security is the rule and freedom the exception. Security is our security and could imply an unfreedomisation of others, the suspension of their rights, but always in the name of more freedoms); and the fascist view (security is the only principle – order and obedience are better values than freedom).

[67] C Gearty, 'The State of Freedom in Europe' (2015) 21(6) *European Law Journal* 712.

[68] The Maastricht Treaty replaced the fragmented approach adopted up to that moment, which had seen the proliferation of a number of Ad Hoc Working Groups, focusing on the fight against drugs, immigration and judicial cooperation. See on this Denza, *The Intergovernmental Pillars of the European Union*, n 50 above, 64–84.

[69] Mitsilegas, Monar and Rees, *The European Union and Internal Security*, n 54 above, 24–25.

[70] See M Jachtenfuchs, J Friedrichs, E Herschinger and C Kasack, *Policing Among Nations. Internationalizing the Monopoly of Force*, Hertie School of Governance – Hertie working papers series, no 28, April 2008, 8 onwards.

[71] See for instance the 1957 European Convention on Extradition (ETS 24), the 1959 European Convention on Mutual Assistance in Criminal Matters (ETS 30) and the 1983 Convention on the

intergovernmental levels (eg the TREVI groups).[72] As of the second half of the 1980s, the EU was under further, massive pressure due to the increase in migration flows.

These major trends were accompanied by the dynamic concerning the completion of the internal market.[73] The abolition of internal frontiers was seen to prompt a common reaction to cross-border crime,[74] including the gradual application of a common policy on borders[75] and harmonisation of laws.[76] Not surprisingly, Member States initially limited free movement to movement of goods, services and capital; checks on persons were lifted through the intergovernmental Schengen agreements,[77] and subsequently incorporated into EU law only by the Amsterdam Treaty.[78] Under the JHA pillar, the EU and Member States could promote cooperation in areas of common interest,[79] such as: asylum and immigration policy; fraud on an international scale; terrorism; drug trafficking; and other serious forms of

Transfer of Sentenced Persons (ETS 112). On these aspects, and for further bibliography, see S Peers, 'Mutual Recognition and Criminal Law in the European Union: Has the Council Got It Wrong?' (2004) 41(1) *Common Market Law Review* 5, 6 onwards.

[72] Terrorism, Radicalism, Extremism and Violence Internationally (TREVI).

[73] See, with regard in particular to citizenship, S Coutts, 'Citizenship of the European Union' in DA Arcarazo and C Murphy (ed), *EU Security and Justice Law. After Lisbon and Stockholm* (Oxford, Hart Publishing, 2014) 92–109.

[74] COM(88) 640 final, printed in HL Select Committee on the European Communities, 22nd Report (1988–89) Appendix 4. This was not an unprecedented dynamic. As early as 1962, the Benelux Treaty on Extradition and Mutual Assistance in Criminal Matters referred to a need for balancing economic union and abolition of frontiers, on the one hand, and enhanced cooperation in criminal matters, on the other.

[75] See the Report from the ad hoc Committee on a People's Europe, Bulletin of the European Economic Community, Suppl 7/85, 1985 (also known as the Adonnino Report): http://aei.pitt.edu/992/1/andonnino_report_peoples_europe.pdf, as well as the 1985 Commission White Paper on Completing the Internal Market, COM(85) 310 final, Brussels, 14 June 1985, at 17 and 18. To a larger extent see G Cornelisse, 'What's Wrong with Schengen? Border Disputes and the Nature of Integration in the Area Without Internal Borders' (2014) 51(3) *Common Market Law Review* 744 onwards.

[76] See the 'Palma Document', drawn up by the 'Coordinators' Group on the Free Movement of Persons' and issued on June 1989: http://www.statewatch.org/semdoc/assets/files/keytexts/ktch1.pdf, at 12; see also Council doc 89/1, 27 June 1989. For further details, see Mitsilegas, *EU Criminal Law*, n 54 above, 6 onwards.

[77] The Schengen *acquis* derived from the 1984 Saarbrucken agreement between France and Germany. Member States announced that they would abolish border controls between the two countries, in order to defuse protests by German commercial truck drivers against border delays. The link between the abolition of border controls on persons and Member States' security concerns is highlighted in E Guild, 'The Single Market, Movement of Persons and Borders' in C Barnard and J Scott (eds), *The Law of the Single Market. Unpacking the Premise* (Oxford, Hart Publishing, 2002) 295–310.

[78] See Protocol (No 2) of the EU Treaty and the EC Treaty integrating the Schengen *acquis* into the framework of the European Union of 2 October 1997, [1997] OJ C340/93, 10.11.1997; see, for the definition of the Schengen *acquis*, Council Decision 1999/435/EC of 29 May 1999, [1999] OJ L176/1, 10.7.1999, corrected by Council Decision 2000/645/EC of 17 October 2000, [2001] OJ L9/24, 13.01.2001. As with the Treaty of Lisbon, see Protocol No 19. See Mitsilegas, Monar and Rees, *The European Union and Internal Security*, n 54 above.

[79] Such a competence was exercised through instruments of international law, mostly Conventions. There were also other instruments in the hands of the EU, namely Joint Actions and Joint Positions.

international crime.[80] The weakness of EU criminal law competence notwithstanding, a great deal of instruments were passed in the post-Maastricht era.[81]

The end of the century saw the adoption of the Treaty of Amsterdam[82] and the Tampere Programme:[83] the former set the objective of the creation of an area of freedom, security and justice in the Union, whereas the latter declared the adoption of the principle of mutual recognition as 'the cornerstone' of judicial cooperation in criminal matters.[84] The EU committed itself to granting people and economic operators legal certainty and a *high level of safety*, by combatting terrorism, trafficking in persons and offences against children, illicit drug trafficking and illicit arms trafficking, corruption and fraud, and by combatting racism and xenophobia.[85]

The terrorist attack on the World Trade Center and the resurfacing of the terrorist threat brought about the toughening up of the EU approach to crime, prioritising important measures among which the most prominent was the Framework Decision on the European Arrest Warrant (EAW FD).[86] The 2004 Hague Programme put a much stronger emphasis on security demands[87] and, as the Tampere Conclusions, paid little attention to individual rights.[88] The 2007 Treaty of Lisbon has eventually brought about the collapse of the pillar-based structure of the EU.

[80] Art K.1 of the Maastricht Treaty.

[81] See for an overview S Miettinen, *Criminal Law and Policy in the European Union* (Abingdon/New York, Routledge, 2014), 34 onwards.

[82] [1997] OJ C340, 10.11.1997.

[83] Tampere European Council, 15 and 16 October 1999, Presidency Conclusions.

[84] Further to this agenda, the Commission published the institution's thoughts on mutual recognition, supporting its application to criminal law. See Communication from the Commission to the Council and the European Parliament, *Mutual Recognition of Final Decisions in Criminal Matters*, Brussels 26.7.2000, COM(2000) 495 Final. See also the *Programme of measures to implement the principle of mutual recognition of decisions in criminal matters*, [2001] OJ C12/10, 15.1.2001.

[85] Former Art 29 TEU.

[86] S Alegre and M Leaf, 'Mutual Recognition in European Judicial Cooperation: A Step Too Far Too Soon? Case Study – The European Arrest Warrant' (2004) 10(2) *European Law Journal* 200–217; Peers, 'Mutual Recognition and Criminal Law in the European Union'; M Fichera, 'The European Arrest Warrant and the Sovereign State: A Marriage of Convenience?' (2009) 15(1) *European Law Journal* 70–97; V Mitsilegas, 'The Constitutional Implications of Mutual Recognition in Criminal Matters in the EU' (2006) 43(5) *Common Market Law Review* 1277–311.

[87] See on the Hague Programme, A Weyembergh, 'Approximation of Criminal Laws, the Constitutional Treaty and the Hague Programme' (2005) 42(6) *Common Market Law Review* 1567–97.

[88] Indeed, the only measure put forward aimed at improving defendants' rights was brushed aside by Member States' resistance in Procedural Safeguards for Suspects and Defendants in Criminal Proceedings throughout the European Union, Brussels, 19.2.2003, COM(2003) 75 final. Walker has argued that the pathway opened up by Maastricht and leading up to The Hague can partially be explained as follows: 'the development of institutional strength and policy capacity in FSJ was preceded, accompanied, and endorsed by a policy attitude and language that sought to address or contain new or extended threats to the security of the European Union in the form of new types or intensities of transnational crime and new "push" and "pull" factors in the sphere of immigration and asylum'. N Walker, 'In Search of the Area of Freedom Security and Justice. A Constitutional Odyssey' in Walker (ed), *Europe's Area of Freedom, Security, and Justice*, n 50 above, 12.

Security of free movement of law-abiding EU citizens is a key driver to the Union action involving deprivation of liberty. As the following chapters highlight, this concerns the adoption of measures in substantive and procedural EU criminal law. A broader tendency has been discerned over recent years towards the designation of categories of offenders as monstrous 'others', from which law-abiding citizens should be protected.[89] This can be seen in Article 83(1) TFEU, which identifies serious areas of crime worthy of 'approximation'; and in secondary law and policy statements, with a number of documents adopting an attitude of 'fight' and 'combat' against major threats, such as corruption, sexual exploitation of children, terrorism and drug trafficking.

The same may hold true in the application of mutual recognition to criminal matters, ie one of the most visible examples of the influence of the free movement paradigm on the EU approach to deprivation of liberty. The 1999 Tampere Council supported the adoption of that principle as the cornerstone of judicial cooperation in criminal matters within the EU by reference to the need to ensure the *safe* exercise of free movement on the part of Union citizens and businesses.

Relatedly, security has become a powerful tool in the area of citizenship rights as well. An overstretched understanding of public security and the need to avoid the abuse of free movement justify the denial or withdrawal of rights on the basis of sentencing to custodial penalties, or time spent in detention.

C. Enhancing Compliance with EU Law

Effectiveness is another key component of the present story. While the principle of effectiveness is used differently according to the specific area considered, in the Union context it broadly assumes the meaning of compliance with Union law. How is this relevant to the deprivation of liberty in EU law?

Effectiveness was the main argument supporting the Member States' obligation stated in the seminal *Greek Maize* judgment, generally marking the dawn of EU criminal law competences *ante litteram*. At first, the *Greek Maize* formula required states to impose effective, dissuasive and proportionate penalties.[90] The Union legislature has subsequently added to that formula the specific call for sanctions involving the deprivation of liberty. Since then, imprisonment has been the EU's exclusive punitive option, due to its – allegedly – stronger 'effectiveness potential'. Relatedly, effectiveness lay at the basis of the *Environmental Crime* and *Ship-Source Pollution* cases.[91] There, the CJEU famously stated the competences to

[89] D Garland, *The Culture of Control: Crime and Social Order in Contemporary Society* (Oxford, Oxford University Press, 2001); J Young, *The Exclusive Society: Social Exclusion, Crime and Difference in Late Modernity* (London, Sage, 1999).

[90] *Commission v Greece*, above n 3.

[91] Respectively, Case C-176/03, *Commission v Council*, [2005] ECR I-7879 and Case C-440/05, *Commission v Council*, [2007] ECR I-9097. For commentaries on the judgments, see V Mitsilegas,

approximate the definition of criminal offences under the law of the Community Pillar, if essential to the effective implementation of a Union policy. This wording would then be literally translated into what is Article 83(2) TFEU, establishing one of the possible legal bases for the adoption of rules in substantive EU criminal law. These are landmark rulings, as the Court used a policy objective (protection of the environment) to empower the EU with a specific competence – approximation of the definition of offences in criminal law – that the Treaty had provided only under the law of the 'third' pillar. As we know, the latter was based on intergovernmental legislative procedures, as opposed to the Community method under the law of the first pillar.

Similarly, the step up in judicial cooperation promoted by mutual recognition rested on the need to ensure the safe exercise of free movement. With that in mind, mutual recognition has been a way to achieve higher effectiveness of law and the compliance with it. The action of mutual recognition – and its flagship, the EAW especially – is twofold. On the one hand, it operates *post delicto*, to ensure that the integrity of the Union as a borderless area is preserved without zones of impunity. On the other, it performs an important deterrent function *ante delicto*. Closer cooperation in criminal justice significantly increases the likelihood of 'being caught'. Potential offenders are then discouraged from activities exploiting the loopholes offered by the absence of internal frontiers and the differences amongst Member States' laws. Security and effectiveness must therefore be understood as complementary, rather than alternative.

Effectiveness emerges from other episodes of the present story, such as immigration detention. EU rules on the administrative detention of migrants are laid down both in the context of asylum and return procedures. While subject to different rationales and specific legal regimes, both sets of provisions use detention to secure the transfer of the migrant to the state responsible for the asylum claim, in one case, or, the completion of the expulsion, and effectiveness of the Union return policy in its broad sense.

EU Criminal Law, n 54 above, 70 onwards; E Symeonidou-Kastanidou, 'Ship-Source Marine Pollution: the ECJ Judgements and their Impact on Criminal Law' (2009) 17 *European Journal of Crime, Criminal Law and Criminal Justice* 335–57; S Peers, 'The European Community's Criminal Law Competence: the Plot thickens' (2008) 33 *European Law Review* 339–407; M Hedemann-Robinson, 'The EU and Environmental Criminal Liability: A Legal analysis in the light of the Recent Ruling of the European Court of Justice on EC Competence' (2005) 13 *Environmental Liability* 149–67; from the same author, also for an assessment of environment criminal policy within the EU, see 'The EU and Environmental Crime: The Impact of the ECJ's Judgment on Framework Decision 2005/667 on Ship-Source Pollution' (2008) 20(2) *Journal of Environmental Law* 279–92. For considerations about the judgments with respect to the principle of subsiarity, see E Herlin-Karnell, 'Subsidiarity in the Area of EU Justice and Home Affairs Law – A Lost Cause?' (2009) 15(3) *European Law Journal* 351–61; C Tobler, *Case Note* (2006) 43 *Common Market Law Review* 835–54; MJ Borgers and M. Kookimans, 'The scope of Community's competence in the field of criminal law' (2008) 16 *European Journal of Crime, Criminal Law and Criminology* 379–95. For a broader critique on the development EU power in criminal law, see J Öberg, 'Union regulatory criminal law competence – scope, limits and judicial review', Stockholm: Swedish Institute for European Policy (SIEPS 2015:4).

IV. Conclusions

The chapter has set the scene for, and introduced some of the key characters of, the story told in this book on EU law and the deprivation of liberty. The main setting of this story is the internal market, and the creation and preservation of the Union as an area without internal frontiers. This being the horizon, a number of issues emerge that will be found in all the subsequent Parts. Broadly, we have seen how the main framework – the Union as an area of free movement – resulted in a close connection between free movement and deprivation of liberty, with the latter being functional to the former. This is the perfect showcase for the integration–fundamental rights protection dynamic acting as the background of the present story.

If the use of free movement as pole star may result in positive consequences for individuals (restriction on states' use of custodial penalties), it can also come with pitfalls and conundra. The two examples provided here – principle(s) of proportionality and the current Article 49 CFREU – express the legal questions constituting the *fil rouge* of the entire book. Firstly, the involvement of the EU – new legal order of international law – in state-related legal phenomena such as deprivation of liberty imposes a rethink of the traditional understanding of fundamental rights and principles. They cannot be transposed at EU law level as they have been conceived in national traditions but have to be adjusted to the peculiarities of the Union legal order. Secondly, principles and rights can bear different – and sometimes clashing – understandings, depending on the specific area of law concerned. The principle of proportionality provides a clear example in this regard. If these two considerations seem to bring nothing new to the existing debate, the following Parts reveal how such re-conceptualisation is far from being developed in the case of deprivation of liberty.

As such, a bright and a dark side of EU law and deprivation of liberty emerge not only *within* the internal market (where the latter acts as a laboratory for further development) but also *outside* it. Here, the internal market is a trigger and objective of closer Union cooperation, resulting in the use of deprivation of liberty in different forms. The abolition of internal frontiers is the cause and horizon of these measures. They are required to fight serious crimes fostered by free movement, guarantee a functioning system of allocation of responsibility on asylum claims and ensure stronger control at the external borders: in a nutshell, to provide Union citizens and business with *secure* exercise of free movement and *effectiveness* of EU law. Though they are manifold concepts, they are used consistently, transversally and often simultaneously; the next Part on substantive EU criminal law addresses and expands upon all these issues.

PART II

Substantive EU Criminal Law

2

Deprivation of Liberty and Substantive Criminal Law. Overview

I. Introduction

The present Part focuses on the EU rules of substantive criminal law involving deprivation of liberty. Chapter two provides an overview of the Union's use of imprisonment.[1] It discusses the adoption and application of the minimum-maximum criterion – used by the EU to approximate levels of penalties – by considering: how often and for which types of conduct Member States are required to impose that punishment; how the Union legislature accounts for the use of deprivation of liberty; and what levels of penalty the Union imposes on Member States.

Thereafter, the chapter explains the reasons for the choice of the three case studies, and the benchmarks used for their assessment: the principle of proportionality for exercising competences under Article 5 TEU and the principle of legality and proportionality of penalties as provided for in Article 49 CFREU. Chapter two ends with an outline of the main features of EU criminal policy following the Lisbon Treaty, and the EU competence in substantive criminal law.

The next three chapters present a more detailed analysis of three case studies: Directive 2017/1371/EU on the fight against fraud in the Union's financial interests by means of criminal law (or 'PIF Directive'),[2] the Directive amending Council Framework Decision 2004/757/JHA in order to include new psychoactive substances in the definition of 'drug' and repealing Council Decision 2005/387/JHA (or 'the Anti-Drug Trafficking Directive'),[3] and Directive 2014/57/EU ('the Market Abuse Directive' or 'the MAD').[4] Each of these chapters places the

[1] The term 'imprisonment' is hereby used as opposed to the broader 'custodial penalties'. This reflects the terminology used by the Union legislature and its focus of action, not especially concerned with other forms of custody.

[2] Directive (EU) 2017/1371 of the European Parliament and of the Council of 5 July 2017 on the fight against fraud to the Union's financial interests by means of criminal law, [2017] OJ L198/29, 28.7.2017.

[3] Directive (EU) 2017/2103 of the European Parliament and of the Council of 15 November 2017 amending Council Framework Decision 2004/757/JHA in order to include new psychoactive substances in the definition of 'drug' and repealing Council Decision 2005/387/JHA, [2017] OJ L305/12, 21.11.2017.

[4] Directive 2014/57/EU of the European Parliament and of the Council of 16 April 2014 on criminal sanctions for market abuse (market abuse Directive), [2014] OJ L173/179, 12.6.2014.

legislative instrument in the broader legal and policy context, presents the relevant provisions in the text and assesses the relevant materials against the principle of proportionality and Article 49.

The analysis of substantive criminal law reveals that the Union's stance on deprivation of liberty in this area is highly influenced by the setting and three main characters of the present story: the two souls of EU constitutionalisation (integration and fundamental rights protection), security and effectiveness. While imprisonment emerges as the barycentre of the EU legislature's approach to punishment, the broader rationale underlying choices of punishment – and criminalisation broadly – is closely connected to the Union as a borderless area. Security and effectiveness are visible drivers of the Union action: they underpin the two main legal bases for adopting substantive criminal law in Article 83(1) and (2) TFEU, respectively.

In the background, approximation and harsh (custodial) penalties are justified as follows. Firstly, reducing differences between Member State laws is required to prevent potential offenders from exploiting free movement and choosing the legal forum more favourable to their criminal activities. Secondly, penalties that are different and too low make existing law insufficiently deterrent and effective. Thirdly, approximation is meant to facilitate mutual recognition in criminal matters (another example of the role of the internal market as a paradigm of integration).

What is the role, in such a context, for fundamental rights (in this specific case, Article 49 CFREU)? Do fundamental rights and integration pull in the same, or opposite, directions? The assessment of the overall EU approach to deprivation of liberty, and the case studies specifically, reveal problems in terms of legal certainty and proportionality. However, this is not at all connected to an excess of integration. Quite the contrary is true. The need to keep approximation at a minimum level due to political sensitiveness leads to the paradoxical results that EU measures might have detrimental effects on individuals. Furthermore, the combination between approximation and use of imprisonment as punishment, on the one hand, and the structural characteristics of the Union legal order on the other, poses challenges to Article 49. The uniqueness of the EU raises thorny questions concerning the interaction between sources of law, and the extent of EU powers to impose penalties involving the deprivation of liberty.

II. The Use of Imprisonment in EU Substantive Criminal Law. Reasons and Methods

The first reference to custodial penalties in EU law can be found in the Convention on the protection of the European Communities' financial interests (or 'PIF Convention') and its First Protocol (or 'First PIF Protocol').[5] In that case, the EU

[5] Art 2, Convention on the protection of the European Communities' financial interests of 26 July 1995, [1995] OJ C316/49–57; Article 5, Protocol to the Convention on the protection of the European Communities' financial interests of 27 September 1996, [1997] OJ C313/2–10.

required Member States to punish specific forms of conduct with penalties involving deprivation of liberty (at least in serious cases). The same formula was used in the Convention on corruption of EC or Member States' officials.[6] Those references were rather vague, and included in instruments of international law.

The Amsterdam Treaty equipped the EU with a more effective tool in criminal law, the Framework Decisions. As a matter of fact, the first instance of a more specific reference to detention may be seen in FD 2000/383/JHA on money counterfeiting,[7] requiring that

> Each member state shall take the necessary measure to ensure that the conduct referred to in Articles 3 to 5 is punishable by effective, proportionate and dissuasive criminal penalties, including penalties involving deprivation of liberty which can give rise to extradition. The offences of fraudulent making or altering of currency provided for [in Article 3(1)(a)] shall be punishable by terms of imprisonment, the maximum being not less than eight years.[8]

Therefore, the *Greek Maize* formula was used in combination with specific levels of penalties approximated through the minimum-maximum criterion. The latter criterion, however, was formally adopted only in the 2002 Council Conclusions on approximation of penalties.[9] Four levels of minimum-maximum penalty to be established and applied were identified, depending on the seriousness of the conduct: level 1 (penalties with a maximum of at least one to three years' imprisonment); level 2 (penalties with a maximum of at least two to five years' imprisonment); level 3 (penalties with a maximum of at least five to ten years' imprisonment); level 4 (penalties with a maximum of at least ten years' imprisonment). The minimum-maximum guides EU and national legislatures, and Member States' judges in sentencing.

Since FD 2000/383/JHA, the EU has adopted a plethora of instruments in substantive criminal law. All of these measures require the use of imprisonment. The only exceptions are Directives 2008/99/EC and 2009/52/EC,[10] which contain a generic reference to the *Greek Maize* formula.[11] Custodial penalties are used in

[6] Art 5, Convention on the fight against corruption involving officials of the European Communities or officials of Member States of the European Union of 26 May 1997, [1997] OJ C195/2–11.

[7] Council Framework Decision 2000/383/JHA of 29 May 2000 on increasing protection by criminal penalties and other sanctions against counterfeiting in connection with the introduction of the euro, [2000] OJ L140/1, 14.6.2000.

[8] Ibid, Art 6.

[9] Council document of 25 April 2002 on the approach to apply approximation of penalties, 9141/2002.

[10] Directive 2008/99/EC of the European Parliament and of the Council of 19 November 2008 on the protection of the environment through criminal law, [2008] OJ L328/28, 6.12.2008; Directive 2009/52/EC of the European Parliament and of the Council of 18 June 2009 providing for minimum standards on sanctions and measures against employers of illegally staying third-country nationals, [2009] OJ L168/24, 30.6.2009.

[11] However, there is an explanation for that: these are instances of Community criminal law, passed following the *Ship-Source Pollution* case (Case C-440/05, *Commission v Council*, [2007] ECR I-9097) and prior to the entry into force of the Lisbon Treaty. The *Ship-Source Pollution* judgment stated the

various ways: the *Greek Maize* formula plus the minimum-maximum criterion;[12] the *Greek Maize* formula plus a general requirement to provide for deprivation of liberty in specific or particularly serious cases;[13] the use of the sole minimum-maximum criteria;[14] the *Greek Maize* formula plus a range of minimum-maximum term of imprisonment, eg between one and three;[15] and the use of the sole range of a minimum-maximum term of imprisonment.[16]

While the EU has exercised its competences in particularly serious areas of crime – such as terrorism, trafficking in humans, child pornography – the seriousness of the specific conduct might be questioned.[17] Initiatives have also been taken within the economic ambit, eg money counterfeiting, money laundering, corruption in the private sector, market abuse or fraud. Such activities certainly have a negative impact. The 2004 Commission Green Paper on the approximation

existence of a Community competence in criminal matters, but the CJEU limited such power on given conditions (namely, those established in current Art 83.2). Furthermore, the Court only allowed the Community to approximate the definition of the offences, with the penalties remaining within the realm of the law of the 'third pillar'. On that ground, the relevant Directive made no reference to imprisonment because it would have been unlawful, according to the word of the Court of Justice.

[12] FD 2000/383/JHA; Council Framework Decision 2002/475/JHA of 13 June 2002 on combating terrorism, [2002] OJ L164/3, 22.6.2002; Council Framework Decision 2002/946/JHA of 28 November 2002 on the strengthening of the penal framework to prevent the facilitation of unauthorised entry, transit and residence, [2002] OJ L328/1, 5.12.2002; Directive 2011/36/EU of the European Parliament and of the Council of 5 April 2011 on preventing and combating trafficking in human beings and protecting its victims, and replacing Council Framework Decision 2002/629/JHA, [2011] OJ L101/1, 15.4.2011; Directive 2013/40/EU of the European Parliament and of the Council of 12 August 2013 on attacks against information systems and replacing Council Framework Decision 2005/222/JHA, [2013] OJ L218/8, 14.8.2013; Directive 2014/62/EU of the European Parliament and of the Council of 15 May 2014 on the protection of the euro and other currencies against counterfeiting by criminal law, and replacing Council Framework Decision 2000/383/JHA, 21.5.2014, [2014] OJ L151/1; the Market Abuse Directive.

[13] Council Framework Decision 2001/413/JHA of 28 May 2001 combating fraud and counterfeiting of non-cash means of payment, [2001] OJ L149/1, 2.6.2001; Council Framework Decision 2002/629/JHA of 19 July 2002 on combating trafficking in human beings, [2002] OJ L203/1, 1.8.2002; Council Framework Decision 2003/80/JHA of 27 January 2003 on the protection of the environment through criminal law, [2003] OJ L29/55, 5.2.2003.

[14] Council Framework Decision 2001/500/JHA of 26 June 2001 on money laundering, the identification, tracing, freezing, seizing and confiscation of instrumentalities and the proceeds of crime, [2001] OJ L182/1, 5.7.2001; Directive 2011/92/EU of the European Parliament and of the Council of 13 December 2011 on combating the sexual abuse and sexual exploitation of children and child pornography, and replacing Council Framework Decision 2004/68/JHA, [2011] OJ L335/1, 17.12.2011.

[15] Council Framework Decision 2003/568/JHA of 22 July 2003 on combating corruption in the private sector, [2003] OJ L192/54, 31.7.2003; Council Framework Decision 2005/222/JHA of 24 February 2005 on attacks against information systems, [2005] OJ L69/67, 16.3.2005; Council Framework Decision 2005/667/JHA of 12 July 2005 to strengthen the criminal-law framework for the enforcement of the law against ship-source pollution, [2005] OJ L255/164, 30.9.2005.

[16] Council Framework Decision 2004/68/JHA of 22 December 2003 on combating the sexual exploitation of children and child pornography, [2004] OJ L13/44, 20.1.2004.

[17] This is especially the case for attempts, aiding and abetting. Furthermore, it should be noted that there is no consistent definition nor criteria to identify what a serious crime is. See A Paoli, A Adriaenssen, VA Greenfield and M Conickx, 'Exploring Definitions of Serious Crime in EU Policy Documents and Academic Publications: A Content Analysis and Policy Implications' (2017) 23(3) *European Journal of Criminal Policy & Research* 269–85.

of criminal sanctions[18] endorses the use of sanctions other than deprivation of liberty (financial penalties, disqualifications and confiscation).[19] Though alternative penalties are sporadically mentioned, the barycentric role of imprisonment has never been questioned. A negative consequence of such a use of imprisonment is that states are obliged to impose deprivation of liberty in areas or for conduct they did not before.

In terms of specificity,[20] the question arises: why is there a need to establish a range for a minimum-maximum term of imprisonment? Such a criterion imposes on Member States a limit below which they shall not go, as far as the highest term of imprisonment is concerned. However, it grants national authorities a generous margin for manoeuvre. Far from being an effective medium of harmonisation, it leaves states with their minimum (if any is provided in Member States for that specific crime) and some discretion as to the maximum term of punishment, since they can still use higher terms of imprisonment.

The maximum levels of penalty laid down in substantive EU criminal law are generally true to those envisaged by the Council.[21] As for the rationale behind imprisonment, the overriding reason is the need to address state laws' differences, and to contribute to the development of efficient judicial and law enforcement cooperation against crime. Not surprisingly, the accent is heavily on (general and specific) prevention. Imprisonment aims to increase compliance with the law,[22] and has a strong deterrent effect. Occasionally, general prevention is flanked by the retributive element.[23] The Union never engages with the actual reach of such a deterrent effect, or with the possibility that the latter might work better on some conduct, and worse on others.

Furthermore, the use of the minimum-maximum criterion as a method of approximation of the levels of penalty reveals the pragmatic nature of the EU approach to deprivation of liberty in substantive criminal law: facilitating judicial

[18] Commission Green Paper on the approximation, mutual recognition and enforcement of criminal sanctions in the European Union, Brussels, 30.04.2004 COM(2004) 334 final.

[19] Ibid, 15 onwards.

[20] It may be observed that only in two circumstances does the instrument at stake generally mention deprivation of liberty without introducing a specific threshold. At any rate, these are rather old instruments, and the well-established praxis is to issue Directives (earlier FDs) with a specific indication of the minimum-maximum sentence of imprisonment that Member States should introduce.

[21] The FD on corruption in the private sector provides for one or three years, depending on circumstances. The Market Abuse Directive imposes two or four years' imprisonment, whereas the Money-Counterfeiting Directive features five or eight years. The FD on trafficking in human beings punishes conduct with five or 10 years' imprisonment, the FD on unauthorised entry, with eight years, the Directive on terrorism, eight or 15 years.

[22] See in particular Directive 2008/99/EC, recital 3 and Directive 2009/52/EC, recital 21.

[23] The retribution element may be used in a generic way, where the EU instrument requires punishment of more serious violations with imprisonment. This is especially the case of the first FDs enacted, such as FD 2001/413/JHA. Otherwise, the reference may be specific. Think of all those instruments providing for aggravated penalties where the offence is committed in the context of a criminal organisation, or where the crime is conducted on a large scale, affecting a significant number of persons, or it causes serious damage (see eg Directive 2013/40/EU, recital 13).

cooperation between Member States. Judicial cooperation and mutual recognition in the EU can take place as long as there are offences punishable by the law of the issuing Member State with a custodial sentence or a detention order for a maximum period of at least 12 months. The minimum-maximum criterion is the real *fil rouge* which ties substantive to procedural criminal laws at EU level. The following chapters cast doubt on the soundness of the use of imprisonment and its possible impact in terms of legal coherence.

III. The Case Studies: Rationales and Criteria of Analysis

The case studies analysed in the following chapters are comparable – though not identical – examples of post-Lisbon use of imprisonment by the EU legislature. Three main reasons support the choice of these specific instruments.

Firstly, they are upheld by the European Commission as instances of a more coherent approach to criminal law following the Lisbon Treaty.[24] Secondly, the case studies stem from different rationales underlying criminalisation and the use of imprisonment pursuant to the Lisbon Treaty:[25] *securitised criminalisation* under Article 83(1) TFEU, allowing for approximation to fight particularly serious areas of cross-border crime (such as terrorism, organised crime, etc); *functional criminalisation* under Article 83(2) TFEU, where minimum rules are essential to ensure the effective implementation of EU policy which has already been subject to harmonisation; and possible and contested forms of criminalisation outside the AFJS, with the most prominent expression being Article 325 TFEU on the protection of the EU's financial interests.[26]

Thirdly, they are in line with the viewpoint of this book. They cover areas where EU criminal law measures are required in relation to the maintenance of the Union as a borderless area.[27] The connection materialises in the need to facilitate judicial cooperation and preserve the integrity of the internal market. This goes without saying for the MAD and the PIF Directive, but also with regards to the Anti-Drug

[24] See the European Commission Memo and related documents, *The Future EU Justice and Home Affairs Agenda: Questions and Answers*, Strasbourg, 11 March 2014; see also http://ec.europa.eu/justice/newsroom/effective-justice/news/140311_en.htm.

[25] V Mitsilegas, *EU Criminal Law after Lisbon: Rights, Trust and the Transformation of Justice in Europe* (Oxford, Hart Publishing, 2016).

[26] See for instance V Mitsilegas, ibid; S Miettinen, 'Implied ancillary criminal law competence after Lisbon' (2013) 3(2) *European Criminal Law Review* 194–219.

[27] On the principle guiding the use of Art 83(2) TFEU, see Communication from the Commission to the European Parliament, the Council, the European Economic and Social Committee and the Committee of Regions, Towards an EU criminal policy: Ensuring the effective implementation of EU policies through criminal law, Brussels 20.9.2011, COM(2011) 573 final.

Trafficking Directive. Indeed, trafficking in narcotic and illicit substances allows perpetrators to make huge profits, which in turn are re-introduced into the legal market. In this respect, EU action on money laundering and freezing, recovery and confiscation of crime proceeds is explicitly related to drug trafficking.[28] The Anti-Drug Trafficking Directive is connected to the internal market also by virtue of the Regulation on the market of new psychoactive substances within the EU.[29] The Regulation sets up a system of control on new psychoactive substances. The Directive represents the *armed branch* of regulation, requiring Member States to criminalise conduct related to the use and selling of substances bearing risk to health and security.

The recourse to deprivation of liberty in EU substantive criminal law is analysed by answering the following questions: is the Union legislature's use of imprisonment justified? Are the rules on offences and levels of punishment clear and proportionate? The answer to the first question is one of proportionate exercise of competences, and is therefore tested against Article 5 TEU. The analysis considers the documents underlying the legally binding texts as strictly understood: communications, reports, impact assessments (IA), as well as the preambles of the Directives. Paying attention to Union soft law, conclusions are drawn on why the Union resorts to deprivation of liberty. This is the method suggested by scholars to discern the main traits of the European criminal law policy.[30] The compliance of the instruments with Article 5 TEU *tout court* is not questioned. The discussion, however, highlights flaws and a lack of elaboration in the legislature's choice of criminal law and imprisonment, especially with regards to other legislative options.

The second question comes with an assessment under Article 49 CFREU, entitled *Principles of legality and proportionality of criminal offences and penalties*.[31]

[28] Furthermore, the EU is revising its tools on this topic, as revealed by Directive (EU) 2018/843 of the European Parliament and of the Council of 30 May 2018 amending Directive (EU) 2015/849 on the prevention of the use of the financial system for the purposes of money laundering or terrorist financing, and amending Directives 2009/138/EC and 2013/36/EU [2018] OJ L 156/43 19.6.2018, and Directive 2014/42/EU of the European Parliament and of the Council of 3 April 2014 on the freezing and confiscation of instrumentalities and proceeds of crime in the European Union, [2014] OJ L127/39, 29.4.2014.

[29] Regulation 2017/2101 amending Regulation (EC) No 1920/2006 as regards information exchange on, and an early warning system and risk assessment procedure for, new psychoactive substances. The Directive aims to amend Council Framework Decision 2004/757/JHA in order to include new psychoactive substances in the definition of 'drug', and to repeal Council Decision 2005/387/JHA.

[30] A Klip, *European Criminal Law: An Integrative Approach* (Cambridge, Intersentia, 2012), 218 onwards.

[31] See, among many, V Mitsilegas, 'Article 49' in S Peers and others (eds), *The EU Charter of Fundamental Rights. A Commentary* (Oxford, Hart Publishing, 2014) 1351–71. C Murphy, 'The Principle of Legality in Criminal Law under the ECHR' (2010) 2 *European Human Rights Law Review* 192 onwards. A Klip, *European Criminal Law*, n 30 above; A Bernardi, 'Riserva di legge e fonti europee in materia penale' (2006) *Annali dell'Università di Ferrara* 1–90; and, 'I principi di sussidiarietà e di legalità nel diritto penale europeo' (2012) 25(1)–(2) *Rivista Trimestrale di Diritto Penale dell'Economia* 15–65, 30 onwards.

The principle of legality represents the pre-eminent observation point in the analysis of substantive criminal law.[32] Article 49 reads as follows:

> 1. No one shall be held guilty of any criminal offence on account of any act or omission which did not constitute a criminal offence under national law or international law at the time when it was committed. Nor shall a heavier penalty be imposed than that which was applicable at the time the criminal offence was committed. If, subsequent to the commission of a criminal offence, the law provides for a lighter penalty, that penalty shall be applicable.
> 2. This Article shall not prejudice the trial and punishment of any person for any act or omission which, at the time when it was committed, was criminal according to the general principles recognised by the community of nations.
> 3. The severity of penalties must not be disproportionate to the criminal offence.

The EU principle of legality poses different boundaries to the exercise of public powers: the obligation that a criminal rule be based on the law;[33] the non-retroactivity or adverse/retroactivity of more lenient penal provisions; the requirement that the penalty should be proportionate to the individual conduct. According to the Explanations to the Charter, the rights guaranteed here have the same meaning and scope as the right guaranteed by the ECHR. The ECtHR regards the principle of legality as a principle of legal certainty.[34] According to the Strasbourg Court case-law, 'law' also includes judicial law-making, and is endowed with specific qualities. These qualities are *accessibility*[35] (understood as *material accessibility to* and *clarity of* the norms) and *foreseeability* (regarding both the rules[36] and the judicial interpretation).[37] This means that the boundaries between legal and illegal behaviour must be comprehensible and clearly identifiable in a given legal source, on the one hand (synchronic certainty); on the other, it

[32] From a comparative and international perspective, see K Gallant, *The Principle of Legality in International and Comparative Criminal Law* (Cambridge, Cambridge University Press, 2009); G Hallevy, *A Modern Treatise on the Principle of Legality in Criminal Law* (Berlin, Springer, 2010).

[33] Furthermore, one should notice the reference of Art 49 to the possible legal basis of criminalisation: not only for national law, but also international law.

[34] However, authors such as Bernardi strongly criticised the CJEU case-law on the principle of legality, since the Luxembourg judges would have resorted to the ECtHR case-law only to the smallest extent. See from the author, among many publications, 'Riserva di legge e fonti europee in materia penale', n 31 above, 51 onwards, as well as 'I principi di sussidiarietà e legalità', n 31 above, 40 onwards.

[35] ECtHR, *Sunday Times v the United Kingdom*, Application No 6538/74, judgment of 26 April 1979, para 49; ECtHR, *Silver et al v the United Kingdom*, Applications No 5947/72; 6205/73; 7052/75; 7061/75; 7107/75; 7113/75; 7136/75, judgment of 25 March 1983, para 87; ECtHR, *Achour v Francia*, Application No 67335/01, judgment of 29 March 2006, para 42.

[36] In particular, foreseeability involves considerations on the precision of the norm, the meaning it assumes in the wider legislative context and the characteristics of the addressees. See EComHR, *X v Austria*, Application No 7830/77, 4 December 1978; EComHR, *Crociani et al v Italia*, Applications No 8603/79, 8722/79, 8723/79, 8729/79, 18 December 1980.

[37] ECtHR, *Kokkinakis v Greece*, Application No 14307/88, judgment of 25 May 1993, para 40; ECtHR *Baskaya v OkcËuoglu v Turkey*, Applications No 23536/94 and 24408/94, judgment of 8 July 1999, para 36.

requires that rules are interpreted in a way that is predictable and 'plausible in the context of a particular legal order' (diachronic certainty).[38]

As we know, Directives in criminal law establish minimum rules and require implementation at national level. Issues of legal certainty ensue from peculiar aspects of the Union legal order, rather than from the mere discretion left by the specific instruments. Examples in this regard relate to the interaction between different sources of EU law, direct applicability and the use of umbrella concepts.

The second aspect of Article 49 is criminal law proportionality. The Explanations to the Charter state that the general principle of proportionality between penalties and criminal offences is enshrined in the common constitutional traditions of the Member States and in the case-law of the Court of Justice. This part of the discussion revolves around the levels of punishment imposed by the EU legislature. It is submitted that the application of the minimum-maximum criterion and the use of mitigating circumstances can have significant impact in terms of proportionality under Article 49.

Article 49 CFREU concerns the severity of the penalty in relation to the seriousness of the offence, whereas Article 5 TEU refers to the proportionate exercise of competences in relation to the objective pursued. Article 49 CFREU is used to evaluate the levels of penalty in relation to the offence, whereas Article 5 tests the use of imprisonment in relation to the objective of the specific legislative instrument.

The assessment of substantive criminal law reveals that the EU approach is shaped by its peculiarities as a legal order. Integration in the use of imprisonment is what makes the Union as an area of free movement sustainable. Developments in this area, however, do result in challenges to traditional strongholds of personal liberty such as the principle of legality. Issues concerning interaction between sources of law and direct applicability arise in the context of the Union's constitutional structure, which likewise requires adjustment of those traditional guarantees to answer unprecedented questions raised by the evolutionary nature of the EU.

IV. Deprivation of Liberty and Substantive EU Criminal Law. The Policy Context

The Lisbon Treaty features a different legal basis for the enactment of criminal law legislation. Those measures follow political and legislative guidelines in the AFJS regularly adopted by the Council, as well as area-specific documents (eg protection of the EU's financial interests). The latest example[39] of comprehensive guidelines is

[38] C Peristeridou, *The principle of legality in European criminal law* (Cambridge/Antwerp, Intersentia, 2015) 58–61.

[39] The more recent legislative guidelines provided by the Council in June 2014 are not treated here as a 'programme'. Indeed, the latter cannot be considered properly as a 'programme', as they limit

the 2010–14[40] Stockholm Programme, that being also the policy framework from which the case studies stem.

Consistent with the spirit of the Treaty legal basis, the Stockholm Programme states that minimum rules may be established when they proves essential to ensure the effective implementation of a Union policy which has been subject to harmonisation measures.[41] Attention is also paid to serious areas of crime, such as drug trafficking, terrorism, trafficking in human beings, and the importance of fighting them by tackling the financial gain ensuing from those activities.[42]

As for imprisonment, the Programme states the importance of implementing the European Prison Rules and alternatives to detention, by exploring the possibilities offered by the Lisbon Treaty in this respect.[43]

In the communication 'Towards an EU criminal policy: Ensuring the effective implementation of EU policies through criminal law', criminal law is regarded as a response to citizens' concerns and a tool for the effective implementation of EU policies.[44] In terms of a legal basis for approximation in substantive criminal law, the communication distinguishes between Article 83(1), Article 83(2) and Article 325(4) TFEU, with the latter providing for the possibility to take *measures* (not only Directives) in the field of prevention and fighting against fraud affecting the financial interests of the Union.

As for the use of Article 83(1) TFEU, there is no defined policy test, although references to the impact and nature of the offences as criteria to define their seriousness are regularly mentioned by the EU institutions.[45] With regards to Article 83(2), the rules on the definition of offences and levels of penalty would increase deterrence, and would compensate for Member States' deficiencies in the enforcement of EU policies.[46] The decision on criminalisation should follow a two-step test.[47] Firstly, impact assessments appraise the necessity and proportionality

themselves to outline a very generic framework concerning the AFJS activity for the next five years, with an 'intermediate review' set for 2017. Such self-restraint is expressed through the scant number of issues dealt with (mainly migration control and terrorism) and particularly vague references to the need for guaranteeing an authentic space of security to citizens, as well as the strengthening of individuals' procedural rights. See the document European Council conclusions, EUCO 79/14, Brussels, 27 June 2014. For a comment, see Athina Giannakoula, 'The European Agenda on Security – A Comment' (2016) 6 *European Criminal Law Review* 99.

[40] The Stockholm Programme – An open and secure Europe serving and protecting citizens, [2010] OJ C115/1. For the approach of Commission to the Stockholm Programme, see L Buono, *From Tampere to the Hague and beyond: the Stockholm Programme in the area of freedom, security and justice*, ERA Forum: http://link.springer.com/article/10.1007%2Fs12027-009-0127-2, 4 April 2009.

[41] [2010] OJ C115/1, para 3.3.1.

[42] The Stockholm Programme, n 40 above, [2010] OJ C115/21–24.

[43] Ibid, 14.

[44] COM(2011) 573 final, para 1. For critical remarks on the risks of 'criminal populism', see E Herlin-Karnell, 'Is the Citizen driving the EU's Criminal Law Agenda?' in M Dougan, E Spaventa and N Nic Shuibhne (eds), *Empowerment and Disempowerment of the European Citizen* (Oxford, Hart Publishing, 2012), 19 onwards.

[45] Paoli and others, n 17 above, 280.

[46] COM(2011) 573 final, paras 1–3.

[47] Ibid, para 2.2, p 7 onwards.

of a measure by looking at: the effectiveness of Member States' sanction regimes; and the specificities of the policy area concerned. Should the need for criminal law measures at EU level be demonstrated, the issue arises as to what kind of measure to adopt. Clear factual evidence about the nature and the effect of the crime in question should be brought. As the minimum rules referred to in Article 83 have no direct effect on citizens, the principle of legal certainty requires that EU law state clearly the result to be achieved. Furthermore, the use of sanctions other than imprisonment should be considered.

Both the *pre-* and *post-*Lisbon EU's approach to penalties (and imprisonment as the centre of gravity thereof) focuses on particularly sensitive areas of crime, and on the implementation of important EU extra-criminal policies. Deterrence is the main driver in the Union's action in this area. The case studies show the inconsistency between the stated principles and their implementation through specific legislation. This holds true for the alternatives to imprisonment – formally endorsed but never really espoused by the legislature[48] – and the principles of legal certainty, necessity and proportionality.

V. Deprivation of Liberty and Substantive EU Criminal Law. The Legal Framework

Deprivation of liberty in EU substantive criminal law occurs in the context of approximation of penalties through the minimum-maximum criterion. Member States are required to punish a certain offence with a term of imprisonment that, at its maximum, must not go below a specific threshold.

The issue of deprivation of liberty at Union level is to be placed in the broader context of legal integration in EU law, and criminal law specifically. Harmonisation would entail the abolition of differences amongst Member States' laws, by laying down a unitary legal framework. Approximation would intend to reduce discrepancies, without completely eliminating them. However, scholars seem to consider approximation and minimum harmonisation (or harmonisation *tout court*) as equivalent.[49] Such a conclusion is underpinned by the same TFEU, which seems to use approximation and harmonisation indistinguishably,[50] as also does the CJEU.[51]

[48] For examples of post-Lisbon legislation, and other than the norms hereby assumed as case studies, the Directives relate to attack against information systems, trafficking in human beings and child pornography.

[49] A Bernardi, 'L'armonizzazione delle sanzioni in Europa: linee ricostruttive' in G Grasso and R Sicurella (eds), *Per un rilancio del progetto europeo. Esigenze di tutela degli interessi comunitari e nuove strategie di integrazione penale* (Milano, Giuffrè, 2008) 76–132; A Klip, *European Criminal Law*, n 30 above, 32; A Weyembergh, *L'harmonisation des législations pénales: condition de l'espace pénal européen et révélateur de ses tensions* (Bruxelles, Editions de l'Université de Bruxelles, 2004) 31–36.

[50] See for instance Art 114 TFEU.

[51] Case C-66/04, *United Kingdom v European Parliament and Council* [2005] ECR I-10553, paras 45–50; Case C-217/04 *United Kingdom v European Parliament and Council* [2006] ECR I-3771.

As to the nature of approximation, one can distinguish between:[52] substantive approximation, which relates to norms of substantive criminal law, such as the constituent elements of the conduct, the circumstances, the *mens rea*, the penalty provided and the like; procedural approximation, which in turn may be understood as procedural approximation *stricto sensu* (rules related to national criminal procedure) and procedural approximation *lato sensu* (rules on conditions and procedures for regulating the function of the mutual recognition principle, such as the EAW).

According to Weyembergh, one may distinguish three different facets of approximation in criminal matters at EU level: sources,[53] degrees[54] and functions.[55] However, substantive approximation and procedural approximation *stricto sensu* have encountered difficulties, due to the resistance of Member States in this respect. The same Treaty refers to the requirement that EU criminal law be

[52] C Janssens, *The principle of mutual recognition in EU Law* (Oxford, Oxford University Press, 2013) 186.

[53] A Weyembergh, 'The functions of approximation of penal legislation within the European Union' (2005) 12(2) *Maastricht Journal of European and Comparative Law* 149–72. The author identifies three kinds of sources. Firstly, texts which directly and expressly aim to approximate penal laws. Secondly, marginal sources of approximation. Such a category encompasses instruments that are intended to have judicial cooperation, but that have an approximation effect, insofar as they introduce similar provisions into the different internal judicial system. Hereby the CoE Conventions, and EU instruments such as the EAW FD may be included. Thirdly, there are indirect sources of approximation of law, that is to say the ECHR, as well as the ECtHR's and CJEU's case-law.

[54] A Weyembergh, *L'harmonisation des législations pénales*, n 49 above. The main difference lies between coordination and cooperation, harmonisation or approximation, unification. Under the first sort of integration mentioned, 'les droit nationaux demeurent en principe ce qu'ils sont'. On the other side, harmonisation 'implique des adaptations de droit nationaux en fonction d'objectifs ou de résultats définis et imposés. Harmoniser des systèmes normatifs différentes consiste à établir entre eux des analogies ou des similitudes en fonction d'un objectif concerté en éliminant celles de leurs divergences qui sont incompatibles'. Furthermore, 'l'harmonisation permet en principe de maintenir une certaine souplesse et s'adapte, dans une certaine mesure du moins, aux spécificités locales'. The deepest means of integration is represented by unification, which 'répond a une volonté de systématiser le droit [et] implique … la substitution d'une règle commune nouvelle à des règles nationales préexistantes et correspond ainsi à l'hypothèse de transfert de compétence'.

[55] A Weyembergh, 'Approximation of criminal laws, the Constitutional Treaty and the Hague Programme' (2005) 42 *Common Market Law Review* 1574 onwards; A Weyembergh, 'The functions of approximation of penal legislation within the European Union', n 53 above. Concerning those functions, one may identify auxiliary functions and autonomous functions. Under the first category, approximation may be seen: as a tool for a smooth judicial cooperation mechanism (and especially mutual recognition); as a condition for the establishment of European actors in criminal matters. According to the autonomous functions, approximation is needed for improving the fight against crime ('sword' function), but also to protect individuals against the potential Member State abuses ('shield' function). Furthermore, it would be conducive to free movement across the EU, by providing citizens with legal transparency and certainty, as well as to reduce differences between European legal subjects. A similar stand is taken by A Bernardi, 'Politiche di armonizzazione e sistema sanzionatorio penale' in T Rafaraci (ed), *L'area di libertà sicurezza e giustizia: alla ricerca di un equilibrio fra priorità repressive ed esigenze di garanzia* (Milano, Giuffrè, 2007) 199 onwards. For further in-depth analysis from the same author, see among many 'L'armonizzazione delle sanzioni in Europa linee ricostruttive', n 49 above; and 'I tre volti del diritto penale comunitario' (1999) *Rivista Italiana di Diritto Pubblico Comunitario* 333–79.

minimum, thereby causing a heated debated about the actual meaning and reach of such a requirement.[56]

As a general principle, Article 67(3) TFEU envisages approximation in criminal law only *if necessary*. Article 83 TFEU provides two legal bases for approximation. Article 83(1) empowers the EU to

> establish minimum rules concerning the definition of criminal offences and sanctions in areas of particularly serious crime with a cross-border dimension, resulting from the nature or impact of such offences or from a special need to combat them on a common basis.[57]

Pursuant to Article 83(2) TFEU,

> if the approximation of criminal laws and regulations of the Member States proves essential to ensuring the effective implementation of a Union policy in an area which has been subject to harmonisation measures, directives may establish minimum rules with regards to the definition of criminal offences and sanctions in the area concerned.

The wording of the legal basis caused uncertainty. The notion of *particularly serious crime*, as well as the meaning of *cross-border dimension* in Article 83(1) TFEU is not straightforward.[58] As Mitsilegas argues,[59] the reference to a *cross-border dimension* seems not to require that the criminal phenomena at stake be inherently transnational. Furthermore, Article 83(1) refers to *areas* of crime rather than specific conducts, so that the provision might turn out to be on a 'catch-all' basis.[60] The Directive on confiscation is an example of a 'generous' use of the Article 83(1) legal basis, which allows for establishment of minimum rules on (1) definition of offences and (2) levels of penalty. The Directive aims to approximate the use of confiscation of proceeds of conducts committed in the context of organised crime. On the one hand, the definitions of the offences are not approximated; on the other, confiscation is treated as a measure rather than a penalty, so that the object of approximation in using Article 83(1) (definition of offences and levels of penalties) seems not to be fulfilled.

Article 83(2) establishes three conditions for the enactment of substantive criminal law.[61] The instrument must be (1) *essential* to ensure the (2) *effective* implementation in an area (3) *already subject to harmonisation measures*. Effectiveness is

[56] However, for an interpretation of 'minimum criminalisation' as 'maximum criminalisation', see A Klip, *European Criminal Law*, n 30 above.

[57] These areas include: terrorism, trafficking in human beings and sexual exploitation of women and children, illicit drug trafficking, illicit arms trafficking, money laundering, corruption, counterfeiting of means of payment, computer crime and organised crime.

[58] See for commentaries, Asp, *The substantive criminal law competence of the EU* (Skrifter utgivna av Juridiska fakulteten vid Stockholms Universitet, 2012) 73–78; A Suominen, 'Effectiveness and Functionality of substantive EU criminal law' (2014) 5(3) *New Journal of European Criminal Law* 388, 390 onwards; H Satzger, *International and European Criminal Law* (Oxford, Hart Publishing, 2012) 72–76.

[59] V Mitsilegas, *EU Criminal Law After Lisbon*, n 25 above.

[60] Ibid, 117.

[61] E Herlin-Karnell, 'EU Competence in Criminal Law after Lisbon' in A Biondi, P Eeckhout and S Ripley (eds), *EU Law After Lisbon* (Oxford, Oxford University Press, 2012) 333.

a foundational principle of EU law,[62] used in the context of seminal judgments of EU criminal law.[63] This cannot be a surprise, since Union law is inherently dependent on Member States' implementation.[64]

The 'essentiality' test examines whether criminal laws are more effective than non-criminal laws in enforcing the EU policy in the terms just specified.[65]

For its part, effectiveness has been relied on to set aside national legislation conflicting with EU law,[66] but also to incentivise legislative actions[67] and promote consistent interpretation. Effectiveness aims to achieve higher compliance with the Union rules. In the context of criminal penalties, we have seen how the *effectiveness* requirement goes hand in hand with *proportionality* and *deterrence*. The use of notions such as effectiveness and dissuasiveness is consistent with the deterrence-oriented approach to (custodial) penalties in EU law sketched above:[68] 'The efficiency-driven EU criminal policy clearly represents utilitarian philosophy [for inducing members of the community to abide by the law] but from an integration-oriented approach'.[69] To this end, the dissuasiveness of criminal penalties should result in higher effectiveness of (compliance with) EU law. However, scholars have criticised the *effectiveness* requirement of Article 83(2) TFEU as an unsuitable orienting criterion for EU competences in criminal law, due to its 'huge constitutional slipperiness'. Furthermore, it would fail to take into account other enforcement mechanisms under Union law and national law.[70]

Other than being effective and dissuasive, penalties must be proportionate. The Court has not elaborated on the precise meaning of this test, the reason why both proportionality tests under Articles 49 and 52 CFREU are relied on in this episode.

VI. Conclusions

The development of the EU's use of imprisonment occurs against the integration–fundamental rights protection dynamic. The main view is that approximation of

[62] See among many Cases C-6/90 and C-9/90 *Francovich and Francovich v Italian Republic*, [1991] ECR I-5357.

[63] E Herlin-Karnell, 'Effectiveness and constitutional limits in European criminal law' (2014) 5(3) *New Journal of European Criminal Law* 267–73.

[64] M Accetto and S Zleptnig, 'The Principle of Effectiveness: Rethinking Its Role in Community Law' (2005) 11 *European Public Law* 375.

[65] J Öberg, 'Do we really need criminal sanctions for the enforcement of EU law?' (2014) 5(3) *New Journal of European Criminal Law* 370–87.

[66] Case C-106/77, *Amministrazione delle Finanze dello Stato v Simmenthal SpA*, [1978] ECR 629.

[67] Case C-91/02, *Hannl + Hofstetter Internationale Spedition GmbH v Finanzlandesdirektion für Wien, Niederösterreich und Burgenland*, [2003] ECR I-2077, para 17.

[68] S Melander, 'Effectiveness in EU criminal law and its effects on the general part of criminal law' (2014) 5(3) *New Journal of European Criminal Law* 274–300.

[69] M Huomo-Kettunen, 'EU criminal policy at a crossroads between effectiveness and traditional restraints for the use of criminal law' (2014) 5(3) *New Journal of European Criminal Law* 314 onwards.

[70] E Herlin-Karnell, *The Constitutional Dimension of European Criminal Law*, 1st edn (Oxford, Hart Publishing, 2012) 57–65.

offences and penalties is necessary to the preservation of the Union as a borderless area: namely, preventing potential offenders from exploiting free movement and from choosing the best legal forum to engage in criminal activities.

The legal bases for criminalisation in the Treaties crystallise the story of legal integration in this area, as they revolve around the fight against cross-border crime (*securitised criminalisation*), and support the effective implementation of EU law and policies (*functional criminalisation*). The policy guidelines issued by the Union's institutions state two priorities: that criminalisation and harmonisation of penalties should be pursued in compliance with the principle of proportionality and legal certainty; and that the use of penalties other than imprisonment should be considered by the legislature.

Firstly, the overview provided in the present chapter highlights that the Union never renounces the recourse to deprivation of liberty, and this holds true for post-Lisbon instruments as well. Secondly, it was shown that the criterion adopted to approximate penalties (the minimum-maximum) lends itself to incentivising an increase in level of imprisonment. The three case studies analysed over the next three chapters expand on these issues. With the overarching framework of the story in mind, they bring to the fore the critical aspects of the EU approach to deprivation of liberty in substantive criminal law.

3

The PIF Directive

I. Introduction

The protection of the Union's financial interests has been key to pursuing outstanding changes in EU (criminal) law. Such a development was promoted by the Court, which endowed specific provisions of the Treaties with unexpected legal force. In the *Greek Maize* case, the CJEU introduced the obligation on Member States to provide for *effective, proportionate* and *dissuasive sanctions*, if needed to ensure implementation of a fundamental EC policy (protection of financial interests of the EC). On fraud, there was focus on the *Corpus Iuris*, a sort of mini-criminal code unifying state laws.[1] The project never saw the light of day, and was replaced by the Convention for the protection of the financial interests of the European Communities and accompanying protocols ('the PIF Convention').[2] Other initiatives were taken in this respect, with the Commission pushing in vain for the adoption of criminal rules against fraud by using a 'first pillar' legal basis.[3] The issue of the legal basis – central to the 2005 and 2007 CJEU judgments – is still relevant even after the communitarisation of criminal law.

The protection of the EU's financial interests, and the PIF Directive specifically, embody the EU's quest for expansion of competences through policy. In the Commission's communications on criminal policy and the protection of the EU's financial interests by criminal law,[4] combating fraud was related to the legal basis: Article 325(4) TFEU would provide for 'the specific possibility to take measures

[1] See, inter alia, M Delmas-Marty (ed), *Corpus Juris introducing penal provisions for the purpose of the financial interests of the European Union* (Paris, Editions Economica, 1997); M Delmas-Marty and JAE Vervaele (eds), *The Implementation of the Corpus Juris in the Member States: penal provisions for the protection of European finances* (Utrecht, Intersentia, 2000).

[2] Convention of 26 July 1995 [2005] OJ C316/49, 27.11.1995) (fraud); First Protocol of 27 September 1996 ([1996] OJ C313, 23.10.1996, p. 2) and Convention of 26 May 1997 ([1997] OJ C195, 25.6.1997) (corruption); Protocol of 29 November 1996 ([1997] OJ C151, 20.5.1997, p 2); Second Protocol of 19 June 1997 ([1997] OJ C221, 19.7.1997, p 12).

[3] 'Proposal for a Directive of the European Parliament and the Council on the criminal-law protection of the Community's financial interests', Brussels 23.5.2001, COM(2001) 272 final.

[4] Communication from the Commission to the European Parliament, the Council, the European Economic and Social Committee and the Committee of Regions, on the protection of the financial interests of the European Union by criminal law and by administrative investigations. An integrated policy to safeguard taxpayers' money, Brussels 26.5.2011, COM(2011) 293 final.

in the field of the prevention of and the fight against fraud affecting the financial interests of the Union'.[5] Pursuant to that provision, the EU 'shall adopt the necessary measures in the fields of the prevention of and fight against fraud'. Article 325(4) TFEU refers to *measures* rather than Directives, and deletes the prohibition, present in its previous version, according to which such measures '[would] not concern the application of national criminal law or the national administration of the justice'.[6]

Shortly after the introduction of the *Greek Maize* formula, the EU legislature flanked the requirement of proportionate, dissuasive and effective penalties with the obligation for Member States to use custodial penalties in the most serious cases. The need to ensure effectiveness of Union-specific law and policies has paved the way to the adoption of coercive measures imposed by EU law. While the protection of financial interests is not the only policy used to support the expansion of the Union's powers, it constitutes a privileged observation point.

The recent *Taricco* saga confirmed the importance of the EU constitutional context to better understanding its approach to (custodial) penalties. Based on the effective protection of the EU's budget through appropriate sanctions, the Court found for the direct applicability of Article 325(4) TFEU and the subsequent disapplication of national rules on discontinuation of criminal proceedings that could jeopardise the objective of that provision.[7] This finding resulted in serious issues of legal certainty and legality, which the CJEU tried to assuage in *Taricco II*.[8]

The PIF Directive has been negotiated and enacted within the integration–fundamental rights protection dynamic. On the one hand, the reasons underlying the legislative proposal confirm the importance of the Union's borderless area as the main horizon; on the other, further harmonisation on grounds of effectiveness of a Union-specific policy raises thorny questions in terms of proportionality and legal certainty.

[5] Ibid, para 1.

[6] Art 280(4) EC. The same has happened to Art 33 TFEU and its predecessor (Art 135 EC).

[7] Case C-105/14, *Criminal proceedings against Ivo Taricco and Others*, Judgment of the Court (Grand Chamber) of 8 September 2015. For comments, see Emmanouil Billis, 'The European Court of Justice: A "Quasi-Constitutional Court" in Criminal Matters? The Taricco Judgment and its Shortcomings' (2016) 7 *New Journal of European Criminal Law* 20; M Caianiello, 'Dum Romae (et Brucsellae) Consulitur …: Some considerations on the taricco judgment and its consequences at National and European level' (2016) 24 *European Journal of Crime, Criminal Law and Criminal Justice* 1; Stefano Manacorda, 'The Taricco saga: A risk or an opportunity for European Criminal Law?' (2018) 9 *New Journal of European Criminal Law* 4; Vittorio Manes, 'Some lessons from the Taricco saga' (2018) 9 *New Journal of European Criminal Law* 12; Valsamis Mitsilegas, 'The evolving relationship between European criminal law and national constitutional law: Lessons from the Taricco litigation' (2018) 9 *New Journal of European Criminal Law* 3; M Timmerman, 'Balancing effective criminal sanctions with effective fundamental rights protection in cases of VAT fraud: Taricco' (2016) 53 *Common Market Law Review* 779; Francesco Viganò, 'Melloni overruled? Considerations on the 'Taricco II' judgment of the Court of Justice' (2018) 9 *New Journal of European Criminal Law* 18.

[8] Case C-42/17, *Criminal proceedings against MAS and MB*, Judgment of the Court (Grand Chamber) of 5 December 2017, EU:C:2017:936.

The chapter is structured as follows. Firstly, the Directive is described. Secondly, the text and preparatory documents are tested against the principle of proportionality and Article 49 CFREU. The assessment homes in on the function attached by the EU legislature to criminal law and imprisonment and the dispute over the appropriate legal basis on which to adopt the Directive. The dispute over the legal basis is directly connected to the broader issue – discussed in the *Taricco* rulings – of the use of policy legal basis to establish criminal liability 'directly' on the basis of EU law. Furthermore, the potential establishment of a minimum threshold of punishment in EU law is dealt with. The conclusions reveal that the Directive presents some lights but also various shadows, in terms of sanctions provided.

II. The Directive

Three preparatory documents explain the EU's view on the PIF Directive: the Impact Assessment (IA),[9] the explanatory memorandum of the proposal and the European Parliament (EP) report.[10] The IA starts with a remark on the strong obligation for the EU and the Member States to protect the Union's financial interests. The shortcomings of the current legal framework would lie in the little dissuasive effect of the existing provisions and the uneven level of enforcement and implementation. The goal of effectiveness by deterrence is to be achieved by: extending the range and types of offences; and harmonising the sanctions – currently too low and diverse amongst Member States.[11] The foregoing summarises the Union approach to the use of criminal law and imprisonment. On the one hand, an area of free movement is sustainable so long as a common set of rules is established. Potential wrongdoers are therefore deprived of the choice of forum: namely, the possibility to move to where offending is more convenient due to low enforcement rates, mild penalties or narrowly defined punishable conduct. On the other, criminal law can unfold its deterring potential through the threat of harsh sanctions such as imprisonment.

The Commission identified a Directive and a Regulation as the two most appropriate legislative instruments to be adopted.[12] While the former was eventually

[9] See in particular Commission Staff Working Document Executive summary of the Impact Assessment Accompanying the document Proposal for a Directive of the European Parliament and the Council on the protection of the financial interests of the European Union by criminal law, SWD(2012) 196 final; https://ec.europa.eu/anti-fraud/sites/antifraud/files/docs/body/impact_assessment_en.pdf.

[10] EP report on the proposal for a Directive of the European Parliament and of the Council on the protection of the euro and other currencies against counterfeiting by criminal law, and replacing Council Framework Decision 2000/383/JHA (COM(2013)0042 – C7-0033/2013 – 2013/0023(COD)), A7-0018/2014, 10.1.2014.

[11] SWD (2012) 196, n 9 above, paras 1–3.

[12] To be thorough, the options initially presented were five, with three of them being ruled out due to their inefficacy (see ibid, para 4).

preferred because less intrusive, the latter – and the enactment of EU directly applicable rules in criminal law – was not regarded as unlawful. Quite the contrary, a regulation would comply with the EU law proportionality principle, owing to the great relevance of the interests at stake.[13]

That being so, the Commission's proposal opted for Article 325(4) TFEU as its legal basis, stating that 'The fight against illegal activities affecting the Union's financial interests is a very specific policy area [where] the Union has a broad array of tools at its disposal'.[14] The EP voiced its disagreement,[15] and secured a change of the legal basis to Article 83(2) TFEU in the final version of the text. The EP considered Article 83(2) TFEU to be *lex specialis* to Article 325(4) TFEU. The *travaux préparatoires* of Article 83(2) TFEU show that the latter provision was considered an appropriate legal basis 'in the context of the protection of the EU's financial interests'.[16] Additionally, Article 86 TFEU contains a provision on the establishment of a European Public Prosecutor's office 'in order to combat crimes affecting the financial interests of the Union'. The protection of the EU's financial interests, therefore, is by no means covered under the sole Article 325 TFEU.

The disappearance, in Article 325 TFEU, of the mentioned prohibition provided by Article 280(4) EC can be explained by the communitarisation of criminal law competence. Preventing EU measures on fraud from affecting national criminal systems would not make sense within the current institutional framework. Opting for a different legal basis would result in eluding the procedural guarantees set out in Article 83(2) TFEU.[17] The dispute over the legal basis reveals the importance of policy legal basis outside the provisions in the Treaties strictly devoted to criminal law. The IA reveals that the issue behind that discussion concerns the possible direct application of EU rules in criminal law and the circumvention of the constraints posed by the EU legislature in Article 83 TFEU. This results in issues of proportionality – which the Commission complied with – and legal certainty.

Another important reason for friction lay in the Commission's initial proposal to establish minimum terms of imprisonment for particularly serious offences, in order to ensure consistency in deterrence throughout the Union and contest fraud in an effective and equivalent manner. Such a provision was objected to by the EP, which argued that

> Minimum penalties do not respect the diversity of legal systems and the need for judicial discretion. Introducing them here would also not be consistent with the position

[13] Although, the document clarifies, 'the intrusiveness and fundamental rights impact is higher than [a Directive] for no noticeably higher positive financial impact' (ibid, para 4.1.).

[14] See Proposal for a Directive of the European Parliament and of the Council on the fight against fraud to the Union's financial interests by means of criminal law, COM(2012) 363 final, 11.7.2012, para 3.1.

[15] See the EP report, n 10 above, 30 onwards.

[16] Ibid, para 3.

[17] Namely, the requirements for harmonising measures to be essential, to establish only minimum rules and to be subject to the so-called 'emergency brake' provided by Art 83(4).

> Parliament has taken as regards the draft Directive on the protection of the euro and other currencies against counterfeiting in criminal law.

In that case, the EP had opposed a rule of the same kind, by stating that

> Given the substantial disparities between Member States the danger exists that the introduction of minimum penalties for counterfeiting the euro and other currencies might lead to lack of uniformity regarding minimum penalties within one and the same national legal system.[18]

Consistent with this approach, the EP added to that provision the following clause: 'This paragraph shall not affect the discretion of courts and judges in Member States in determining the most appropriate and proportionate sentence in any individual case'. The approved text of the Directive thus provides no harmonised minimum penalties, but only the requirement for Member States to impose maximum penalties consisting of imprisonment for the offences stated in Articles 3 and 4. The maximum penalty must be of at least four years when the offence involves considerable damage or gain[19] In cases of an offence involving damage of less than EUR 10,000 and gain of less than EUR 10,000, sanctions other than criminal penalties may be provided for. No financial penalties are provided, whereas the Directive features freezing and confiscation of the proceeds and instrumentalities of crimes.[20]

The Commission explained the choice of imprisonment and a minimum threshold of deprivation of liberty by arguing that 'Economic crime is typically an area where criminal sanctions can have a particularly deterrent effect, as potential perpetrators can be expected to make a certain calculation of risks before deciding to engage in such criminal activities'.

Article 12 provides that Member States shall take the necessary measures to enable the investigation, prosecution, trial and judicial decision of those offences which are punishable by a maximum sanction of at least four years' imprisonment, for a period of at least five years from the time when the offence was committed. Furthermore, Member States shall take the necessary measures to enable the enforcement of: a penalty of more than one year's imprisonment; or, alternatively, a penalty of imprisonment in the case of a criminal offence which is punishable by a maximum sanction of at least four years' imprisonment.

Article 11(3) allows states to extend their jurisdiction over offences committed outside their territory where the offender is a *habitual resident* in their territory. Such a provision offers a glimpse of what will follow in the next Parts of the story. EU law is reshaping the traditional connection between public powers and the individual, with residence taking over the pre-eminent role of the nationality bond in the areas of prosecution, reintegration and citizenship.[21]

[18] See amendment to recital 16, EP report, n 10 above.

[19] The considerable damage or advantage is presumed in specific cases stated in Art 7(3).

[20] Anti-Fraud Directive, Art 10.

[21] See the chapter on criminal law and EU citizenship, as well as L Mancano, 'Criminal conduct and lack of integration in the society under EU citizenship: This Marriage Is not to Be Performed' (2015) 7 *New Journal of European Criminal Law* 53.

III. EU Law Proportionality

The function attached to custodial penalties reveals the EU stance on deprivation of liberty in substantive criminal law, and works as a *trait d'union* between the latter and the broader horizon of the present story. The investigation in terms of EU Law proportionality under Article 5 TEU comes with an assessment of the reasons whereby the legislature justifies the use of criminal law and imprisonment, as opposed to other instruments and sanctions. The three centrepieces of the analysis are therefore the objective stated by the EU, the means proposed and the rationale underlying that choice. This shows that the roots of the EU approach rest on the preservation of the Union as a borderless area, and the effectiveness of EU-specific policies.

The use of criminal law is based on reasons of general prevention, underpinned by the argument that 'potential perpetrators can be expected to make a certain calculation of risks before deciding to engage in such criminal activities'. Offenders are therefore perfectly rational agents who make choices on the basis of a cost–benefit analysis – an approach emerging from the other case studies as well. Such a risk calculation concerns the decision as to *whether* and *where* to offend. The creation of a legal level playing-field aims to eliminate any possible 'impunity heaven' within the EU. Removing the opportunity for crime is key to fighting these phenomena. This understanding of opportunity as the root of illegal activities lies at the heart of the so-called Rational Choice Theory (RCT) of crime, a criminological theory building on economic theory of crime and deterrence-based, utilitarian approaches to punishment. Similarly, the use of custodial penalties is justified by their great dissuasive power, which can compensate for deficient implementation of the PIF Convention.[22]

Rational choice theory and opportunity theory of crime – the latter, in turn, being mostly influenced by the former[23] – are deeply rooted in the economic analysis of criminal law:[24]

> Crudely put, rational choice theory models behaviour by assuming that humans act intentionally and rationally; that they are purposive and goal-orientated; that they have sets of hierarchically ordered preferences, or utilities; and that, in deciding how to behave, they seek to maximize utility.[25]

The opportunity theory of crime claims that the main cause of crime is opportunity. Opportunities are highly specific to the offence at stake, are concentrated

[22] Commission communication on the protection of financial interests, n 4 above, para 4.2. onwards.

[23] See B Hindess, 'Rational Choice Theory' in W Outhwaite and T Bottomore (eds), *Blackwell Dictionary of Twentieth-Century Social Thought* (Oxford, Blackwell Publishers, 1993) 542.

[24] The economic analysis to crime was famously championed by Gary Becker. See G Becker, 'Crime and Punishment: An Economic Approach' (1968) 76(2) *Journal of Political Economy* 169–217.

[25] L Zedner, 'Opportunity Makes the Thief-Taker: The Influence of Economic Analysis on Crime Control' in T Newburn and P Rock (eds), *The Politics of Crime Control* (Oxford, Oxford University Press) 150.

in time and space, and are contingent on the day-to-day activities of potential perpetrators and victims.[26] A powerful tool to increase the rational agent's compliance with the law[27] and to make criminal behaviour less attractive from a cost–benefit perspective, deterrence can be achieved by appropriately harsh penalties established by law, and a higher likelihood, for the criminal, of being caught. Such an approach assumes that potential wrongdoers have complete information about the enforcement parameters such as the likelihood and severity of punishment.[28]

In the market for crime,[29] where all rational agents act to optimise behaviour, opportunities are given by the interaction between a likely offender, a suitable target and the absence of a capable guardian.[30] A number of authors have pointed to the connection between such a managerial, risk-based and effectiveness-oriented approach and neo-liberal forms of governance characterising western democracies over the last decades, where the principles of rational calculation and interest maximisation feed the denial of any forms of irrationality.[31] Thereby, decision-making of individuals is divested of normativity, and compliance with the law by such a de-moralised model of offender is exclusively based on costs–benefits analysis.[32] With personal, demographic and social considerations kept out of sight,[33] these accounts are more concerned with crime control through a short-term strategy – the 'here-and-now of everyday life' – rather than macro-level socio-political intervention.[34]

[26] M Felson, *Crime and Everyday Life* (London, Sage, 2002).

[27] D Earnhart and L Friesen, 'Can Punishment Generate Specific Deterrence Without Updating? Analysis of a Stated Choice Scenario' (2013) 56(3) *Environmental and Resource Economics* 379–97.

[28] This harm can be considered the harm to society minus the benefit to the criminal. See T. Fisher, 'Economic analysis of criminal law' in *The Oxford Handbook of Criminal Law* 38–59. Other authors who are in the same thread, like Posner address the specifics of criminal law doctrine and its key elements of *actus reus* and *mens rea*. See R Posner, 'An Economic Theory of the Criminal Law' (1985) 85(6) *Columbia Law Review* 1193–231.

[29] As scholars put it, the 'market for crime' has not be considered a 'physical setting where illegitimate transactions are contracted, but … a market in which the aggregate behavior of suppliers and demanders is coordinated and made mutually consistent through adjustments in relevant prices'. See I Ehrlich, 'Crime, Punishment, and the Market for Offences' (1996) 10(1) *Journal of Economic Perspectives* 45.

[30] As noted, 'Given this sustained interest in the causal influence of situational/environmental factors, SCP practitioners began to draw on commensurate developments in the (related) field of Routine Activity Theory (RAT). Like RCT [Rational Choice Theory], RAT proceeds with the belief that criminal motivation is a given … it is concerned with *three* core concepts: "likely (motivated) offenders", "suitable (soft) targets", and (the absence of) "capable guardians" …' See K Hayward, 'Situational Crime Prevention and its Discontents: Rational Choice Theory versus the "Culture of Now"' (2007) 40(3) *Social Policy and Administration* 232, 235.

[31] D Garland, *The Culture of Control* (Oxford, Oxford University Press, 2001).

[32] E Eide, 'Economics of Criminal Behaviour' in B Douckaert and G De Geest (eds), *Encyclopedia of Law and Economics* (Cheltenham, Edward Elgar, 2000) 345.

[33] N Tilley and G Laycock, 'Working out What to Do: Evidence-based Crime Reduction', *Crime Reduction Series Paper 11* (London, Home Office, 2002) 30.

[34] M Felson and RV Clarke, 'Opportunity Makes the Thief: Practical Theory for Crime Prevention', *Police Research Series* No 98 (London, Home Office, 1998) 33. However, the denial of irrationality is not a refusal to acknowledge the existence of subjects whose capacity for rational calculation is

The unquestioned use of imprisonment builds on two extremely controversial assumptions: capacity for risk-assessment by potential offenders and effective deterrence of the sole threat of punishment.[35] On the one hand, the effectiveness of 'protection by deterrence' invoked by the Commission is not supported by any evidence. The threatened punishment in itself is a weak tool in fighting crime, without significant influence on individuals' behaviour.[36] On the other, the anthropological model of the criminal as a perfectly rational agent is open to criticism. Even considering economic crime as an area where potential offenders are less exposed to impoverishment of their capacity for rational calculation – which is a rather strong assumption – the imposition of imprisonment as the appropriate punishment cannot be taken for granted.

While the Commission advocated for the use of penalties other than imprisonment in its communication on a European criminal policy, all instruments of EU substantive criminal law require the imposition of deprivation of liberty. There is not much *favor libertatis* in the Union's legislative approach to custodial penalties, which might have been promoted without the obligation of imprisonment, and use of – possibly even more – dissuasive financial penalties.

Related to such concerns is the choice of the legal basis. The Commission considers criminal law as the only effective instrument,[37] and Article 325(4) TFEU as the appropriate and effective legal basis. The use of Article 325 might have paved the way to other forms of effectiveness-based criminalisation outside the AFSJ, such as Articles 114 and Article 192 TFEU.[38] Such criminalisation would avoid the limits posed by the Treaty in the case of Article 83 TFEU, ensuring the use of criminal law as *extrema ratio*. For this reason, the EP preference for Article 83 TFEU – followed in the final draft – should be welcome.

IV. Legal Certainty

Issues of legal certainty arise from the dispute on the legal basis and the thresholds of punishment laid down in the Directive. The use of Article 325 TFEU was meant

impoverished. Rather, 'These groups tend to be demonized as distinct dangerous classes who must be managed and contained in the mass penal warehouses that are the hallmark of late modern penalty. Penal incapacitation denies such people the opportunity of choice of action and in so doing denies them also the opportunity to re-join the moral consensus by desisting from crime'. See L Zedner, n 25 above, 165.

[35] For references to criminological and law and economic literature on these two aspects see J Öberg, 'Do we really need criminal sanctions for the enforcement of EU law?' (2014) 5(3) *New Journal of European Criminal Law* 370–87.

[36] D Dölling and others, 'Is Deterrence Effective? Results of a Meta-Analysis of Punishment' (2009) 15 *European Journal of Criminology and Research* 201–24.

[37] S Melander, 'Effectiveness in EU criminal law and its effects on the general part of criminal law' (2014) 5(3) *New Journal of European Criminal Law* 274–300.

[38] Namely, the establishment and functioning of the internal market, and environmental policy, respectively.

to promote the enlargement of EU competences in criminal law through the effectiveness of the Union's policies;[39] a dynamic well-known from the *Greek Maize*, the *Environmental Crimes* and *Ship-Source Pollution* cases. While this debate might appear as pure speculation after the Directive was adopted pursuant to Article 83 TFEU, recent developments suggest that quite the opposite is true. The recourse to a policy-based – rather than area-specific – legal base is not limited to Article 325 TFEU.[40]

In a 2014 judgment[41] concerning Directive 2011/82/EU[42] on exchange of information between Member States on specific driving offences, the CJEU ruled in favour of the Commission and stated that the Directive should have been adopted pursuant to Article 91 TFEU, rather than Article 87(2) TFEU. The two legal bases cover transport policy and police co-operation respectively. The CJEU's consistent preference for the policy legal basis – rather than the criminal-law-specific one – should not be overlooked.

More closely related to the protection of the Union's financial interests, the *Taricco* saga on Article 325 TFEU has revamped the debate on direct applicability of EU law resulting in the establishment of individual criminal liability. The judicial saga concerned the Italian law of limitations on prosecution of VAT offences. The CJEU stated that a short limitation period like the one laid down in the Italian law would affect Member States' obligations under Article 325(1) and (2) TFEU, where that law would: prevent the imposition of dissuasive and effective penalties in a considerable number of cases; and provide a longer limitation period for prosecution of fraud against the financial interest of the state. The Court stated the obligation for national judges to disapply those rules, if needed to ensure the effectiveness of Article 325(1) and (2) TFEU. The judgment sparked a fierce debate, with – especially Italian – lawyers concerned that the ruling might result in the direct establishment of criminal liability through EU law and circumvention of the principle of legal reserve (or *nulla poena sine lege parlamentaria*) established in Article 25(2) of the Italian Constitution.[43]

The issue arrived before the Italian Constitutional Court, which referred three questions to the CJEU asking – as far as is relevant here – whether the

[39] As far as the relationship between the legal basis and the extension of competence at EU level more in general goes, see S Prechal, 'Competence Creep and General Principle of Law' (2010) 3(1) *Review of European and Administrative Law* 5 onwards. As to the competence creep, see S Weatherhill, 'Competence creep and competence control' (2004) 23(1) *Yearbook of European Law* 1–55.

[40] For a complete reconstruction of the argumentats concerning the relationship between Art 325 and Art 83 TFEU, see M Böse, 'La sentenza della Corte costituzionale tedesca sul Trattato di Lisbona e il suo significato per la europeizzazione del diritto penale' (2009) *Criminalia* 267–301.

[41] Case C-43/12, *European Commission v European Parliament and Council*, 6 May 2014, EU:C:2014:298.

[42] Directive 2011/82/EU of the European Parliament and of the Council of 25 October 2011 facilitating the cross-border exchange of information on road safety-related traffic offences, [2011] OJ L288/1, 5.11.2011.

[43] The principle is a corollary of the principle of legality and is a constitutional rule in many Member States. See M Muñoz de Morales Romero, 'In Pursuit of Basics for a New Principle of Legal Reserve in Supranational Criminal Law' (2012) 3 *European Criminal Law Review* 252–75.

obligation to disapply national rules, stated in *Taricco*, should be upheld even where that would be at variance with the overriding principles of the constitution of the Member State concerned or with the inalienable rights of the individual conferred by the constitution of the Member State. The CJEU reaffirmed the obligation, unless that disapplication entailed a breach of the principle that offences and penalties must be defined by law because of the lack of precision of the applicable law or because of the retroactive application of legislation imposing conditions of criminal liability stricter than those in force at the time the infringement was committed.[44] While the Court seemed to retreat from this in *Taricco II*, it did so without relying on the principle of legal reserve. Consistently with its case-law,[45] the CJEU focused on foreseeability, legal precision and non-retroactivity.[46]

The adoption of a criminal law Regulation – expressly regarded as proportionate by the Commission[47] – and the scenario envisaged in *Taricco*, are different. They both, however, reveal the uniqueness of penalties in EU law: imposition of imprisonment terms through direct application of Union rules for reasons of effectiveness. The CJEU argued that criminal liability deriving from direct applicability of Article 325 TFEU/disapplication of rules on limitation periods have a procedural effect, whereas the principle of legality would regard substantive criminal law. The argument is too formalistic. Furthermore, it might be objected that the obligation refers to effective and dissuasive sanctions broadly. The previous discussion revealed, however, that no penalties are considered as effective and dissuasive as those entailing deprivation of liberty.

The reasons underlying the use of imprisonment highlight the importance of the setting of this research: namely, the creation of the Union as an area of free movement. The dispute over the legal base and the *Taricco* cases show that the constitutional structure of the EU and its multi-level system of governance pose challenges to a stronghold of personal liberty such as the principle of legality. The case of the EU's financial interests brings to the fore the connection between direct applicability of EU law, consequences in terms of individual liability, and different understandings of legality at Union and national level. Horizontal (approximation of levels of punishment) and vertical (direct applicability) integration on levels of imprisonment, with free movement in mind, causes constitutional dilemmas.

[44] *MAS* and *MB*, n 8 above, para 62.

[45] Case C-80/86, *Criminal proceedings against Kolpinghuis Nijmegen BV*, [1987] ECR 3969, para 13; Case C-68/95, *Criminal proceedings against Arcaro*, [1996] ECR I-6065, paras 36–37; joined Cases C-74/95 and 129/95, *Criminal proceedings against X*, [1996] ECR I-6609, para 25; Case 384/02 *Criminal proceedings against Grøngaard and Bang*, [2005] ECR I-9939, paras 29–30; Joined Cases 387/02, 391/02, 403/02, *Criminal proceedings against Berlusconi and other*, [2005] I-3565, para 74.

[46] *MAS and MB*, n 8 above, para 49.

[47] See on such a possibility Mitsilegas, *EU Criminal Law After Lisbon: Rights, Trust and the Transformation of Justice in Europe* (Oxford, Hart Publishing, 2016) 118–21; S Miettinen, 'Implied ancillary criminal law competence after Lisbon' (2013) 3(2) *European Criminal Law Review* 194–219.

An EU-specific principle of legality cannot overlook the peculiarities of the Union. For the time being, the CJEU has accommodated the divergence concerning the role of legal reserve in Italian law, but the story seems to be far from over.[48]

As we know, the legal reserve ensures the accountability and the public debate on the choices of criminalisation, and guarantees the link between criminal law and its centrepieces: the national cultural and societal context from which those rules ensue; and popular sovereignty channelled through a parliamentary representative enacting criminal law.[49] The role and function of legal reserve – which enjoys a different legal status throughout the Union – raises broader questions on the nature of the Union legislature as a fully-fledged democratic one;[50] concerns epitomised by the German Constitutional Court's judgment on the Lisbon Treaty,[51] and reaffirmed years later apropos of the German Law on the election of the EP.[52] The introduction of the ordinary legislative procedure has made the EP a proper co-legislator, and the first two additional protocols to the Treaty empower the national parliaments to exercise a deeper ex ante and ex post control on EU law. Still, the issue of the Union's suitability for imposing custodial penalties is bound to be one of the thorniest issues to be addressed by institutional actors within the EU.

[48] To be thorough, EU law has significantly contributed to the erosion of the legal reserve over recent decades, especially through the interaction between Union Regulations (describing conduct allowed or forbidden) and national criminal provisions. For a detailed discussion of some of these examples, see V Manes, 'Metodo e limiti dell'interpretazione conforme alle fonti sovranazionali in materia penale' (2012) *Diritto Penale Contemporaneo* 13; M Bosi and C Sotis, 'Il bizzarro caso dei pesci "in malam partem"' (2011) *Diritto Penale Contemporaneo*; A Colella, 'Una nuova ipotesi di applicazione diretta in *malam partem* del diritto della UE' (2011) *Diritto Penale Contemporaneo*.

[49] While the ECtHR has consistently found that the existence of a formal parliamentary law is not a lone guarantee of compliance with legal certainty, it constitutes a core principle in many Member States. See, among many, ECtHR, *Sud fondi srl v Italia*, Application No 75909/01, judgment of 20 January 2009.

[50] With particular regard to European criminal law and democratic deficit, see for an overview and references C Grandi, 'The "Qualities" of Criminal Law – Connected to National and European Law-making Procedures' (2011) 3 *European Criminal Law Review* 285–309.

[51] Judgment of 30 June 2009 – 2 BvR 1010/2008, 2 BvR 1022/08, 2 BvR 1259/08, 2 BvR 5/08 e 2 BvR 182/09, available at: www.bverfg.de/entscheidungen/es20090630. The aim of the present work is neither to elaborate on the debate on the arguments in favour and against the democratic nature of the EP, nor to analyse the reasoning of the German Constitutional Court. However, among the countless comments on the *Lissabon Urteil*, see M Böse, 'La sentenza della Corte costituzionale tedesca sul Trattato di Lisbona', n 40 above; M Wendel, 'Lisbon Before the Courts: Comparative Perspectives' (2011) 7 *European Constitutional Law Review* 96–137; B Zwingmann, 'The Continuing Myth of Euro-Sceptisism? The German Federal Constitutional Court Two Years After Lisbon' (2012) 61 *International and Comparative Law Quarterly* 665–95; D Grimm, 'Defending Sovereign Statehood Against Transforming the Union Into a State' (2009) 5 *European Constitutional Law Review* 353–73; T Lock, 'Why the European Union is Not a State. Some Critical Remarks' (2009) 5 *European Constitutional Law Review* 407–20; D Halberstam and C Möllers, 'The German Constitutional Court Says "'Ja zu Deutschland!'"' (2009) 10(8) *German Law Journal* 1241 onwards.

[52] See for an in-depth analysis, G Delledonne, 'Il *Bundeverfassungsgericht*, il Parlamento Europeo e la soglia di sbarramento del 5%: un (altro) ritorno del *Sonderweg*?' (2012) 1 *Rivista AIC*.

V. Criminal Law Proportionality

Proportionality under Article 49 CFREU has a retributive meaning, as compared to the utilitarian logic of Article 52 CFREU. The Commission proposed the introduction of a minimum level of punishment, with a view to ensuring consistency in deterrence throughout the Union. The EP expunged such provisions, since they would not respect the diversity of legal systems and the need for judicial discretion. They would cause a lack of uniformity regarding minimum penalties within one and the same national legal system.

To this end, the distinction between ordinal and cardinal proportionality in criminal law comes in handy.[53] The former concerns the question of how severely specific crimes should be punished, as compared to others. The latter concerns what overall level of severity should be adopted as reference for the system of penalties. In this regard, the proportionality of a system goes hand in hand with its own coherence.

The EU system of criminal penalties is not easily assessed, since sanctions are approximated by the minimum-maximum criterion. The four levels identified in the Council conclusions provide some guidance. However, criminal law is holistic in nature and requires high inner consistency. Thresholds of punishment may not be evaluated in isolation, but are to be placed in the broader context, where murder is punished more than unlawful bill posting, and unlawful bill posting is punished less than robbery. The duty of coherence involves both the legislative[54] and judicial (sentencing) levels.[55] The EP rightly suggests that a piecemeal intervention in criminal penalties would affect the uniformity of penalty systems in Member States.

If coherence and proportionality are two sides of the same coin, serious doubts can be raised on the appropriateness and legitimacy of the minimum-maximum. This is the only harmonising criterion adopted by the EU conceived to facilitate judicial cooperation without reducing Member States' discretion. However, it seems not to be able to endow EU criminal law with an adequate level of consistency, and is significantly out of touch with the overall constitutional evolution of the Union since its adoption in 2002. Furthermore, the discussion on the Market Abuse Directive shows that such a method of approximation might contribute to the increase in imprisonment rates in the EU.

[53] See in particular A von Hirsch, 'Proportionality in the Philosophy of Punishment' (1992) 16 *Crime and Justice* 55, 75 onwards; A Ashworth and A von Hirsch, *Proportionate sentencing: Exploring the Principles* (Oxford, Oxford University Press, 2005) 137 onwards.

[54] See on it P Asp, 'The Importance of the Principles of Subsidiarity and Coherence in the Development of EU Criminal Law' (2011) 1 *European Criminal Law Review* 44, 47 onwards.

[55] See R Miklau, 'Approximation of Sanctions within the European Union' in T Daems, D van Zyl Smit and S Snacken, *European Penology?* (Oxford, Hart Publishing, 2013) 115 onwards, where it is stated that 'the duration of prison sentences and the actual period of time served in prison are determined by national traditions, local practices, judicial perceptions and pragmatic considerations such as prison capacity and the (un)availability of alternative sentencing options and (early) conditional release, as well as pardon and amnesty practices. The time spent in prison varies accordingly'.

The use of other criteria such as mandatory minimum penalties might be problematic as well. The Lisbon Treaty has dropped the declaration annexed to the Treaty of Amsterdam, according to which the EU could not oblige the Member States to adopt a common minimum threshold of penalties. The EP, however, raises legitimate concerns, as not all Member States provide for minimum thresholds of punishment.[56] Furthermore, the margin for judicial discretion in sentencing varies significantly across the EU national systems.[57] The formula used to approximate penalties stipulates that Member States shall take the necessary measures to ensure that specific offences shall be *punishable* by a maximum penalty of at least, for example, five years' imprisonment. That reasonably means that such a level of penalty must be included in national law, which must not make impossible *in concreto* the imposition of that punishment; for example, by providing one-size-fits-all sentences.

The establishment of a rigid minimum level of imprisonment alone might create issues of proportionality, with the judge potentially obliged to impose too harsh a penalty in light of the specific circumstances of the case. Once again, the holistic nature of criminal law reveals the need to act on the bigger picture. The use of the minimum-maximum criterion on its own might facilitate judicial cooperation. It nonetheless raises more questions than answers if not considered as an intervention encompassing not only minimum penalties, but also consideration of circumstances and the extent of judicial discretion to be left to national judges. These issues are expanded upon over the following Parts of this book, where the discussion of further aspects of approximation of penalties sheds further light on the intricacy of custodial penalties in EU law.

VI. Conclusions

The PIF Directive highlights the importance of the dynamic integration-fundamental rights protection in shaping the EU approach to the use of deprivation of liberty in substantive criminal law. The pursuit of further integration rests on the need to keep an area of free movement sustainable. The aims, means and rationale of that action pose challenges to a stronghold of personal liberty enshrined in Article 49 CFREU, as well as a pillar of the EU constitutional structure such as Article 5 TEU. Those issues are triggered and emphasised by the peculiarities of the Union legal order.

On the one hand, the exercise of competences in the shape of criminalisation and imprisonment builds on the assumption that approximation serves

[56] S Melander, n 37 above.

[57] Jannemieke Ouwerkerk, 'Criminal Justice beyond National Sovereignty. An Alternative Perspective on the Europeanisation of Criminal Law' (2015) 23 *European Journal of Crime, Criminal Law and Criminal Justice* 11.

to deprive the wrongdoers of the choice of forum – potentially fostered by free movement – and to enhance deterrence. This line of reasoning relies on a debatable anthropological model of potential offenders making a rational calculation on whether and where to offend. On the other hand, a link is made between approximation and the facilitation of judicial cooperation. Doubts can be raised with regard to the very justification of imprisonment, where extremely abstract and weakly-founded reasons of deterrence flank the pragmatism of facilitating judicial cooperation.

On closer inspection, the analysis brings to the fore concerns of legal certainty and proportionality. Effectiveness of the protection of the Union's financial interests and (potential) use of directly applicable rules of criminal law are inextricably linked. This emerged from the Commission IA and proposal to base the Directive on Article 325 TFEU (criminalisation outside the AFSJ and the constraints of Article 83 TFEU). It was also relied on by the CJEU, when stating the direct applicability of Article 325 TFEU and the related duty of Member States to disapply their rules on prescription. Both situations give rise to a scenario where EU law can – to a variable extent – directly impact on determination of criminal liability. The resulting concerns in terms of legality and legal certainty led the CJEU to mitigate its stance in *Taricco II*.

Deprivation of liberty in substantive EU criminal law materialises in the approximation of the levels of penalty through the minimum-maximum criterion. That criterion reinforces the link between action in substantive criminal law and fostering judicial cooperation. Furthermore, it results in issues of coherence and proportionality of criminal law systems. The next chapters highlight that the use of the minimum-maximum criterion alone might: create a race to the top, with a state obliged to introduce or raise imprisonment rates considerably; create more problems than it solves if not used in conjunction with rules on circumstances and room for judicial discretion.

4

The Anti-Drug Trafficking Directive

I. Introduction

The Anti-Drug Trafficking Directive fits with the narrative of this research. While adopted pursuant to Article 83(1) TFEU – the legal base for the so-called securitised criminalisation – the instrument is closely connected to the functioning of the internal market. This allows for the assessment of a coherent and homogeneous array of instruments of substantive criminal law. Furthermore, the legislative technique deserves attention. Directive 2017/2103 is to be jointly read with Regulation 2017/2101, issued by virtue of Article 168(5) TFEU. Drug trafficking is a highly sensitive subject to the EU, with actions taken a long time before the Treaty of Maastricht.[1] The attention of the Union's institutions was confirmed in multi-annual programmes concerning the AFJS,[2] as well as the inclusion of drug trafficking amongst the serious areas of cross-border crime under Article 83(1) TFEU.

The Regulation and the Directive hereby considered are intended to amend and replace three older instruments, and form an integral part of a broader EU strategy on drugs.[3] According to the Commission, the efficient fight against drug trafficking should ensure that 'any measures to prevent the diversion of drug precursors must strike a balance between ensuring an effective control of diversion without disrupting lawful trade in such substances'.[4] Such a strategy – which

[1] See G Estievenart, *Policies and strategies to combat drugs in Europe: the Treaty on European Union: Framework for a new European strategy to combat drugs?* (Dordrecht, Martinus Nijhoff Publisher, 1995). Concerning previous instruments, see for instance Joint Action 96/698/JHA of 29 November 1996 adopted by the Council on the basis of Article K.3 of the Treaty on European Union, on cooperation between customs authorities and business organisations in combating drug trafficking, [1996] OJ L322/3, 12.12.96. See also Council Regulation (EC) No 111/2005 of 22 December 2004 laying down rules for the monitoring of trade between the Community and third countries in drug precursors, [2005] OJ L22/1, 26.1.2005; Regulation (EC) No 273/2004 of the European Parliament and of the Council of 11 February 2004 on drug precursors, [2004] OJ L47/1, 18.2.2004.

[2] Namely, the Tampere, the Hague, the Stockholm and now, albeit very vaguely, the Ypres Programmes.

[3] Council EU Drugs Strategy (2013–20), [2012] OJ C 402/01, 29.12.2012; Council EU Action Plan on Drugs (2013–2016), [2013] OJ C 351/01, 30.11.2013; Communication from the Commission to the European Parliament and the Council, *Towards a stronger European response to drugs*, Brussels, COM(2011) 689/2.

[4] Communication, *Towards a stronger European response to drugs*, n 3 above, 5.

includes actions on confiscation and money laundering – aims primarily to tackle financial gain,[5] and builds on three circumstances: the innovative techniques of smuggling drugs into and within the EU, facilitated by new technologies; the fast emergence of new and harmful psychoactive substances; Member States' difficulties in reining in the spread of drugs without effective cooperation.

Many new psychoactive substances are not provided for in UN Conventions, which in turn represent the basis of EU legislation in the field. That being so, a Regulation and a Directive were adopted. The former regulates market restrictions of new psychoactive substances, the latter establishes minimum rules of a criminal nature. The Directive leaves untouched the Framework Decision (FD) it is meant to replace, and extends its scope of application to new psychoactive substances.[6] For this reason, the following analysis refers to the text of the FD. Firstly, the Regulation is presented. Thereafter, the discussion moves onto the Directive, followed by an assessment in light of proportionality and Article 49 CFREU.

II. The Regulation

A significant rise in the number of new psychoactive substances available on the market has occurred over recent years. These substances present two main characteristics: they are not covered by UN Conventions on Drugs, or by EU legislation; they are marketed for legitimate purposes[7] but are increasingly used recreationally. Member States treat conduct connected to new psychoactive substances as administrative or criminal offences.

The relevant EU instrument was a 'third pillar' Decision, considered ineffective by the Commission.[8] The Regulation was adopted with the view to establishing a level playing-field, and addressing possible obstacles to trade arising from the presence of many different legal regimes within the Union. The Regulation provides that, where a majority of Member States, the European Monitoring Centre for Drugs and Drug Addiction (EMCDDA) or the Commission, considers that information on a new psychoactive substance collected in one or more Member States

[5] Communication, *Towards a stronger European response to drugs*, n 3 above, 6 onwards.

[6] See for an analysis see R Kert and A Lehrer, 'Content and impact of approximation – The case of drug trafficking' in F Galli and A Weyembergh (eds), *Approximation of substantive criminal law in the EU: The way forward* (Bruxelles, Editions de l'Université de Bruxelles, 2014) 169–88.

[7] Commission Staff Working Document Impact Assessment Accompanying the document Proposal for a Regulation of the European Parliament and of the Council on new psychoactive substances and proposal for a Directive of the European Parliament and of the Council amending Council Framework Decision 2004/757/JHA of 25 October 2004 laying down minimum provisions on the constituent elements of criminal acts and penalties in the field of illicit drug trafficking, as regards the definition of drug, Brussels 17.9.2013, SWD(2013) 319 final, 20 onwards.

[8] See the Report from the Commission on the assessment of the functioning of Council Decision 2005/387/JHA on the information exchange, risk assessment and control of new psychoactive substances, Brussels, 11.7.2011 COM(2011) 430 final.

gives rise to concerns that the new psychoactive substance may pose health or social risks at a Union level, the Centre shall draw up an initial report on the new psychoactive substance.[9]

Within two weeks of receipt of an initial report, the Commission may request the Centre to assess the potential risks posed by the new psychoactive substance and to draw up a risk assessment report, where there are indications in the initial report that the substance may pose severe public health risks and, where applicable, severe social risks.[10] The Regulation provides that no risk assessment shall be carried out, eg when the substance in question has already been (or is being) assessed by the United Nations system and the World Health Organization.[11]

This mechanism has to be jointly read with the amended Directive, as explained in the following section.

III. The Directive

The Directive is significantly inspired by a general-prevention logic, as clarified by the proposals[12] and the Impact Assessment. Criminal sanctions are considered more *effective* than administrative sanctions,[13] and would reduce availability and demand of substances due to their deterrent effect.

The Directive extends the scope of application of the FD, so that the analysis is carried out by referring to the numeration of the Articles in the FD. In Article 1, the FD clarifies the meaning of 'drugs', by referring to: the UN Single Convention on narcotic drugs (adopted in 1961 and amended in 1972); and the 1971 Vienna Convention on Psychotropic Substances. As far as precursors are concerned, these amount to any substances scheduled in the Community legislation giving effect to the obligations deriving from Article 12 of the 1988 Convention against the Illicit Traffic in Narcotic Drugs and Psychotropic Substances. According to Article 1a, based on a risk assessment, the Commission

> shall adopt a delegated act in accordance with Article 8a amending the Annex to [the FD] in order to add the new psychoactive substance or substances to it and provide that the new psychoactive substance or substances pose severe public health risks and, where applicable, severe social risks at Union level …

[9] Regulation (EU) 2017/2101 of the European Parliament and of the Council of 15 November 2017 amending Regulation (EC) No 1920/2006 as regards information exchange on, and an early warning system and risk assessment procedure for, new psychoactive substances, Art 5b.

[10] Ibid, Art 5c.

[11] Ibid, Art 5d.

[12] Proposal for a Regulation of the European Parliament and of the Council on new psychoactive substances, COM(2013) 619 final, 6; Proposal for a Directive of the European Parliament and of the Council amending Council Framework Decision 2004/757/JHA of 25 October 2004 laying down minimum provisions on the constituent elements of criminal acts and penalties in the field of illicit drug trafficking, as regards the definition of drug, COM(2013) 618 final on drug trafficking, 2 onwards.

[13] Impact Assessment, n 7 above, 35.

The Commission shall take into account whether the impact of the new psychoactive substance on social functioning and public order is such as to disrupt public order, or cause violent or anti-social behaviour. Member States are required to extend the provisions of the FD to the newly added substances.

The FD rules may be grouped in two main clusters of norms: the criminalised conduct and the penalties provided. The conduct to be criminalised includes:

(a) the production, manufacture, extraction, preparation, offering, offering for sale, distribution, sale, delivery on any terms whatsoever, brokerage, dispatch, dispatch in transit, transport, importation or exportation of drugs;
(b) cultivation of opium poppy, coca bush or cannabis plant;
(c) the possession or purchase of drugs with a view to conducting one of the activities listed in (a); [and]
(d) the manufacture, transport or distribution of precursors, knowing that they are to be used in or for the illicit production or manufacture of drugs.

At the same time, the FD requires that incitement, attempt, and aiding and abetting of mentioned conduct were treated as criminal offences in Member States.[14]

The FD features different thresholds of penalties. The basic punishment for violations of the contemplated conducts is established in a minimum-maximum term of imprisonment between one and three years. With the exception of (d), imprisonment is raised to a maximum term of at least between five and 10 years' imprisonment when: a large quantity of drugs, or particularly harmful drugs are involved; or when serious damage to the health of a number of persons is brought about. Another range (of at least 10 years' imprisonment) is required when the offence is committed in the context of a criminal organisation as defined by Joint Action 98/773/JHA. Under the same circumstances, conduct described in (d) is required to be punished with a minimum-maximum term between five and 10 years' detention.[15] However, Member States are authorised to introduce more lenient penalties, when the offender renounces criminal activity related to trafficking in drugs and precursors, or when the person concerned provides the authorities with information helping to prevent or mitigate the effects of the offence, to identify or bring to justice the other offenders, to find evidence, or to prevent further offences referred to in the FD.[16]

IV. EU Law Proportionality

The Directive is in line with the overall approach to substantive criminal law and imprisonment. Effectiveness underlies a general deterrence-based approach,

[14] See the Framework Decision 2004/757/JHA, Arts 2 and 3.
[15] Ibid, Art 4.
[16] Ibid, Art 5.

according to which criminal law prompts individuals to comply with law. However, that criminal law creates greater effectiveness is far from a straightforward proposition. The Commission does not go much further, and in a sort of tautological argument states that criminal measures are more effective because they induce people to abide by the law. To defend such a position is to claim that general-prevention is the right choice because it works, and adds not much substance to the reasons underlying the use of custodial penalties.

Two studies carried out by the European Criminal Law Academic Network (ECLAN) at the request of the Commission come in handy. These are a report on the evaluation of the implementation and impact of the Framework Decision 2004/757/JHA on drug trafficking and a preparatory study for an impact assessment on a new legislative instrument replacing the Council Framework Decision 2004/757/JHA on illicit drug trafficking.[17] The studies reveal scepticism on the real possibility of measuring the effectiveness of the abstract threat of imprisonment in fighting drug-related crimes.[18] To this end, much importance lies in the concrete risk of being caught and convicted, and the penalties actually inflicted. Studies have shown an inverse correlation between the crime rate and the *probability* of being punished, while a relationship between the crime rate and the *severity* of sanctions provided in the law has not been ascertained.[19]

While a real assessment of the need for imprisonment does not emerge from the documents or the text of the instrument, the initiative seems to mainly be driven by the establishment of a common legal framework to facilitate judicial cooperation.

V. Legal Certainty

Possible issues of legal certainty arise from the interaction between the Regulation, the Directive and the national law implementing those instruments. Member States are required to criminalise certain conduct related to any new psychoactive substance identified by a Commission. The Commission does so by means of a delegated act. According to Article 290 TFEU, a legislative act may delegate to the Commission the power to adopt non-legislative acts of general application to supplement or amend certain non-essential elements of the legislative act.

[17] Report on the evaluation of the transposition and impacts of the Framework Decision 2004/757/JHA on drug trafficking (March 2013) and Preparatory study for an impact assessment on a new legislative instrument replacing the Council Framework Decision 2004/757/JHA on illicit drug trafficking (March 2013), available at: http://bookshop.europa.eu.

[18] See the preparatory study for an impact assessment, n 17 above, 50.

[19] M Gottfredson, 'Sanctions, situations, and agency in control theories of crime' (2011) 8(2) *European Journal of Criminology* 128–43; A Harrel and J Roman, 'Reducing Drug Use and Crime among Offenders: The Impact of Graduated Sanctions' (2001) 31(1) *Journal of Drug Issues* 210; A Pagliaro, 'Empirical Verification of the Effects of General Prevention and Incapacitation' (2003) 11(4) *European Journal of Crime, Criminal Law and Criminal Justice* 406.

The objectives, content, scope and duration of the delegation of power shall be explicitly defined in the legislative acts. The essential elements of an area shall be reserved for legislative acts and accordingly shall not be the subject of a delegation of power.

The other main example of delegated powers to be exercised by the Commission relates to the adoption of implementing acts, laid down in Article 291 TFEU and specifically governed by Regulation 182/2011/EU.[20]

Unlike implementing acts, however, Article 290 TFEU does not require the adoption of any binding instrument of secondary legislation to ensure its implementation. The provision is sufficient in itself and contains all the elements required by the legislator for defining, case-by-case, the scope, content and practical arrangements for delegating power.[21] The only guidance in the area is provided by an interinstitutional agreement between the EP, the Council and the Commission on better law-making.[22] Other than not being legally binding, the document offers no specific details on the procedures for adopting delegated acts. A lack of transparency and clarity of delegated and implementing acts has been strongly criticised.[23]

The extent to which such acts will be known and easily accessible to individuals could be debated. In the example of anti-drug trafficking, the delegated act establishes which psychoactive substances are to be criminalised by Member States. Thereby, the criminal conduct sanctioned by national law would be grounded on a Directive, with the latter eventually delegating through an executive act of the EU. The original source of criminalisation would be the delegated act.

Two main questions are raised in this regard. Firstly, there is the issue of the applicability of a delegated act adding a new psychoactive substance to the list of those that must be punished with custodial penalties. Would the person be liable, even though the Member State has failed to update its legislation? Secondly, delegated acts can merely supplement or amend legislative acts. The compliance between the function formally attributed to them by the Treaty, on the one hand, and the substantive criminalising role taken on in the case of the Directive, on the other, is not entirely clear. While delegation through administrative regulations

[20] Regulation (EU) No 182/2011 of the European Parliament and of the Council of 16 February 2011 laying down the rules and general principles concerning mechanisms for control by Member States of the Commission's exercise of implementing powers, [2011] OJ L55/13, 28.2.2011.

[21] COM(2009) 673 final.

[22] [2016] OJ L123/1, 12.5.2016.

[23] See among many P Craig, 'Delegated Acts, Implementing Acts and the New Comitology Regulation' (2011) 36 *European Law Review* 671; S Peers and M Costa, 'Accountability for Delegated and Implementing Acts after the Treaty of Lisbon' (2012) 18(3) *European Law Journal* 427–60; D Ritleng, 'The dividing line between delegated and implementing acts: The Court of Justice sidesteps the difficulty in Commission v. Parliament and Council (Biocides)' (2015) 52 *Common Market Law Review* 243–58; J Mendes, 'Delegated and Implementing Rule Making: Proceduralisation and Constitutional Design' (2013) 19(1) *European Law Journal* 22–41; T Christiansen and M Dobbels, 'Non-Legislative Rule Making after the Lisbon Treaty: Implementing the New System of Comitology and Delegated Acts' (2013) 19(1) *European Law Journal* 42–56.

in criminal law is not an entirely new phenomenon at national level, it certainly is in the case of the EU. The challenges that manifold interaction between sources of Union and Member State law might pose in terms of legal certainty should not be underestimated, especially when this is directly connected to the obligation to impose deprivation of liberty on the persons concerned.

VI. Criminal Law Proportionality

The Directive creates no further harmonisation, as compared to the FD. In terms of conducts, drug-related crimes are linked to the peculiarities of a national context. Specific inputs from the EU concerning the meaning of concepts such as a *large quantity* or *particularly harmful* drugs, or the *serious damage* to a *number of persons*, are unrealistic.

The same goes for the penalty system set up by the FD. Firstly, almost all Member States already provide higher terms of imprisonment than those of the FD, so they need not amend their legislation in this respect.[24] Secondly, the question remains as to whether the minimum-maximum is suitable for approximating (custodial) penalties. Member States can still provide for longer terms of imprisonment, which results in significant discrepancies throughout the EU. Thirdly, harsh penalties *result in* and *depend on* numerous factors related to the specific national law. On the one hand, threatened high penalties can allow for the use of particularly intrusive means of investigation, recourse to longer terms of pre-trial detention and the like. On the other, punishment can be significantly influenced by the application of aggravating and mitigating circumstances. In both cases, the legal regimes within the EU vary considerably as to what constitutes a large quantity, serious harm to health, personal consumption, facts of minor severity and voluntary withdrawal from the offence.[25]

In this respect, more specific references to the treatment of minor or petty offences might have rendered the Directive more in compliance with the principle of proportionality. The ECLAN preparatory study argued that the lowering of penalties while maintaining the minimum-maximum criterion would have a limited positive impact on individuals.[26] Furthermore, the report proposed making Article 5 FD (the provision on mitigating circumstances) mandatory, as well as adding two mitigating circumstances on 'drug mules' and addicted offenders. None of those suggestions were followed. The question arises as to whether the

[24] At the time of writing, 12 Member States impose life imprisonment for drug offences: nine when committed in the context of a criminal organisation, and three for marketing a large quantity of drugs. The first group includes AT, CY, EE, FR, GR, IT, MT, SK and UK, whereas the second features CY, GR, HU, IE, SK and UK.

[25] See the ECLAN report, n 17 above, 9 onwards.

[26] See the ECLAN preparatory study, n 17 above, 96.

minimum rule clause under Article 83 TFEU prevents the Union from imposing the application of mitigating circumstances upon Member States at all.

From a systematic perspective, the answer would be negative. Not only has the EU imposed the obligation of criminalisation on Member States in areas where they did not formerly provide penal sanctions, but the cases of driving licences and immigration (will) show that the CJEU has imposed decriminalisation through general principles, such as proportionality and effectiveness. In light of the foregoing, the introduction of mandatory mitigating circumstances seems to be compatible with the Treaties. This is even more so when considering that this would not impose any form of decriminalisation, and that the specific discipline concerning the operation of those circumstances would be still governed by national law.

VII. Conclusions

The Anti-Drug Trafficking Directive confirms, and builds on, the key features of the EU approach to deprivation of liberty as punishment, discussed in previous chapters. Similarly to the Anti-Fraud Directive, the establishment of a level playing-field and facilitation of judicial cooperation are the two main drivers of an approximation endeavour whose main goal is the reinforcement of the Union as a borderless area. The use of imprisonment epitomises the pursuit of effectiveness through deterrence.

The Directive on anti-drug trafficking cases adds further substance to the concerns in terms of legal certainty and criminal law proportionality emerging from the protection of the Union's financial interests. Firstly, the analysis brought to the fore the interaction of sources of EU law as a possible issue of legal certainty. When comitology acts are entrusted with the role of drawing the boundaries of criminal law and founding the imposition of high terms of imprisonment, the accessibility and foreseeability of those norms must be subject to the closest scrutiny. This would require, inter alia, enhanced transparency and clarity underpinning the adoption of those acts.

Secondly, the effective role for the Union in promoting proportionality of penalties arises. On the one hand, the Directive confirms that the minimum-maximum bears insufficient approximation potential. On the other, it strengthens the need for a holistic approach where levels of penalty must be conceived of jointly with, inter alia, tailored provisions on circumstances. To this end, it is submitted that the non-imposition of mandatory mitigating circumstances concerning small quantities of drug mules is a missed opportunity. The final case study on market abuse builds on these issues and completes the picture of the use of deprivation of liberty in EU substantive criminal law. The overall conclusion goes in the direction of reconceptualisation of the EU legality and proportionality that takes into account the peculiarities of the EU legal order.

5

The Market Abuse Directive

I. Introduction

Market abuse is a long-standing item on the EU agenda. Directive 89/592/EEC[1] first required Member States to introduce effective, proportionate and dissuasive sanctions against insider trading.[2] A second Directive[3] was adopted in 2003, defining conduct of insider trading and market manipulation.[4] As in the case of the first Directive, Member States were left free to decide which kinds of penalty to apply.[5]

The 2008 Executive Summary of the Committee of European Securities Regulators (CESR)[6] analysed the effects of this legislation. Firstly, only two countries did not punish insider trading with deprivation of liberty, and only four states exclude custodial penalties for market manipulation. Secondly, the terms of detention can vary considerably. The maximum thresholds concerning insider trading offences range from one year (Belgium) to 15 (Latvia), while market manipulation is punished with a maximum in the range of two years (Belgium) to 15 years (Latvia).

[1] Directive 89/592/CEE of the Council coordinating regulations on insider trading, [1989] OJ L334/30, 13.11.1989.

[2] See for analysis also from a comparative perspective L Foffani, *Infedeltà patrimoniale e conflitto d'interessi nella gestione d'impresa. Profili penalistici* (Milano, Giuffrè, 1997) 360–61, fn 225.

[3] Directive 2003/6/EC of the European Parliament and of the Council of 28 January 2003 on insider dealing and market manipulation (market abuse), [2003] OJ L96/16, 12.4.2003.

[4] Though the Directive in question was not an instrument of criminal law, it has had significant implications in terms of criminal law principles in EU law. To this end the Case C-45/08, *Spector Photo Group NV and Chris Van Raemdonck v Commissie voor het Bank-, Financie- en Assurantiewezen (CBFA)*, [2009] ECR I-12073 should be mentioned. In that judgment the Court stated that once the (objective) constituent elements of insider dealing are satisfied, it is possible to assume intention on the part of the performer of that transaction.

[5] EU law on market abuse consisted (and still consists, to some extent) of a multi-levelled and comprehensive set of provisions. See on this MM Siems, 'The EU Market Abuse Directive: A Case-Based Analysis' (2008) 2 *Law and Financial Markets Review* 39–49.

[6] Committee of European Securities Regulators, Executive Summary to the Report on Administrative Measures and Sanctions as well as the Criminal Sanctions available in Member States under the Market Abuse Directive (MAD), available at: www.cesr-eu.org.

The Stockholm Programme,[7] and the Commission communications on criminal policy[8] and on reinforcing the sanctions regime in the financial services sector[9] confirm the importance of market abuse to the EU. By means of a familiar argumentative pattern, the EU found the need for new EU instruments on market abuse due to the differences amongst Member States' laws, with specific regard to types and ranges of penalty. Dissuasiveness and effective application of sanctions may ensure compliance with EU financial services rules. However, the Commission states that penalties involving deprivation of liberty should be introduced only for the most serious violations, and only where this would prove essential to ensure the effective implementation of EU legislation.

On those grounds, the EU adopted Regulation 596/2014 on market abuse (the Market Abuse Regulation or 'MAR')[10] and a Directive on criminal sanctions for market abuse.[11] The former establishes detailed administrative rules on market abuse and related sanctions. The latter – enacted on the basis of Article 83(2) TFEU – introduces criminal sanctions against market manipulation and insider dealing.[12]

II. The Regulation

The Regulation provides definitions of many aspects of market abuse, such as that of 'financial instrument' or 'market operator'. The MAR points out the

[7] The Stockholm Programme – An open and secure Europe serving and protecting citizens, [2010] OJ C115/124.

[8] Communication from the Commission to the European Parliament, the Council, the European Economic and Social Committee and the Committee of Regions, *Towards an EU criminal policy: Ensuring the effective implementation of EU policies through criminal law*, Brussels 20.9.2011, COM(2011) 573 final, 10 onwards.

[9] Communication from the Commission to the European Parliament, the Council, the European Economic and Social Committee and the Committee of the Regions, *Reinforcing sanctioning regimes in the financial services sector*, Brussels, 8.12.2010 COM(2010) 716 final.

[10] Regulation (EU) No 596/2014 of the European Parliament and of the Council of 16 April 2014 on market abuse (market abuse regulation) and repealing Directive 2003/6/EC of the European Parliament and of the Council and Commission Directives 2003/124/EC, 2003/125/EC and 2004/72/EC, [2014] OJ L173/1, 12.6.2014.

[11] The EU package on market abuse even goes beyond the Regulation and the Directive mentioned. In particular, the Union has adopted Regulation (EU) No 600/2014 of the European Parliament and of the Council of 15 May 2014 on markets in financial instruments and amending Regulation (EU) No 648/2012, [2014] OJ L173/84, 12.6.2014, and Directive 2014/65/EU of the European Parliament and of the Council of 15 May 2014 on markets in financial instruments and amending Directive 2002/92/EC and Directive 2011/61/EU, [2014] OJ L173/349, 12.6.2014. See on it R Kert, 'The relationship between administrative and criminal sanctions in the new market abuse provisions' in F Galli and A Weyembergh, *Do labels still matter?* (Bruxelles, Editions de l'Université de Bruxelles, 2014) 95–108.

[12] See on it E Herlin-Karnell, 'White-collar crime and European financial crises: getting tough on EU market abuse' (2012) 37(4) *European Law Review* 481–94; L Foffani, 'Politica criminale europea e sistema finanziario: l'esempio degli abusi di mercato' (2014) 3–4 *Diritto Penale Contemporaneo* 65–72; M Siems and M Nelemans, 'The Reform of the EU Market Abuse Law: Revolution or Evolution?' (2012) 19 *The Maastricht Journal of European and Comparative Law* 195–205.

activities falling within the meaning of market manipulation, insider dealing, and unlawful disclosure of inside information, as well as those which are accepted market practices. Chapter 5 of the Regulation lays down the sanctions,[13] with the Member States required to empower competent authorities to sanction the conduct provided for in the Regulation, unless they already punish such conduct as criminal offences. The MAR features three groups of penalties: sanctions directed to violations committed either by legal and natural persons;[14] financial penalties framed through the minimum-maximum criterion; and financial penalties against legal persons, also identified through the minimum-maximum. As far as sentencing is concerned,[15] Member States shall ensure that competent authorities take into account all relevant circumstances, including the gravity and duration of the infringement, the degree of responsibility of the person responsible for the infringement, and previous infringements by the person responsible.

III. The Directive

The Impact Assessment to the Market Abuse Directive (MAD)[16] identified three main reasons for the approximation of criminal laws in this area. Firstly, the different legal regimes on the definition of offences and penalties against market abuse made the penalty system within the EU lead to insufficient dissuasiveness and ineffective enforcement. Secondly, (custodial) penalties have a strong deterrent effect. Thirdly, common minimum rules for the most serious market abuse offences would facilitate law enforcement cooperation.

In terms of definition of conduct, the MAR and MAD are very similar. Article 3 MAD and Article 8 MAR deal with insider dealing, the only difference being that Article 3 MAD requires criminalisation in serious cases and when the offence is committed intentionally. The same holds true for Articles 4 MAD and 10 MAR on the unlawful disclosure of inside information. Article 4 MAD specifies that that provision applies in accordance with the need to protect the freedom of the press and the freedom of expression. Articles 5 MAD and 12 MAR focus

[13] See in particular Arts 30 and 31 of MAR.

[14] Such sanctions are, for example: an order requiring the person responsible for the infringement to cease the conduct and to desist from a repetition of that conduct; withdrawal or suspension of the authorisation of an investment firm; or maximum administrative pecuniary sanctions of at least three times the amount of the profits gained or losses avoided because of the infringement, where those can be determined (Art 30(2)).

[15] MAR, Art 31.

[16] Commission Staff Working Paper Impact Assessment Accompanying the document Proposal for Regulation of the European Parliament and of the Council on insider dealing market manipulation (market abuse) and the Proposal for a Directive of the European Parliament and of the Council on criminal sanctions for insider dealing and market manipulation, Brussels, 20.10.2011 SEC(2011) 1217 final.

on market manipulation. The MAR extends the meaning of market manipulation to a number of forms of conduct not mentioned in MAD. A partial coincidence of definitions between the two instruments remains, save for the additional requirement of the seriousness and intentional nature of the conducts featured in the MAD.

The MAR establishes that for some of the conduct falling under the meaning of market manipulation, 'Annex I defines non-exhaustive indicators relating to the employment of a fictitious device or any other form of deception or contrivance, and non-exhaustive indicators related to false or misleading signals and to price securing'. The Commission is empowered to adopt delegated acts to specify such indicators.[17] As for the sanctions, the Directive establishes a maximum term of imprisonment of at least four years for insider dealing and market manipulation. The unlawful disclosure of inside information is to be punished by Member States with a maximum term of imprisonment of at least two years.[18]

IV. EU Law Proportionality

The two measures were justified through the differences amongst Member States' legislation on market abuse. Criminal sanctions and imprisonment would increase deterrence and facilitate law enforcement cooperation. Enacted pursuant to Article 83(2) TFEU, the Directive aims to ensure the effectiveness of EU law and policy in an area outside criminal law and already subject to harmonisation.

The lack of dissuasiveness brought about by the legal discrepancies across the EU is dealt with mostly by administrative sanctions in the MAR. Nonetheless, the question arises as to whether the arguments founding the MAD and the rules contained therein are sufficiently solid. Firstly, one should consider whether criminal law was necessary at all. Secondly, the need for custodial penalties should be assessed. Criminal law may be considered the right choice to avoid 'labelling frauds'. Particularly serious penalties deserve an appropriate qualification. Individuals are better protected where harsh measures are labelled as criminal, since the latter are required to comply with much higher standards, from a substantive and procedural viewpoint. However, the MAR and MAD offer little clarification as to the meaning of *seriousness*, and an essential aspect of criminalisation is referred to Member States.

As for the use of custodial penalties, the Commission proposal only required effective, dissuasive and proportionate sanctions, with the EP adding the mentioned provisions on imprisonment.[19] The EU co-legislator justified the amendment by

[17] MAR, Arts 12(3) and 12(5) respectively.

[18] Ibid, Arts 7(2) and 7(3) respectively.

[19] European Parliament Report on the proposal for a Directive of the European Parliament and of the Council on criminal sanctions for insider dealing and market manipulation (COM(2011)0654 – C7-0358/2011 – 2011/0297(COD)), A7-0344/2012, 19.10.2012.

arguing that 'if the need for this legal instrument lies on the fact that Member States sanctioning regimes are in general weak and heterogeneous, sanctions should be to a certain extent harmonised'. The latitude left to Member States by the Commission would have been more favourable to personal liberty. Member States could still resort to imprisonment even though they are not required to do so by EU law. Leaving discretion to Member States on this would have been more consistent with the 'open' approach established by the Directive.

Seen from another perspective, Mitsilegas argued that the interplay between criminal and administrative law at EU level, on the one hand, and the principle of effectiveness, on the other, may result in decriminalisation. Article 82 TFEU on approximation of procedural criminal law allows Member States to maintain or introduce a higher level of protection for individuals. The same provision is absent in Article 83, so that the establishment of a national regime harsher than that provided at EU level seems to be precluded. The double channel implies that Member States cannot choose to treat the administrative offences in the Regulation as criminal offences. In this sense, the effectiveness argument implies that the use of criminal law might jeopardise the effective implementation of EU law.[20] Secondly, the CJEU is now empowered to carry out a double-proportionality test: an EU law proportionality test, as provided for in Article 52 CFREU; and a criminal law proportionality test, required by Article 49 CFREU.

V. Legal Certainty

The MAD requires Member States to criminalise insider dealing, unlawful disclosure of information and market manipulation *at least in serious cases* and when such actions are committed *intentionally*. The final text reached a compromise following inter-institutional dialogue: The Commission proposed criminalisation only in case of intentional offence; the EP added conduct recklessly perpetrated; the Council put forward measures *at least in serious cases*.[21] Guidance on how to assess the seriousness of the conduct is provided in recitals 11 and 12.[22]

[20] V Mitsilegas, *EU Criminal Law After Lisbon: Rights, Trust and the Transformation of Justice in Europe* (Oxford, Hart Publishing, 2016) 121 onwards.

[21] Proposal for a Directive of the European Parliament and of the Council on criminal sanctions for insider dealing and market manipulation (MAD) – Presidency Compromise Text, DROIPEN 133, 2011/0297 (COD), Brussels, 5 October 2012.

[22] The Council's proposal was to include these in the text of the Directive. As to insider dealing, the Council proposal identified that the offence should be considered serious at least in the following cases: when the value of the financial instruments acquired or disposed, at the time of the conduct, is considered high by Member States in accordance with their national law; when the agent has obtained the inside information as a result of the exercise of his employment, profession or duties; when the agent has obtained the inside information as a result of the exercise of a public office or of an office or profession in a regulatory or supervisory body, or of a position directly connected to a public office or regulatory or supervisory body; when the inside information has been obtained as a

Other than being unclear, seriousness is not even a precondition for criminalisation. Imprisonment is required *at least* in serious cases; which means that Member States can impose deprivation of liberty for actions that are not so serious.

The EU has repeatedly stated that approximation in substantive criminal law aims to overcome divergence of Member States' legal regimes, for the benefit of legal certainty and effectiveness of EU policy. Key aspects of criminalisation and coordination between the MAR and the MAD remain rather obscure. Possible overlap and blurred boundaries heighten the risk of cases of violations of *ne bis in idem* in the area of market abuse,[23] repeatedly deplored by the ECtHR.[24] This is even more the case as the CJEU, by means of very problematic reasoning, has recently found that an interference with *ne bis in idem* can be justified if proportionate to a legitimate aim.[25]

In terms of legal certainty, and similarly to the Anti-Drug Trafficking Directive, concerns arise from Article 12(3) MAR. That provision empowers the Commission to specify aspects of the conduct which falls under the definition of market abuse, through delegated acts. The delegated act is key to drawing the boundaries of penal intervention. However, the procedures of adoption of delegated acts present serious problems of accessibility and transparency. To this end, one may raise concerns of the same kind as those voiced apropos of the implementing acts and Anti-Drug Trafficking Directive, in terms of transparency and accessibility.

VI. Criminal Law Proportionality

Other than issues of legal certainty, a possible overlap between the MAR and the MAD can have repercussions in terms of proportionality between the seriousness of the offences and the severity of penalties. The '*at least in serious cases*' clause

result of criminal activity of the agent, alone or in conjunction with other persons. Concerning market manipulation, the following circumstances were selected: when the conduct relates to a benchmark, or a significant number of financial instruments or related spot commodity contracts, or causes effects, or is likely to cause effects, on financial instruments or related spot commodity contracts traded on a significant number of trading venues in different Member States; when the conduct is performed in the exercise of the agent's employment, profession or duties, or of the exercise of a public office or of an office or profession in a regulatory or supervisory body, or of a position directly connected to a public office or regulatory or supervisory body.

[23] As to the relationship between *ne bis in idem* and legal certainty, see among many J Lelieur, 'Transnationalising *Ne Bis In Idem*: How the Rule of *Ne Bis In Idem* Reveals the Principle of Personal Legal Certainty' (2013) 9(4) *Utrecht Law Review* 198–210.

[24] See ECtHR, *Grande Stevens and Others v Italy*, Applications No 18640/10, 18647/10, 18663/10, 18668/10 and 18698/10, judgment of 4 March 2014.

[25] Case C-524/15, *Criminal proceedings against Luca Menci*, judgment of 20 March 2018, EU:C:2018:197; Case C-537/16, *Garlsson Real Estate SA v Commissione Nazionale per le Società e la Borsa (Consob)*, judgment of 20 March 2018, EU:C:2018:193.

might result in criminalisation of minor offences. The discretion left to Member States regarding the cases of criminalisation is not in agreement with the penalty system outlined by the MAD. States are obliged to introduce minimum-maximum terms of imprisonment. This means that, should a member treat a *not so serious* violation as a criminal offence, it would have to punish that violation with imprisonment.

The MAD provides a minimum-maximum term of four years' imprisonment for market manipulation, which forces Member States such as Belgium to raise their penalties significantly. The text sums up the intentional nature of the offences (proposed by the Commission) with the '*at least in serious cases*' clause (expression of the Council) and the specific provisions on imprisonment (put forward by the EP).[26] Criminal law is not the result of an arithmetic sum, but should reflect a more coherent stance. On the one hand, the Commission and the Council had conceived open rules (so leaving the choice to Member States) on the definition of offences and penalties. One the other, the EP report provided for no '*serious cases*' clause.

The possible consequences ensuing from this *melange* confirm that proportionality and coherence may not be dissociated. On the basis of the MAD, a Member State can criminalise conduct which is not particularly serious, but then it would have to apply a maximum term of at least two years' (or four) imprisonment.

VII. Conclusions

Similarly to the case study on psychoactive substances, the approximation of offences and penalties carried out by the MAD must be read in conjunction with the establishment of key definitions on market abuse and administrative penalties laid down in the MAR. Once again, the EU justifies its choice on criminalisation and use of custodial penalties by reference to the ineffectiveness caused by the diversity of legal regimes within the Union.

The MAR and the MAD require punishment of the same conduct, the only difference being the requirement that criminal penalties regard *at least serious cases* of conducts committed intentionally. No extensive guidance is provided as to what should be understood as *serious offences*. The Member States seem not to be bound to the requirement of gravity, since they are allowed to criminalise the conduct that they consider appropriate. Furthermore, and in a way akin to the Anti-Drug Trafficking Directive, key aspects of the offence will be defined by a delegated act.

The interaction between sources of the EU is twofold. It regards the MAD and the MAR, on the one hand, and those instruments and the delegated act,

[26] To be thorough, the initial proposal of the EP on the penalties for market manipulation and insider dealing was even higher than that eventually agreed, namely five years' imprisonment.

on the other. This causes concern in terms of legal certainty and proportionality. Firstly, the blurred boundaries between the administrative, and criminal, systems of penalties might be prone to cases of double punishment. This is even more so in light of the recent case-law of CJEU, which relaxes the constraints set by Article 50 CFREU. Secondly, the MAD leaves Member States free to impose penalties other than in serious cases, save when requiring the punishment of those actions with imprisonment.

While the main view of the use of deprivation of liberty in substantive EU criminal law is straightforward (protection of free movement), the justifications of that action and the implementation of the approximation strategy creates challenges to one of the strongholds of personal liberty. The peculiarities of the Union legal order are key to emphasising the seriousness of those issues, requiring a re-conceptualisation of the EU legality and proportionality in criminal law.

Concluding Remarks on EU Substantive Criminal Law and Deprivation of Liberty

The Union's approach to imprisonment builds on the fundamentals of EU law involvement in deprivation of liberty as highlighted in Part I. According to the legislature, integration in criminal law and with regard to the levels of penalty specifically is essential to the preservation of the Union as an area without internal frontiers. The emergence of use of deprivation of liberty in substantive criminal law, however, raises an issue in terms of fundamental rights protection.

The Treaties provide for two legal bases, embodying decades of legal and political development: on the one hand, criminalisation to fight serious areas of cross-border crime; and on the other, approximation essential to ensure implementation of the Union's policies through *effective*, *dissuasive* and *proportionate* penalties. These being the two main rationales for substantive criminal law, key features in the use of deprivation of liberty come to the surface.

Firstly, approximating offences and penalties would serve to make EU law more effective. According to the legislature, a borderless area needs balance: a level playing-field aimed at fighting against exploitation of legal differences and loopholes. Secondly, criminal sanction is a synonym for deprivation of liberty, since the EU legislature never renounces imprisonment. Thirdly, and relatedly, the threat of harsh penalties is preferred because it would bear a strong dissuasive effect, which in turn will contribute to effectiveness. Fourthly, approximation is needed as it fosters judicial cooperation.

There is now a proper body of law of deprivation of liberty in substantive EU criminal law. The Union has increasingly stepped into an area historically reserved for state sovereignty. Against that background, the peculiarities of the EU legal order not only determine the nature and extent of legal integration (effectiveness, mutual recognition, free movement), but also the impact of such developments on strongholds of personal liberty.

The first issue – conceptually speaking – on the EU approach to deprivation of liberty in this area is one of legitimacy. The Union legislature is driven by both abstract, and pragmatic, reasons like general deterrence and judicial cooperation. The suitability of these grounds for justifying a general and irreducible requirement for imprisonment in all instruments of substantive criminal law can be doubted. This is even more so considering that, in some cases, the EU will impose an increase in the levels of penalty at state law level.

The second and related problem is one of legal certainty and proportionality. In the background, there is the question of competences and the unresolved conundrum of what 'minimum rules' means. Does this clause preclude the introduction of mandatory mitigating circumstances? A systemic interpretation would suggest an answer in the negative. Does the minimum rules requirement preclude the use of a stronger approximating criterion than the minimum-maximum? It was shown that the latter was conceived to serve the purposes of judicial cooperation, and lives at the expense of proportionality and coherence.

The unprecedented interaction between different sources of law creates new challenges in terms of legal certainty. This concerns the emerging use of 'comitology' to ultimately establish what should be subject to custodial penalties, and foundational doctrines of EU law such as direct applicability. The former case results in concerns of accessibility and foreseeability due to: opaque procedures for adoption of delegated acts; and the possible lack of clarity in national law ensuing from the interaction between these different forms of cross-references.

Direct applicability raises doubts on new horizons that could be reached by the use of deprivation of liberty and EU criminal law, broadly. The example of the protection of the EU's financial interests makes clear that the issue of directly applicable rules in this area is vividly in debate. In conclusion, the EU's approach to the deprivation of liberty shows that the Union involvement in this area takes the shape of legal integration and has free movement as a trigger and aim of its action. This, however, creates challenges to a stronghold of personal liberty such as the principle of legality and proportionality of penalties. The argument that approximation of levels of penalty facilitates mutual recognition reinforces the importance of a holistic approach. It introduces the issue of the combined use of static (approximation of substantive criminal law) and dynamic (judicial cooperation) rules involving deprivation of liberty, meant to preserve free movement (and the borderless area, broadly) through the forced movement of people. In line with the foregoing considerations, the next Part moves on to the analysis of the EU approach to the deprivation of liberty in procedural criminal law and mutual recognition.

PART III

Procedural Criminal Law and Mutual Recognition

6

EU Procedural Criminal and Mutual Recognition. Overview

I. Introduction

This Part is devoted to procedural criminal law and instruments of mutual recognition in criminal law at EU level. The first two Parts of this book brought to the fore the two souls of EU constitutionalisation (integration and fundamental rights protection) as the overarching framework in which the EU's involvement in the deprivation of liberty came into being and developed. Against that background, the threefold role of free movement as trigger, paradigm and laboratory surfaced. The construction and preservation of the Union as a borderless area stood out as the main horizon of the Union's action. That being the perimeter of the story, the key characters of this research (security, effectiveness and free movement) manifested their manifold roles across Union law. The emergence of strong connections amongst different areas of EU law confirms the appropriateness of a holistic approach. For example, the analysis of substantive criminal law showed that the criterion for approximation of custodial penalties (the minimum-maximum) ties that realm to judicial cooperation, which is activated when a specific minimum-maximum threshold of punishment is involved. The Part on mutual recognition and EU procedural criminal law reinforces the idea of the Union's understanding of deprivation of liberty as one developed through building blocks added to foundational concepts.

Mutual recognition – the barycentre of judicial cooperation and, as shown below, EU procedural criminal law – has fostered integration in criminal justice, but has posed challenges to fundamental rights protection. 'Borrowed' from the law of the internal market, it applies the principle of free movement to judicial decisions. It implies that a judicial order issued in one Member State is recognised and executed in another Member State without further formality. By doing so, it means to substitute the previous system of extradition with smoother inter-state cooperation in criminal matters, with a view to preventing the existence of any criminals' safe heavens within the EU and ensuring the *safe* exercise of free movement by the Union's citizens and businesses.

There are significant implications in terms of fundamental rights. Firstly, the higher level of automaticity brought about by mutual recognition rests on a legal fiction. This fiction is the principle of mutual trust, ie the presumption that

Member States respect fundamental rights throughout the Union. Not surprisingly, such a presumption has been highly contested over recent years, not least because of important judgments showing how critical this fiction can be.[1] To make mutual recognition sustainable, the Union has adopted Directives aimed at establishing a level playing-field of individual rights in criminal proceedings. These are trust-building measures, so that Member States' compliance with fundamental rights is not just presumed but also based on factual elements.[2]

Secondly, mutual recognition aims to enforce judicial decisions against individuals, with a strong emphasis being placed on state demands.[3] This has led to paying higher attention to the effectiveness of judicial cooperation at the expense of individual rights protection.[4] We have seen this particularly in the case-law of the CJEU on the European Arrest Warrant Framework Decision (EAW FD).[5] Thirdly, a number of mutual recognition instruments in EU law involve the deprivation of liberty.

Automaticity and effectiveness of judicial cooperation place the right to liberty under pressure, so that its content and protection in the Union is carefully assessed. The right to liberty is indeed the first and core fundamental right coming into play in this area, requiring that deprivation of liberty is carried out in the *cases* and *according to the procedures* established by the law. This Part distinguishes between a 'default right to liberty' and an 'evolutionary right to liberty'. Chapter six outlines the 'default right to liberty', as shaped by: The Charter and its Explanations; the ECHR as interpreted by the ECtHR. As clarified by the Explanations, the CFREU and ECHR-relevant provisions on the right to liberty have the same meaning and scope. The 'evolutionary right to liberty' is the product of the interaction between the 'default right to liberty' and its interpretation by the CJEU in the context of

[1] See ECtHR, *MSS v Belgium and Greece*, Application no 30696/09, (2011) 53 EHRR 2; C-411/10, *NS v Secretary of State for the Home Department*, and C-493/10, *ME and Others v Refugee Applications Commissioner and Minister for Justice, Equality and Law Reform*, EU:C:2011:865. See E Brouwer, 'Mutual Trust and the Dublin Regulation: Protection of Fundamental Rights in the EU and the Burden of Proof' (2013) 9(1) *Utrecht Law Review* 135; V Mitsilegas, 'The Limits of Mutual Trust in Europe's Area of Freedom, Security and Justice: From Automatic Inter-State Cooperation to the Slow Emergence of the Individual' (2012) 31(1) *Yearbook of European Law* 319.

[2] Valsamis Mitsilegas, *EU Criminal Law after Lisbon: Rights, Trust and the Transformation of Justice in Europe*, Hart Studies in European Criminal Law, 1st edn (Oxford, Hart Publishing, 2016) 153.

[3] It should be recalled, however, that mutual recognition has also been applied to limit states' coercive powers, as testified to by the CJEU's case-law on Article 54 CISA and transnational *ne bis in idem*. See Anne Weyembergh and Inés Armada, 'The principle of ne bis in idem in Europe's Area of Freedom, Security and Justice' in M Bergstrom V Mitsilegas, T Konstadinides (ed), *Research Handbook on EU Criminal Law* (Cheltenham, Edward Elgar, 2016).

[4] V Mitsilegas, 'Mutual Recognition, Mutual Trust and Fundamental Rights After Lisbon' in V Mitsilegas and others (eds), *Research Handbook on EU Criminal Law* (Cheltenham, Edward Elgar, 2016) 148–77; V Mitsilegas, 'The Symbiotic Relationship Between Mutual Trust and Fundamental Rights in Europe's Area of Criminal Justice' (2015) 7(4) *New Journal of European Criminal Law* 457.

[5] C-237/15 PPU, *Minister for Justice and Equality v Francis Lanigan*, EU:C:2015:474, para 28; C-192/12 PPU, *Melvin West*, EU:C:2012:404, para 54; C-399/11, *Stefano Melloni v Ministerio Fiscal*, EU:C:2013:107, para 36; C-168/13 PPU, *Jeremy F v Premier ministre*, EU:C:2013:358, para 34.

mutual recognition. As the evolutionary right to liberty logically presupposes the default right to liberty, the latter is outlined in the first place.

Part III tests EU law on mutual recognition and criminal procedure involving detention against the right to liberty, and is organised as follows. Chapter six explains the main aspects underlying the analysis: mutual trust, mutual recognition, the right to liberty in EU law and its connection to the principle of proportionality. Chapter seven uses those benchmarks to discuss: the EAW FD, three Directives on the right to translation and interpretation,[6] information[7] and the access to the lawyer[8] in criminal proceedings and EAW procedures. Chapter eight focuses on the FDs on the transfer of prisoners (2008/909/JHA),[9] probation measures (2008/947/JHA),[10] and pre-trial measures alternative to detention (2009/829/JHA, or European Supervision Order Framework Decision).[11] Finally, Chapter nine draws some conclusions from the previous chapters.

While the link between the right to liberty and the materials in Chapter seven (EAW and the Directives) is self-evident, the connection to the other FDs is subtler. Firstly, those FDs feature rules *allowing for* or *regulating* deprivation of liberty. Secondly, they are instruments of mutual recognition in criminal matters, whose object is judicial decisions in criminal law. Criminal procedure and mutual recognition heavily influence each other. The latter is inextricably linked to the former, without being formally a part of it. The result is a legal framework of an undefined nature, which has a great impact on the right to liberty but provides few individual guarantees.

The two substantive chapters highlight the unbalanced relationship between the smoothness of judicial cooperation on the one hand, and the level of protection of the right to liberty on the other. The impact on that right is twofold. Firstly, the legal framework concerned lacks legal certainty. If deprivation of liberty shall be carried out in the *cases* and according to the *procedures* established by the law,

[6] Council Directive (EU) No 2010/64 [2010] OJ L280/1. R Vogler, 'Lost in Translation: Language Rights for Defendants in European Criminal Proceedings' in S Ruggeri (ed), *Human Rights in European Criminal Law* (Switzerland, Springer, 2014) 95–110.

[7] Council Directive (EU) No 2012/13 [2012] OJ L142/1. S Quattrocolo, 'The Right to Information in EU Legislation' in S Ruggeri (ed), n 6 above.

[8] Council Directive (EU) No 2013/48 [2013] OJ L294/1. See L Bachmaier Winter, 'The EU Directive on the Right to Access to a Lawyer: A Critical Assessment' in S Ruggeri (ed), n 6 above.

[9] Council Framework Decision 2008/909/JHA of 27 November 2008 on the application of the principle of mutual recognition to judgments in criminal matters imposing custodial sentences or measures involving deprivation of liberty for the purpose of their enforcement in the European Union, [2008] OJ L327/27, 5.12.2008.

[10] Council Framework Decision 2008/947/JHA of 27 November 2008 on the application of the principle of mutual recognition to judgments and probation decisions with a view to the supervision of probation measures and alternative sanctions, [2008] OJ L337/102, 16.12.2008.

[11] Council Framework Decision 2009/829/JHA of 23 October 2009 on the application, between Member States of the European Union, of the principle of mutual recognition to decisions on supervision measures as an alternative to provisional detention, [2009] OJ L294/20, 11.11.2009.

the rules *authorising* (the *cases*) and *governing* (the *procedures*) deprivation of liberty must be clear, accessible and foreseeable. This seems especially not to be the case when it comes to the materials discussed in Chapter eight. Furthermore, the uncertain nature of mutual recognition procedures gives rise to a double standard of protection, whereby individual rights are better safeguarded in criminal proceedings than in the context of judicial cooperation.

Secondly, the current EU approach to the right to liberty leaves detention conditions outside its scope. Requiring that 'one shall be deprived of liberty [only] in accordance with a procedure established by law' logically involves the phase of enforcement: so long as deprivation of liberty is ongoing, clear and accessible legal procedures must apply. Detention conditions are inherent in the *established procedures*, and therefore constitute part of a test on violations of the right to liberty.

The conclusion is that integration through the paradigm of the internal market and with free movement in mind creates tensions with fundamental rights, and the right to liberty specifically. That right is to be redefined, to tailor its content to the peculiarities of the Union legal order and the framework ensuing from integration in this area.

II. Mutual Recognition and Mutual Trust in EU Law

As is known, mutual recognition in criminal matters is a principle borrowed from the law of the internal market, where it was introduced by the *Cassis de Dijon* judgment of the CJEU.[12] It requires that a product lawfully produced and marketed in one Member State, should be capable of being marketed in another Member State, unless grounds for refusal apply.[13] The 1999 Tampere Council adopted the principle of mutual recognition as the cornerstone of judicial cooperation in criminal matters. In criminal law, mutual recognition is used to step up judicial cooperation between Member States within the EU: according to this principle, a judicial order issued by one Member State is to be recognised and executed by another Member State, save where grounds for refusal apply. However, the principle of mutual recognition had already been applied to judicial cooperation in civil

[12] Case 120/78, *Rewe-Zentral AG v Bundesmonopolverwaltung für Branntwein (Cassis de Dijon)*, EU:C:1979:42; K Armstrong, 'Mutual Recognition' in C Barnard and J Scott (eds), *The Law of the Single European Market. Unpacking the Premises* (Oxford, Hart Publishing, 2002) 225–68; J Snell, 'The Internal Market and the Philosophies of Market Integration' in C Barnard and S Peers (eds), *European Union Law* (Oxford, Oxford University Press, 2004) 300–323.

[13] A Rosas, 'Life after Dassonville and Cassis: Evolution but No Revolution' in M Maduro and L Azoulai (eds), *The Past and Future of EU Law: The Classics of EU Law Revisited on the 50th Anniversary of the Rome Treaty* (Oxford, Hart Publishing, 2010) 433–46; C Barnard, *The Substantive Law of the EU: The Four Freedoms*, 4th edn (Oxford, Oxford University Press, 2013) 171–77; C Janssens, *The Principle of Mutual Recognition in EU Law* (Oxford, Oxford University Press, 2013) 31 onwards.

justice, where a number of international law instruments had been adopted over the previous decades.[14] Examples in this respect are the 1968 Brussels Convention on jurisdiction and the enforcement of judgments in civil and commercial matters, and the 1988 Lugano Convention, which extended the application of the Brussels Convention to certain state members of the European Free Trade Association.[15]

The principle of mutual recognition streamlines the previous system of extradition, by introducing a higher level of automaticity in inter-state cooperation in criminal matters.[16] It does so by means of three main novelties: firstly, it abolishes the principle of dual criminality (although not in all cases); secondly, it allocates the responsibility for the surrender of judicial rather than political authorities; thirdly, it (almost completely) drops the prohibition on a state extraditing its own nationals (also referred to as the 'nationality exception' or 'nationality ban').[17] The cooperation on a given order (arrest warrant, probation measure, custodial sentence and the like) is regulated by specific legislative instruments adopted at EU law level. In the cases analysed in this chapter, the recognition of the judicial decision results in the coercive transfer of the person concerned from the issuing Member State to the executing Member State. The application of mutual recognition to criminal law has drawn criticism over the years, with major concerns being voiced about the inadequate level of individual safeguards.[18]

Indeed, mutual recognition in criminal matters implies the extraterritoriality of Member States' rules and standards, as well as a higher level of automaticity in judicial cooperation.[19] This may happen only in the context of a general feeling of

[14] Council Draft Programme of measures for implementation of the principle of mutual recognition of decisions in civil and commercial matters [2001] OJ C12/1, 2 onwards.

[15] Brussels Convention on jurisdiction and the enforcement of judgments in civil and commercial matters [1968] OJ L299/32.

[16] For a diachronic analysis, see S Miettinen, 'Onward Transfer under the European Arrest Warrant: Is the EU Moving Towards the Free Movement of Prisoners?' (2013) 5(1) *New Journal of European Criminal Law* 99.

[17] M Fichera, 'The European Arrest Warrant and the Sovereign State: A Marriage of Convenience?' (2009) 15(1) *European Law Journal* 79; M Platcha, 'Non-Extradition of Nationals: A Never-Ending Story?' (1999) 13(1) *Emory International Law Review* 77; Z Deen-Racsmány and R Blekxtoon, 'The Decline of the Nationality Exception in European Extradition? The Impact of the Regulation of (Non-) Surrender of Nationals and Dual Criminality under the European Arrest Warrant' (2005) 13(3) *European Journal of Crime, Criminal Law and Criminal Justice* 317.

[18] G Vernimmen-Van Tiggelen and others (eds), *The Future of Mutual Recognition in Criminal Matters in the European Union* (Brussels, Editions de l'Université de Bruxelles, 2009); V Mitsilegas, 'The Constitutional Implications of Mutual Recognition in Criminal Matters in the EU' (2006) 43(5) *Common Market Law Review* 1277; S Peers, 'Mutual Recognition and Criminal Law in the European Union: Has the Council Got It Wrong?' (2004) 41(1) *Common Market Law Review* 5; S Lavenex, 'Mutual Recognition and the Monopoly of Force: Limits of the Single Market Analogy' (2007) 14(5) *Journal of European Public Policy* 762.

[19] On mutual recognition and extraterritoriality, see K Nicolaidis and G Shaffer, 'Transnational Mutual Recognition Regimes: Governance without Global Government' (2005) 68(3) *Law and Contemporary Problems* 263.

mutual trust among Member States.[20] Broadly speaking, mutual trust refers to a sociological perspective, which sees trust as a tool to deal with social complexity, when there are certain values shared within a community, so as to create an expectation of regular and honest behaviour.[21] In EU criminal law, mutual trust rests on the presumption that Member States habitually act in compliance with fundamental rights.[22] To this end, Article 6 Treaty on European Union (TEU) stipulates that the Charter has the same value as the Treaty on the one hand; and on the other, fundamental rights, as guaranteed by the ECHR and as they result from the constitutional traditions common to the Member States, shall constitute general principles of the Union's law.[23]

In the context of this threefold system of fundamental rights protection (CFREU, ECHR and national traditions), the importance of mutual recognition materialises at three levels: a vertical perspective, which raises the issue as to which kind of fundamental rights standard should be applied (that of the Union or that of the Member State); a horizontal dimension, posing the question as to whether a presumption of compliance with fundamental rights by the Member State may be maintained; and the EU level, where a Union norm is reviewed against the yardstick of fundamental rights. In the vertical dimension, the most problematic issue has so far been the definition of the scope of the application of the Charter: whether it binds Member States when they *implement* EU law (as stated in Article 51(1) CFREU), or when they act *within the scope of* Union law (according to the wording of the Explanations).[24] A heated debate flourished, fuelled by highly contested judgments of the Court of Justice.[25] The horizontal dimension

[20] Case 46/76, *WJG Bauhuis v The Netherlands State*, EU:C:1977:6; Case C-25/88, *Criminal proceedings against Esther Renée Bouchara, née Wurmser, and Norlaine SA*, EU:C:1989:187; Case C-5/94, *The Queen v Ministry of Agriculture, Fisheries and Food, ex parte Hedley Lomas (Ireland)*, EU:C:1996:205.

[21] N Luhmann, *La Fiducia* (Bologna, il Mulino, 2002); F Fukuyama, *Trust: The Social Virtues and The Creation of Prosperity* (London, Penguin, 1995); G Majone (ed), *Regulating Europe* (New York, Routledge, 1996).

[22] D Flore, 'La Notion de Confiance Mutuelle: L' "alpha" Ou L' "omėga" D'une Justice Pénale Européenne?' in G De Kerchove and A Weyembergh (eds), *La Confiance Mutuelle Dans L'espace Pénal Européen – Mutual Trust in the European Criminal Area* (Brussels, Editions de l'Université de Bruxelles, 2005), 17–28; V Mitsilegas, see n 1 above.

[23] S Douglas-Scott, 'The European Union and Human Rights after the Treaty of Lisbon' (2011) 11(4) *Human Rights Law Review* 645; F Fabbrini, *Fundamental Rights in Europe* (Oxford, Oxford University Press, 2014).

[24] See, among many, A Knook, 'The Court, the Charter and the Vertical Division of Powers in the European Union' (2005) 42(2) *Common Market Law Review* 367; K Lenaerts, 'Exploring the Limits of the EU Charter of Fundamental Rights' (2012) 8 (3) *European Constitutional Law Review* 375; JHH Weiler, 'The Transformation of Europe' (1991) 100(8) *Yale Law Journal* 2403; P Eeckhout, 'The EU Charter of Fundamental Rights and the Federal Question' (2002) 39(5) *Common Market Law Review* 945.

[25] *Melloni v Ministerio Fiscal*, EU:C:2013:107; C-617/10, *Åklagaren v Hans Åkerberg Fransson*, EU:C:2013:105; C-206/13, *Cruciano Siragusa v Regione Sicilia–Soprintendenza Beni Culturali e Ambientali di Palermo*, EU:C:2014:126. F Fontanelli, 'Implementation of EU Law through Domestic Measures after Fransson: the Court of Justice Buys Time and "Non-preclusion" Troubles Loom Large' (2014) 39(5) *European Law Review* 782; L Besselink, 'The Parameters of Constitutional Conflict after Melloni' (2014) 39(4) *European Law Review* 531; A Torres Pérez, 'Melloni in Three Acts: From Dialogue

takes the form of the duty, for the executing Member State, to recognise the standard of fundamental rights protection of the issuing Member State as equivalent to its own standard.[26] However, the CJEU has found that this presumption is a rebuttableone, and that a conclusive presumption would be incompatible with EU law.[27] As shown below, the Court has confirmed this approach in the *Căldăraru* judgment.[28] In this case, the Luxembourg judge acknowledged the possibility to postpone and not implement the EAW FD, where there is a serious risk that the person concerned will be subject to inhumane treatment in the issuing Member State. The third scenario concerns the possible review of EU law against the benchmark of fundamental rights. Here, the compliance of EU norms with fundamental rights is at stake. For the purposes of this chapter, the *Advocaten voor de Wereld* case is worth mentioning.[29] The Court upheld the compatibility of the EAW FD with Article 6(2) TEU, and in particular with the principle of legality. The CJEU argued that the aim of the FD is to provide Member States with a *procedural* instrument, and not to harmonise national regimes of substantive criminal law. Indeed, it is still for Member States to define criminal offences and related penalties.[30]

to Monologue' (2014) 10(2) *European Constitutional Law Review* 308; G Cavallone, 'European Arrest Warrant and Fundamental Rights in Decisions Rendered in Absentia: The Extent of Union Law in the Case C-399/11 Melloni v Ministerio Fiscal' (2014) 4(1) *European Criminal Law Review* 19; N de Boer, 'Addressing Rights Divergences under the Charter: Melloni' (2013) 50(4) *Common Market Law Review* 1083.

[26] See in particular, Cases C-187/01 and C-385/01, *Criminal proceedings against Hüseyin Gözütok and Klaus Brügge*, EU:C:2003:87, para 33.

[27] See *NS and ME*, EU:C:2011:865, para 190.

[28] Cases C-404/15 and C-659/15, *Pál Aranyosi and Robert Căldăraru v Generalstaatsanwaltschaft Bremen*, PPU, EU:C:2016:198. KHP Bovend'Eerdt, 'The Joined Cases *Aranyosi* and *Căldăraru*: A New Limit to the Mutual Trust Presumption in the Area of Freedom, Security, and Justice?' (2016) 32(83) *Utrecht Journal of International and European Law* 112–21; Szilárd Gáspár-Szilágyi, 'Joined Cases Aranyosi and Căldăraru: Converging Human Rights Standards, Mutual Trust and a New Ground for Postponing a European Arrest Warrant' (2016) 24 *European Journal of Crime, Criminal Law and Criminal Justice* 197; Mathias Hong, 'Human Dignity, Identity Review of the European Arrest Warrant and the Court of Justice as a Listener in the Dialogue of Courts: *Solange-III* and *Aranyosi*: BVerfG 15 December 2015, 2 BvR 2735/14, *Solange III*, and ECJ (Grand Chamber) 5 April 2016, Joined Cases C-404/15 and C-659/15 PPU, *Aranyosi and Căldăraru*' (2016) 12(3) *European Constitutional Law Review* 549–63.

[29] G De Burca, 'After the EU Charter of Fundamental Rights: The Court of Justice as a Human Rights Adjudicator?' (2013) 20(2) *Maastricht Journal of European and Comparative Law* 13; F Fontanelli, 'National Measures and the Application of the EU Charter of Fundamental Rights – Does Curia.eu Know Iura.eu?' (2014) 14(2) *Human Rights Law Review* 231; F Fontanelli, 'The Implementation of European Union Law by Member States Under Article 51(1) of the Charter of Fundamental Rights' (2014) 20(2) *Columbia Journal of European Law* 194.

[30] Case C-303/05, *Advocaten voor de Wereld VZW v Leden van de Ministerraad*, EU:C:2007:261, paras 53 and 59. F Geyer, 'European Arrest Warrant: Advocaten Voor de Wereld VZW v. Leden van de Ministerraad' (2008) 4(1) *European Constitutional Law Review* 149; D Leczykiewicz, 'Constitutional Conflicts and the Third Pillar' (2008) 33(2) *European Law Review* 230; E Cloots, 'Germs of Pluralist Judicial Adjudication: Advocaten Voor de Wereld and Other References from the Belgian Constitutional Court' (2010) 47(3) *Common Market Law Review* 645; D Sarmiento, 'European Union: The European Arrest Warrant and the Quest for Constitutional Coherence' (2008) 6(1) *International Journal of Constitutional Law* 171.

Having set the scene on the legal framework concerning fundamental rights protection (with specific regard to mutual recognition in criminal matters), the next section presents the content of the right to liberty in EU law.

III. The Right to Liberty in Europe

The materials are tested against the principle of proportionality and the right to liberty.[31] The combination of Articles 6 and 52 CFREU requires that *grounds for* and *procedures of* deprivation of liberty are drafted, enacted and enforced in an accessible and foreseeable way (legal certainty), and in compliance with the principle of proportionality. To ensure proper protection of the right to liberty, *certainty* and *proportionality* of deprivation of liberty should be tested across a spectrum of situations that goes *from* the legislative adoption of norms authorising detention *to* enforcement – mainly, prison rules and compliance with them.[32] This assessment concerns EU and Member States' laws and practices, as these are subject to the Charter when they act within the scope of the application of EU law.

While the analysis of the following chapters reveals that mutual recognition can result in issues of proportionality under Article 49 CFREU as well, it is argued that the application of Article 52 CFREU can offer wider protection of the right to liberty.

Article 6 CFREU states that 'Everyone has the right to liberty and security of the person'. According to the Praesidium's Explanations to the Charter, Articles 6 CFREU and 5 ECHR have the same meaning and scope.[33]

Under Article 5 ECHR, 'Everyone has the right to liberty and security of person. No one shall be deprived of his liberty save in the following cases and in accordance with a procedure prescribed by law'. Other than deprivation of liberty of minors, or of persons of unsound mind, alcoholics or drug addicts (Article 5(1)(d) and (e) ECHR), the grounds for deprivation of liberty are: enforcement of a custodial penalty, the lawful arrest or detention of a person for non-compliance with the lawful order of a court or in order to secure the fulfilment of any obligation prescribed by law; detention on remand; and 'the lawful arrest or detention of a person to prevent him effecting an unauthorised entry into the country or of a person against whom action is being taken with a view to deportation or extradition' – Article 5(1)(f).

[31] On the role of proportionality for limiting mutual recognition see Mitsilegas, *EU Criminal Law after Lisbon: Rights, Trust and the Transformation of Justice in Europe* (Oxford, Hart Publishing 2016) 124 onward.

[32] For an insight into this perspective, see L Mancano, 'The right to liberty in European Union law and mutual recognition in criminal matters' (2016) 18 *Cambridge Yearbook of European Legal Studies* 1–24.

[33] CFREU, Art 52(7).

Article 5(1)(f) ECHR is the reference used by the ECtHR for interpreting and assessing Member States' compliance with the right to liberty in the context of extradition procedures. The test elaborated on by the ECtHR for verifying that state laws and practices have not resulted in arbitrary deprivation of liberty – so violating Article 5 ECHR – requires deprivation of liberty to be: carried out in good faith; closely connected to the grounds of detention relied on by the executing judicial authority; enforced in appropriate places and conditions; and of reasonable length in relation to the purposes pursued. The Strasbourg Court does not require that a decision on deprivation of liberty in this context be necessary and proportionate, but only that extradition procedures be ongoing and carried out with due diligence.[34] Criticised in the context of the ECHR, the dissociation between the arbitrariness test and the principle of proportionality becomes even more controversial in judicial cooperation in criminal matters in EU law. The principle of proportionality is a cornerstone of the CJEU's review of – inter alia – rights restriction, and its application is particularly important due to the high level of automaticity introduced by mutual recognition.

When it comes to judicial cooperation, authorities have mainly been deemed exempt from the duty of carrying out the proportionality test, when issuing or executing a judicial order. This has drawn the attention of the scholars EU institutions and practitioners.[35] With specific regard to the position of the issuing judge in relation to the EAW, the Council found that, although the proportionality check does not constitute a legal obligation on the issuing Member State, the competent authorities have to evaluate the proportionality between the aim of the surrender and the fundamental rights implications. It has been argued that imposing an obligation of this kind on the issuing judge would be difficult, since a major difference exists between two groups of Member States: on the one hand, there are those Member States which feature the principle of legality in their systems of criminal justice (the obligation to investigate and prosecute all criminal offences);[36] on the

[34] R White and C Ovey, *Jacobs, White & Ovey, The European Convention on Human Rights*, 5th edn (Oxford, Oxford University Press, 2010), 122 onward; C Grabenwarter, *The European Convention for the Protection of Human Rights and Fundamental Freedoms: A Commentary* (Beck/Hart Publishing, 2014), 60 onward; A Mowbray, *Cases and Materials on The European Convention on Human Rights*, 2nd edn (Oxford, Oxford University Press, 2007), 245 onward.

[35] J Vogel and JR Spencer, 'Proportionality and the European Arrest Warrant' (2010) 56(6) *Criminal Law Review* 474; E Herlin-Karnell, *The Constitutional Dimension of European Criminal Law* (Oxford, Hart Publishing, 2012); N Keijzer and E van Sliedregt (eds), *The European Arrest Warrant in Practice* (TMC Asser Press, 2005); E Xanthopoulou, 'The Quest for Proportionality for the European Arrest Warrant' (2015) 5(1) *New Journal of European Criminal Law* 32; D Helenius, 'Mutual Recognition in Criminal Matters and the Principle of Proportionality. Effective Proportionality or Proportionate Effectiveness?' (2014) 5(3) *New Journal of European Criminal Law* 349. Report from the Commission to the European Parliament and the Council on the implementation since 2007 of the Council Framework Decision of 13 June 2002 on the European arrest warrant and the surrender procedures between Member States, Brussels, 11.4.2011 COM(2011) 175 final; Council doc 17195/1/10 REV1, 17 December 2010.

[36] For instance, Germany, Italy, Sweden, Croatia and Poland.

other hand, a minor number of Member States apply the opportunity principle, according to which the national judiciary retains a certain margin of discretion in this regard.[37]

Therefore, requiring a proportionality test of the former group of states would significantly affect their legal systems. Besides, the case may be that Member States applying the legality principle suffer from over-criminalisation and extensive use of harsh custodial penalties, which in turn are capable of triggering the issuing of EAWs. The combination of these three elements (mandatory prosecution, diffuse criminalisation and frequent recourse to high levels of imprisonment) makes the introduction of a binding proportionality test rather difficult. Some authors have also argued that 'in certain cases, the problem of disproportionate EAWs is self-regulatory'.[38] The Council's Handbook and the 2011 Commission Evaluation Report urged Member States to deal with the issue of disproportionate EAWs. Following these recommendations, Poland has adopted legislative reforms to bring the national regime into compliance with the principle of proportionality. Growing attention to proportionality concerns in mutual recognition is confirmed by Directive 2014/41/EU, which makes the issuance of a European Investigation Order subject to an assessment in terms of necessity and proportionality.[39] It should also be noted that the UK amended the Extradition Act 2003 (which implements the EAW FD) in 2014, by inserting section 21A, entitled 'Person not convicted: human rights and proportionality'. According to this amendment, the judge called on to execute a EAW is to determine whether the surrender (the text uses the word 'extradition') would be disproportionate, by taking into account the seriousness of the offence, the likely penalty that would be imposed, and the possibility of the relevant foreign authorities taking measures that would be less coercive than the extradition. The judge must order discharge, should s/he decide that the surrender would be disproportionate.

The connection between proportionality and the right to liberty does not just emerge from the joint reading of Articles 6 and 52 CFREU. Proportionality is inextricably linked to legal certainty. Such a right stipulates that deprivation of liberty is to be carried out *in the cases* and *according to the procedures* established by the law. This requires that the legal basis *authorising* and *regulating* deprivation of liberty be of sufficient quality: clear and accessible legislative provisions are to be laid down. Broadly-worded rules allowing for detention, or vague norms establishing procedures for deprivation of liberty may thus result in disproportionate (ab)use of force and thus violation of Article 6 CFREU.[40] The FDs involving deprivation of

[37] eg Belgium, France, The Netherlands and The United Kingdom.

[38] A Weyembergh, I Armada and C Brière, 'European Added Value Assessment. The EU Arrest Warrant. Annex 1: Critical Assessment of the Existing European Arrest Warrant Framework Decision' (2014) Research Paper EAVA 6/2013 (Brussels, European Union, 2014) 35.

[39] Council Directive (EU) No 2014/41 [2014] OJ L130/1.

[40] ECtHR, *Amuur v France*, Application no 19776/92 (1996) 22 EHRR 533, paras 50–54.

liberty leave much to be desired in terms of legal certainty, so resulting in serious concerns over the protection of the right to liberty in EU law.

The overarching question concerning the right to liberty in EU law is one of scope. The higher level of automaticity introduced by mutual recognition calls for an enhanced level of protection of individual rights. In particular, the question arises as to what situations should be included in the scope of the requirement that deprivation of liberty be carried out only in the *cases* and according to the *procedures* established by the law. The *cases* are those situations that can lawfully result in deprivation of liberty. As shown below, mutual recognition of *pre*- and *post*-trial measures alternative to detention results in the transfer of the person from one state to another. However, the national regimes on these measures vary considerably throughout the EU. This has to do, mostly, with the consequences ensuing from the breach of these *pre*- or *post*-trial measures: one state may feature detention, while other states may resort to less harsh sanctions. The inclusion of these situations in the concept of *cases* can significantly improve the content of the right to liberty in EU law.

The same may hold true for the meaning of *procedures*. The doubt here involves the possible inclusion, in this requirement, of the procedures whereby deprivation of liberty is carried out *after* the apprehension of the person concerned: namely, the phase of enforcement. The first requirement of the right to liberty is that no one shall be deprived of liberty save according to the procedures established by the law. Once the individual has been placed in detention, s/he is still being deprived of liberty, and this requires that clear and accessible legal procedures be applied to this continuing deprivation.[41] This means that prison rules, and more generally detention conditions, can be relevant to the right to liberty. This is testified to by the case-law of the ECtHR, which sees detention conditions as a possible signifier of arbitrary detention, so resulting in a violation of the right to liberty.

IV. Conclusions

The maintenance of the Union as a borderless area required the creation of an area of freedom, security and justice, where citizens and businesses can circulate freely and safely thanks to the fight against the emergence of a safe haven for the criminals in the EU. In this sense, security is inextricably linked to effectiveness of (compliance with) law. This is pursued through integration in criminal justice, built around the principles of mutual recognition and free movement of judicial decisions. They significantly streamline inter-state cooperation in criminal matters within the EU, and require major attention to the safeguards protecting the person concerned against arbitrary deprivation of liberty. If the EU as an area

[41] A di Martino, 'La Disciplina dei CIE è Incostituzionale' (12 May 2012) *Diritto Penale Contemporaneo*.

without internal frontiers is the main goal of the EU's involvement in deprivation of liberty in judicial cooperation, the integration–fundamental rights protection dynamic is key to understanding the Union's approach. Integration takes the shape of mutual trust, but the latter is based on the presumption that fundamental rights are complied with in other Member States. While that presumption is being reinforced by actions attempting to establish common standards within the EU, many questions remain unanswered. The peculiarities of the EU as a polity, heavily influencing legal development in this area, pose three main challenges to the right to liberty: proportionality, legal certainty and scope of application. The next two chapters analyse these issues in detail, and put forward a new understanding of the right to liberty more suitable for the Union legal order.

7

The European Arrest Warrant and the Procedural Rights Directives

I. The European Arrest Warrant

A. The European Arrest Warrant Framework Decision

The EAW aims to replace extradition procedures with a smoother and swifter system of surrender between judicial authorities. The introduction of the EAW FD has been ground-breaking for a number of reasons: amongst others, the abolishment of the principle of dual criminality, the allocation of the responsibility for the surrender on judicial rather than political authorities, the (almost complete) drop of the prohibition on a state extraditing its own nationals.

Though the EAW was preceded by previous attempts to streamline inter-state judicial cooperation in criminal matters,[1] the terrorist attack on the World Trade Center on 11 September 2001 urged the Union to put into effect actual *EU* instruments to fight crime. This is confirmed by the circumstance that, before 9/11, the EAW was not the highest priority in the EU's agenda on mutual recognition in criminal matters.[2] The implementation of the EAW FD at national level has had a difficult path,[3] and Constitutional Courts across the EU have had to rule on the compatibility of the EAW FD with their constitutional systems.[4]

[1] Article 66 of the 1990 Convention implementing the Schengen Agreement refers to the possibility for Member States to extradite their nationals without extradition formalities (as long as the surrendered person has agreed before a court and s/he has been informed of his/her right to the extradition procedure). Also the 1996 EU Convention on Extradition between Member States was aimed at limiting the application of the nationality ban.

[2] Concerning the factors leading to the prioritisation of the EAW, scholars also mention the adoption of the Rome Statute of the International Criminal Court (ICC), which distinguishes state-to-state extradition from surrender to the ICC; the latter excluding the possibility of a nationality exception.

[3] For a comparison between the English and French system, see JR Spencer, 'Implementing the European Arrest Warrant: A Tale of How Not to Do It' (2009) 30(3) *Statute Law Review* 184. For a specific analysis of the Italian case, see L Marin, 'The European Arrest Warrant in the Italian Republic' (2008) 4(2) *European Constitutional Law Review* 251.

[4] J Komárek, 'European Constitutionalism and the European Arrest Warrant: In Search of the Limits of Contrapunctual Principles' (2007) 44(1) *Common Market Law Review* 9; Z Deen-Racsmány, 'The European Arrest Warrant and the Surrender of Nationals Revisited: The Lessons of Constitutional Challenges' (2006) 14(3) *European Journal of Crime, Criminal Law and Criminal Justice* 271.

According to the wording of the FD, the EAW is a judicial decision issued by a Member State with a view to the arrest and surrender by another Member State of a requested person, for the purposes of conducting a criminal prosecution or executing a custodial sentence or detention order. While Member States shall execute any EAW on the basis of the principle of mutual recognition, the FD shall not have the effect of modifying the obligation to respect fundamental rights and fundamental legal principles as enshrined in Article 6 TEU.[5]

The final decision on the execution of an EAW should be taken within 60 days of the arrest, a term which can be postponed by a further 30 days. The surrender must be carried out no later than 10 days after the final decision. If the surrender is prevented by circumstances beyond the control of any of the Member States, the executing and issuing judicial authorities shall agree on a new date, and the surrender shall take place within 10 days of the new date. The surrender may exceptionally be temporarily postponed for serious humanitarian reasons, following which the authorities shall find a new date and comply with the 10-day deadline. Upon expiry of those time limits, if the person is still being held in custody s/he shall be released.[6]

The executing judge must decide whether the person arrested must be kept in detention pending the decision on the recognition. Release may be ordered, provided that measures are taken so as to ensure that the person will not abscond.[7] The issuing state must deduct the period of detention already served by the person in the executing state from the total period of detention to be served.[8]

With regard to the rights of the individual in the context of the procedures of recognition and execution, the FD provides the following. The person concerned has the right to be heard by the executing judge in accordance with the law of the executing Member State. In case of an EAW issued for prosecution, the executing judge must either agree that the requested person should be heard, or temporarily transfer him/her to the issuing state. In the first case, the requested person must be heard by a judicial authority, assisted by another person designated in accordance with the law of the Member State of the requesting court. The requested person shall be heard in accordance with the law of the executing Member State and with the conditions determined by mutual agreement between the issuing and executing judicial authorities.[9] In the latter situation, the conditions and duration of the transfer are determined by the states involved, and the person must be able to return to the executing Member State to attend hearings concerning him or her as part of the surrender procedure.

The FD provides that the recognition and execution of the EAW can be refused on the basis of mandatory and optional grounds for refusal of execution.

[5] See Council Framework Decision of 13 June 2002 on the European arrest warrant and the surrender procedures between Member States (2002/584/JHA) [2002] OJ L190/1, 18.2.2002, Art 1(3) and (2).
[6] Ibid, Arts 17, 23 and 24.
[7] Ibid, Art 12.
[8] Ibid, Art 26.
[9] Ibid, Art 18.

Within the first category are included grounds such as the *ne bis in idem*, or the fact that the offence on which the EAW is based is covered by amnesty in the executing Member State.[10] Article 4 establishes optional grounds for refusal, among which is the possibility not to execute the EAW where 'the requested person is staying in, or is a national or a resident of the executing Member State and that state undertakes to execute the sentence or detention order in accordance with its domestic law'.[11]

Having presented the main features of the EAW FD, the analysis moves on to the interpretation given by the CJEU in three preliminary rulings relevant to the right to liberty. In *Radu*, the Court dealt with the possibility to refuse the execution of an EAW on the basis of fundamental rights violation (in particular, the breach of the right to liberty). In that judgment, the CJEU denied that the EAW FD allows for such a possibility. The *Lanigan* and *Vilkas*[12] cases show a different approach on the part of the Court, with higher attention being paid to individual rights. The CJEU clarified that the EAW FD must be interpreted in light of Articles 6 and 52 CFREU. The *Căldăraru* case[13] revolved around the thorny issue of detention conditions and mutual recognition. By this decision, the Luxembourg Court has opened the door to the non-execution of an EAW, should detention conditions in the issuing state prove to be likely to result in inhuman or degrading treatment. In *JZ*,[14] the Court was asked to define the concept of 'deprivation of liberty' under the FD, and did so in light of Articles 6 and 49 CFREU. While the CJEU found that measures such as curfew amount to restriction rather than deprivation of liberty, it left the national judge with the option to apply a higher standard of protection.

B. Execution of the EAW and Fundamental Rights

The case-law of the CJEU on the EAW FD is conspicuous, and contributed to defining essential aspects of the functioning of these instruments. These decisions

[10] Ibid, Art 3.

[11] This provision has given rise to a number of highly discussed preliminary rulings, on the part of the CJEU. See C-66/08, *Proceedings concerning the execution of a European arrest warrant issued against Szymon Kozłowski*, EU:C:2008:437; C-123/08, *Dominic Wolzenburg*, EU:C:2009:616; C-42/11, *Proceedings concerning the execution of a European arrest warrant issued against João Pedro Lopes Da Silva Jorge*, EU:C:2012:517. For comments, see E Herlin-Karnell, 'European Arrest Warrant Cases and the Principles of Non-Discrimination and EU Citizenship' (2010) 73(5) *The Modern Law Review* 824; V Mitsilegas, *EU Criminal Law after Lisbon: Rights, Trust and the Transformation of Justice in Europe*, Hart Studies in European Criminal Law, 1st edn (Oxford, Hart Publishing, 2016) 338 onwards; TP Marguery, 'EU Citizenship and European Arrest Warrant: The Same Rights for All?' (2011) 27(73) *Merkourios* 84; C Janssens, *The Principle of Mutual Recognition in EU Law* (Oxford, Oxford University Press, 2013) 207 onwards.

[12] Case C-640/15, *Minister for Justice and Equality v Tomas Vilkas*, EU:C:2017:39.

[13] Joined Cases C-404/15 and C-659/15 PPU, *Pál Aranyosi and Robert Căldăraru v Generalstaatsanwaltschaft Bremen*, EU:C:2016:198.

[14] Case C-294/16 PPU, *JZ v Prokuratura Rejonowa Łódź – Śródmieście*, EU:C:2016:610.

cover a broad spectrum of highly sensitive issues, such as the specialty rule, the principle of *ne bis in idem*, the right to appeal and to a fair trial.[15] In a number of judgments, the Court has been faced with questions bearing a direct relevance to the right to liberty: refusal of execution of an EAW on the basis of breach of the right to liberty (*Radu*); the relevance of the right to liberty and proportionality to the interpretation of the EAW FD (*Lanigan* and *Vilkas*); the role of detention conditions in the EAW system (*Căldăraru*); and the definition of deprivation of liberty (*JZ*).

In *Radu*, the Court was asked whether the EAW must satisfy the requirements of necessity and proportionality, and whether its execution can be refused in case of (actual or potential) violations of Articles 5 and 6 ECHR or Articles 6, 48 and 52 CFREU. The case concerned the issuance of EAWs against a Romanian national who claimed that his defence rights had been violated.[16] The Advocate General (AG) recalled the arbitrariness test elaborated by the ECtHR (good faith; connection to detention relied on by the judicial authority; appropriate detention conditions; reasonable length), and suggested that the execution of an EAW may be refused on a fundamental rights ground (in particular Articles 5 and 6 ECHR and/or Articles 6, 47 and 48 CFREU). How could this occur where 'the deficiency or deficiencies in the trial process [are] such as fundamentally to destroy its fairness'?[17] Breaches that are remediable would not justify a refusal to transfer the requested person to the Member State where those rights are at risk. The Court, unlike the AG, paid very little attention to the right to liberty. Though acknowledging that the right to be heard is enshrined in Articles 47 and 48 CFREU, it placed much more of an emphasis on the 'enforcement' objectives of the EAW FD, and rejected the possibility for the executing judge to refuse the execution of a EAW on fundamental rights grounds.[18] Admittedly, Mr Radu argued that his rights had been violated because he had not been summoned by the issuing judge before the EAW was issued. On the other hand, the question posed by the referring court had to do, more broadly, with the possibility to refuse the execution of an EAW on the basis of a fundamental rights breach. Granted, references for preliminary rulings always arise from a concrete case, and the violation of fundamental rights in the case of Mr Radu could be questioned. Unlike the AG, the Court seemed to completely close the door, at least at that moment, to considering breaches of fundamental rights as a basis for refusing the execution of an EAW.

[15] See, amongst others, C-261/09, *Gaetano Mantello*, EU:C:2010:683; C-192/12 PPU, *Melvin West*, EU:C:2012:404; C-168/13 PPU, *Jeremy F v Premier ministre*, EU:C:2013:358.

[16] C-396/11, *Proceedings relating to the execution of European arrest warrants issued against Ciprian Vasile Radu*, EU:C:2013:39.

[17] *Radu*, AG's Opinion, EU:C:2012:648, para 83. The AG proposed this test instead of that of the ECtHR, according to which execution may be opposed in case of *flagrant denial* of fair trial in the requested country, or where a potential breach is established 'beyond reasonable doubt'.

[18] *Radu*, EU:C:2013:39, para 43.

Lanigan, *Vilkas* and *JZ* engage with the role of proportionality and the right to liberty in the EAW. The first two judgments do it from the perspective of the executing judge and detention pending recognition, whereas *JZ* revolved around proportionality 'duties' on the issuing judge after surrender. In *Lanigan*, the questions referred concerned the interpretation of Article 17, read in conjunction with Article 15 and Article 12 EAW FD. Articles 17 and 15 establish procedures and time-limits for the decision on the execution of a EAW, whereas Article 12 provides the possibility for the executing judge to order the provisional release of the person concerned during execution procedures.[19] The doubts raised by the national court had to do with: the effects deriving from the executing Member State's failure to comply with the time-limits; and the possibility to envisage a right for the person to be released, in light of that failure. The Court found that the expiry of the deadline neither precludes the execution of the EAW, nor creates a general and unconditional obligation to release the person. Such an interpretation, it said, 'could limit the effectiveness of the surrender system put in place by the Framework Decision and, consequently, obstruct the attainment of the objectives pursued by it'.[20]

However, the CJEU found that Article 1(3) determines an obligation to interpret the EAW FD in compliance with the Charter. As far as that specific case was concerned, the relevant provisions to take into account were Articles 6 and 52 CFREU.[21] As for the right to liberty, the CJEU relied on the ECtHR's case-law on Article 5(1)(f) ECHR (which, however, refers to the right to liberty in the context of *extradition* procedures). In particular, the right to liberty would result in the duty, for the executing judge, to hold that person in custody so long as the procedure for the execution is carried out in a sufficiently diligent manner. In order to ensure that this is the case, the executing judge is required to consider factors such as: the possible failure to act on the part of the authorities of the Member States concerned; any contribution by the requested person to that delay; the sentence potentially faced by the requested person; the potential risk of that person absconding; the fact that the requested person has been held in custody for a period which in total greatly exceeds the time-limits stipulated in Article 17. Should the judge opt for release, s/he should adopt any measures to ensure that the material conditions necessary for the surrender remain fulfilled. Article 52(1) CFREU requires that any limitations of Charter rights must be provided for by law, must respect the essence of those rights and, subject to the principle of proportionality, must be necessary and genuinely meet objectives of general interest.

While the *Lanigan* judgment reveals higher consideration for the right to liberty and the principle of proportionality, the potential reach of the judgment was strongly mitigated in *Vilkas*. The question arose as to whether

[19] C-237/15 PPU, *Lanigan*, EU:C:2015:474.
[20] Ibid, para 50.
[21] Ibid, paras 53 onwards.

Article 23(5) FD – obligation of release on expiry of surrender deadlines – applied to a situation where the new date for surrender agreed under Article 23(3) could not be met because of the continuing resistance by the person concerned to execution of the EAW. While the CJEU confirmed that states are not exempt from the obligation laid down in the FD once the deadline for the new surrender has expired, it also found that there is no obligation of release where the second attempt at surrendering within the deadline is prevented by circumstances beyond Member States' control.[22] The executing judge has discretion under Article 12 FD as to whether the circumstances allow for freeing the person concerned.[23] Thereby, the margin for detaining beyond the terms expressly provided in the FD is considerably broadened. 'Circumstances beyond states' control' is a one-size-fits-all ground for extending deprivation of liberty. The wide leeway left to the state judges is not balanced with clear guidance. The criteria laid down in *Lanigan* do not constitute a proper test for the state authority. It is not clear whether they are cumulative or alternative, or whether any of them should be prioritised. The broad discretion granted by the 'circumstances beyond states' control' should be balanced in such a way that the judge should base the decision to continue detention only on the basis of the individual assessment: namely, the risk of absconding and the penalty potentially imposed.

The connection of the right to liberty concerns not only Article 52 CFREU and the executing judge, but also Article 49 CFREU and the issuing authority. *JZ* concerned the interpretation of the concept of 'detention' under Article 26 EAW FD, according to which the issuing Member State must deduct all periods of detention arising from the execution of an EAW from the total period of detention to be served in the issuing Member State as a result of a custodial sentence or detention order being passed. The referring court asked whether the concept of detention under Article 26 EAW FD, interpreted in light of Articles 6 and 49 CFREU, covers measures applied by the executing Member State consisting of the electronic monitoring of the person to whom the arrest warrant applies at his place of residence, in conjunction with a curfew. Before the referring court, Mr JZ had requested that the period during which he was subject to a curfew in the UK and to electronic monitoring be credited towards his custodial sentence.

Firstly, the Court pointed out that the national judge has to interpret national law, as far as possible, in light of the wording and the purpose of the FD.[24] Article 26(1) makes no express reference to the law of the Member States, which means that its meaning and scope must normally be given an autonomous and uniform interpretation throughout the EU.[25] The terms 'detention' and 'deprivation of liberty' – used interchangeably in the various language versions of

[22] *Vilkas*, n 12 above, EU:C:2017:39, para 74.
[23] Ibid, para 42.
[24] *João Pedro Lopes Da Silva Jorge* (n 11 above) paras 53 and 54.
[25] *Szymon Kozłowski* (n 11 above) para 42; C-108/16 PPU, *Openbaar Ministerie v Paweł Dworzecki*, EU:C:2016:346, para 28.

Article 26(1) – imply a situation of confinement or imprisonment, and not merely a restriction of the freedom of movement. As regards the context of Article 26(1), Article 12 envisages the possibility for the executing judge to order the provisional release of the person concerned, in conjunction with measures to prevent him/her from absconding. The EAW FD therefore provides for *alternatives* to detention to be used in the context of EAW procedures. Concerning the objective of Article 26(1), the Court stated that the deduction obligation under that article aims to meet the general objective of respecting fundamental rights, as referred to in recital 12, and recalled in Article 1(3) EAW FD; in particular, preserving the right to liberty and the principle of proportionality of penalties, protected by Articles 6 and 49 CFREU.[26]

While deprivation of liberty need not take place necessarily in the form of detention, criteria must be taken into account such as the type, duration, effects, manner of implementation and severity of the measure, to understand how the latter can be comparable to imprisonment.[27] This is confirmed by the ECtHR case-law on Article 5 ECHR, which is not concerned with mere restrictions on liberty of movement.[28] In light of the foregoing, the Court found that the measures to which Mr JZ was subject, while surely restricting his liberty, could not be regarded as deprivation of liberty. However, the Court also clarified that Article 26(1) EAW FD *merely imposes a minimum level of fundamental rights protection* (emphasis added). On the basis of its national law, the issuing court is *allowed* to deduct, from the total period of detention which the person concerned would have to serve therein, the period during which that person was subject, in the executing state, to measures involving not a deprivation of liberty but a restriction of it.[29]

The *Căldăraru* case concludes this circular analysis started with the Court's stance in *Radu* on the refusal of execution of EAWs for fundamental rights reasons. *Căldăraru* is a keystone in the interpretation of the EAW. It opens the door to halting the operation of the EAW on grounds other than those established in Articles 3 and 4 EAW FD, and brings to the fore the relevance of detention conditions to judicial cooperation. The CJEU had to deal with the possibility to refuse the execution of an EAW on the basis of the risk of inhumane treatment in the issuing Member States (Romania and Hungary), due to poor detention conditions.[30] The AG's Opinion was characterised by heavy reliance on the principle of mutual trust. The AG stated that introducing a systemic ground for refusal, based on the risk that the person concerned will be subject to inhumane detention conditions in the issuing state, would undermine the mutual trust that founds

[26] *JZ* (n 14 above) para 43.
[27] Ibid, para 47.
[28] ECtHR, 6 November 1980, *Guzzardi v Italy*, Application no 7367/76, Series A no 39 [1980] ECHR 5, para 92; and ECtHR, 5 July 2016, *Buzadji v Republic of Moldova*, Application no 23755/07, para 103. ECtHR, 20 April 2010, *Villa v Italy*, Application no 42559/08.
[29] *JZ* (n 14 above) paras 55–57.
[30] *Aranyosi and Căldăraru*, n 13 above, EU:C:2016:198.

judicial cooperation within the EU. Article 19 CFREU and recital 13 EAW FD state that 'No person should be removed, expelled or extradited to a State where there is a serious risk that he or she would be subjected to the death penalty, torture or other inhuman or degrading treatment or punishment'. On the AG's reading of them, by not mentioning *surrender*, these provisions would reveal the intention of the Union legislature to leave the EAW system outside their scope of application. The Union legislature, when establishing the grounds for refusal enumerated in the FD, did not provide for refusal of execution based on violations of fundamental rights. The application of a systematic check on detention conditions, performed by the executing judge, would be incompatible with the principle of mutual trust, according to which Member States are presumed to respect fundamental rights.[31]

To this end, the issuing and executing Member States have a key role in preserving that trust and the functioning of mutual recognition. On the one hand, and except for the cases laid down in Articles 3 to Article 4a, the executing court is to surrender the person even if the provisions of its national law, including constitutional ones, would provide a higher level of protection of fundamental rights.[32] What the executing judge can (or has to) do in the case of systemic deficiencies is assess, through an exchange of information with the issuing judge, whether the person will be detained in proportionate conditions. Being a general principle of EU law, proportionality could be relied on to refuse the execution of an EAW. Detention conditions would be proportionate where: they do not result 'in the detachment from society of the person concerned', in the case of an EAW issued for execution of sentence purposes; or they remain strictly related to the aim of prosecution, in the case of an EAW issued for that purpose. The issuing judge, on his/her part, is called on to apply a proportionality check, and issue an EAW by taking into account the nature of the offence and the regime of execution. Broadly, the issuing Member State should take all necessary measures, including reforms of criminal policy, to ensure that that person serves his/her sentence in conditions which respect fundamental rights.

The Court decided differently to the AG, by according Article 1(3) a major role for fundamental rights protection. The CJEU found that Article 1(3) obliges Member States to respect the prohibition of inhumane and degrading treatment, as stated in Article 4 CFREU. This implies that where the executing judge has objective, reliable, specific and properly updated evidence showing that there are deficiencies – which may be 'systemic *or* generalised, *or* which may affect certain groups of people, *or* which may affect certain place of detention, with respect to detention conditions in the issuing Member State' – that judge must, pursuant to Article 15(2) EAW FD, request that the issuing judge provide supplementary

[31] Joined Cases C-404/15 and C-659/15 *Pál Aranyosi and Robert Căldăraru v Generalstaatsanwaltschaft Bremen*, PPU, AG's Opinion, ECLI:EU:C:2016:140.

[32] C-399/11, *Melloni v Ministerio Fiscal*, EU:C:2013:107.

information (emphasis added). The evidence at the basis of the request under Article 15(2) may be obtained from, inter alia,

> judgments of international courts, such as judgments of the ECtHR, judgments of courts of the issuing Member State, and also decisions, reports and other documents produced by bodies of the Council of Europe or under the aegis of the UN.

The decision on the surrender must be postponed until supplementary information is obtained, allowing the judge to exclude the risk of inhumane treatment. Should that risk not be discounted within a reasonable timeframe, the executing judge is to decide whether the surrender procedure should be brought to an end. Meanwhile, the person concerned should be held in custody only in so far as the duration of the detention is not excessive, on the basis of the requirement of proportionality laid down in Article 52(1) of the Charter.[33]

C. The EAW and the Right to Liberty

The EAW FD and the interpretation of the CJEU have important implications in terms of the right to liberty and proportionality. Certainty and proportionality being inherent in the right to liberty, they apply to drafting, interpretation and application of laws and practices of detention. Unclear or very broadly worded rules governing the exercise of the use of force by a public authority lend themselves to abuse. This results in a disproportionate use of those powers, and confirms that proper protection of the right to liberty requires a holistic approach.

Two main principles can be inferred from the law of the EAW. Firstly, the FD is to be interpreted in the light of the right to liberty and Article 52 CFREU, which makes restrictions of the Charter rights conditional upon the proportionality principle. Secondly, the execution of an EAW must be postponed – or even abandoned – where there are serious reasons to believe that detention conditions in the issuing state would expose the person concerned to the risk of inhuman or degrading treatment.

That said, the EU approach to the right to liberty as has emerged from the foregoing analysis is flawed in three main respects: legal certainty; the application of the proportionality test; and the role of poor detention conditions in the issuing state.

(i) Legal Certainty

Issues of legal certainty arise from discretion left to states' authorities with regards to the implementation of the EAW system. Firstly, the FD seems to leave to inter-state agreement aspects that can be relevant to the right to liberty. Article 18 allows for the temporary transfer of the person for prosecution purposes, under

[33] *Aranyosi and Căldăraru*, n 13 above, EU:C:2016:198, para 101.

conditions and for a duration determined by mutual agreement between the issuing and executing state. As the discussion below on the ESO reveals, non-residents are much more likely to be subject to pre-trial detention than residents. This means that if the executing state must decide on an EAW issued against a non-resident, the latter would probably be deprived of his/her liberty pending the decision. If this is the case, and the executing state opts for a temporary surrender, the latter will not take place before conditions are agreed, which could result in significantly delaying the transfer, and the possible application of pre-trial measures alternative to detention. This could result in a disproportionate number of cases of deprivation of liberty, in circumstances where the person concerned would have no responsibility for this delay.

Uncertainty stems from the vexed question of possible non-implementation of mutual recognition on the grounds of fundamental rights violations. The Court was rather reluctant to admit such a possibility in earlier judgments, but the latest development has increasingly opened the door to it. Even though fundamental rights violations are not included in the possible grounds for refusal enumerated in the EAW FD, Article 1(3) explicitly states that the FD does not have the effect of modifying Member States' obligations under Article 6 TEU. In other words, the Member States cannot apply the FD, where the latter would result in a fundamental rights violation. Furthermore, the CJEU has explicitly affirmed that EU secondary law may not be implemented, where this can bring about the breach of a general principle of EU law or a Charter right.[34]

Căldăraru made clear that the execution of an EAW may be refused when fundamental rights violations are at stake even when they are not systemic. There are, however, structural questions still on the table related to the very operation of mutual recognition and its foundation. The principle of mutual trust is a presumption, which legally comes with two main considerations.[35] On the one hand, the nature of that presumption must be clarified: following the *NS* judgment, we know that mutual trust constitutes a rebuttable one. On the other hand, the threshold required to overcome that presumption is key. *Radu* and *Căldăraru* highlighted that two main variables must be taken into account: the difference between relative and absolute rights/prohibitions; violations – allegedly – already occurred and potentially invalidating the EAW and prospective breaches perpetrated following the surrender. The CJEU has not addressed the distinction between past and future violations in the EAW FD so far, although Part IV shows that a principle for

[34] L Mancano, 'Another Brick in the Whole. The Case-Law of the Court of Justice on Free Movement and Its Possible Impact on European Criminal Law' (2016) 8(1) *Perspectives on Federalism* 1, 12 onwards.

[35] For legal analysis of the content of mutual trust, see Michael Schwarz, 'Let's talk about trust, baby! Theorizing trust and mutual recognition in the EU's area of freedom, security and justice' (2018) 24 *European Law Journal* 124–41; E Xanthopoulou, 'Mutual trust and rights in EU criminal and asylum law: Three phases of evolution and the uncharted territory beyond blind trust' (2018) 55(2) *Common Market Law Review* 489.

assessing the lawfulness of decisions following breaches of relative rights can be discerned in the Court's law on immigration detention.

While absolute rights can be used to limit the operation of mutual recognition, the same cannot be taken for granted as far as relative rights – included the right to liberty – are concerned. However, the CJEU has recently found in *LM* that non-execution is an option where possible violations of the (relative) right to a fair trial are at stake.[36] That finding was stated in the context of the broader issue concerning the independence of the judiciary in Poland, the respect by that Member State of the EU values under Article 2 TEU, and the Article 7 TEU procedure activated by the European Commission as a reaction thereto.[37] In particular, the ruling concerned the risk of violation of the right to an independent tribunal, and therefore a breach of the essence of the right to a fair trial. After pointing out the key features of judicial independence, the CJEU confirmed the *Căldăraru* two-step test. Firstly, the executing judge must assess, on the basis of material that is objective, reliable, specific and properly updated, whether there is a real risk of such a right being breached. Secondly, the judge must assess specifically and precisely whether, in the particular circumstances of the case, there are substantial grounds for believing that the requested person will run that risk. Furthermore, the executing judicial authority must request from the issuing judicial authority any supplementary information that it considers necessary for assessing whether there is such a risk. If the risk cannot be discounted, the EAW must not be given effect.[38] Therefore, even violations of relative rights can fall under the *exceptional circumstance* clause needed to halt the operation of mutual recognition. The question arises whether and on what conditions the right to liberty would be capable of triggering the clause. It is submitted below that detention conditions are one of the factors that could be relied on for applying the foregoing principle.

(ii) Proportionality

The possible application of the principle of proportionality in the context of the EAW has been heavily debated.[39] Both the issuing and executing state have a key role in protecting the right to liberty. Leaving aside the responsibility of cooperating with each other imposed by the FD in various provisions, the issuing judge comes into play especially before issuing and following the execution of the EAW. Proportionality of penalties under Article 49 CFREU would require the issuing judge not to issue an EAW for particularly petty or tame offences. Furthermore,

[36] C-216/18 PPU, *LM*, EU:C:2018:586.
[37] See the Commission proposal: http://europa.eu/rapid/press-release_IP-17-5367_en.htm.
[38] *LM*, n 36 above, paras 73–79.
[39] A Weyembergh, I Armada and C Brière, 'European Added Value Assessment. The EU Arrest Warrant. Annex 1: Critical Assessment of the Existing European Arrest Warrant Framework Decision' (2014) Research Paper EAVA 6/2013 (Brussels, European Union, 2014).

in *JZ* Articles 49 and 6 CFREU were used to allow the issuing judge to apply the court's own definition of detention, should this amount to a higher level of protection. It should be remembered, however, that such leeway was left in a situation where the enforcement of the EAW had been secured, with the person concerned surrendered to the issuing state. This seems to confirm *a contrario* the *Melloni* principle that higher national standards can be applied as long as they do not jeopardise the effectiveness of the EAW.

More indirectly related to proportionality of penalties is the minimum-maximum, criterion used to trigger judicial cooperation and translated to substantive criminal law to approximate levels of penalty. As shown in Part I, this can boost a race to the top in thresholds of punishment, with serious implications in terms of proportionality. The question arises as to whether the minimum-maximum criterion should be reconsidered, due to its broad repercussions in substantive and procedural terms.

The executing judge must assess the proportionality of detention under Article 52 CFREU. As *Căldăraru* and *Radu* have shown, the evaluation of the executing authority in terms of the right to liberty is twofold. It can – again, with the collaboration of the issuing judge – refuse to recognise or execute the EAW, and decide on detention of the person pending recognition and execution.

The latter scenario is particularly important under Article 52 CFREU. The introduction of rigid time-limits for recognition and surrender has undeniably improved the right to liberty, as compared to extradition. Within and without those limits, the executing judge has an obligation to interpret the EAW in compliance with Articles 6 and 52 CFREU. The executing judge must use those provisions when deciding whether or not to hold the person in detention after s/he has received an EAW. Indeed, it is that authority in charge of the ruling on deprivation of liberty in the first place. The test must *always* be applied. It constitutes a preliminary requirement of any limitations of the Charter rights (and thus also the right to liberty) under Article 52 CFREU, and should relate the proportionality of *opting for detention* to *the aim of ensuring the enforcement of the EAW*. To this end, circumstances such as the seriousness of the offence, the time of its (alleged) commission, as well as the personal situation of the person concerned in the executing Member State (in terms of family, working and social links), should be taken into account.

This being a regular scenario, the question arises as to how to interpret the FD when the system experiences 'hiccups'. *Lanigan* made it clear that the expiry of the terms laid down in the FD gives rise to no right to release for the person concerned. The possible implication of this finding is that the person would still be deprived of liberty for other state authorities' failures. The *Vilkas* case reinforces and broadens such a concern. It is understandable that the Court objected to the application of Article 23(5) FD – obligation to release the person after the expiry of the deadlines laid down in Article 23(2) to (4) – to situations where the delay was caused by the subject's own continuing resistance to the surrender. However, the CJEU more broadly phrased its objection as based on situations beyond Member

States' control, so potentially including cases where the person bears no responsibility. The accent placed in *Vilkas* on Article 12 FD – allowing the executing judge to order release – confirms the role for the executing state in terms of the right to liberty and proportionality, without, however, providing guidance to balance the discretion left by that ground for extended detention.

As shown in the next sub-section, the CJEU stated that detention pending removal must be ended, once the terms established in the Directive have expired. While that case-law concerns persons that have not committed a crime, a similar argument could be made with regard to EAWs for prosecution on the basis of the presumption of innocence stated in Article 48 CFREU.[40]

What should be firmly rejected is the argument put forward by the AG in *Căldăraru*, where the principle of proportionality was used to consider refusal of execution for possible violations of Article 4 CFREU. When breaches of absolute rights/prohibitions are at stake no room for proportionality can possibly be made: the balance inherent in the use of proportionality is incompatible with *absolute* prohibitions. The application of the former to the latter is misleading and unacceptable, as well as legally wrong.

(iii) Detention Conditions

The right to liberty is key to the operation of the EAW not just for decisions on whether to detain the person pending surrender. Past or prospective violations of the right to liberty might limit the very execution of the EAW. The question arises as to which violations – if any – of the right to liberty might invalidate an EAW already issued, or allow for non-execution *tout court*. This comes with a preliminary question on what factors to include in the very concept of the right to liberty. In an endeavour to re-conceptualise the right to liberty in EU law, the analysis of the EAW brings to the fore the importance of detention conditions.[41] The case-law of both the ECtHR and the CJEU has acknowledged that poor detention conditions may result in violations of fundamental rights.[42] The traditional legal reference in this respect is Article 3 ECHR, which prohibits torture and inhuman and degrading treatment. However, this requires a high threshold to be met, and the case may be that bad detention conditions are *too poor* to be lawful, but *not poor enough* for invoking Article 3 ECHR.[43] Another legal anchor is needed,

[40] Debbie Sayers, 'Presumption of Innocence and Right of Defence (Criminal Law)' in Steve Peers and others (eds), *The EU Charter of Fundamental Rights: A Commentary*, 1st edn (Oxford, Hart Publishing 2014) 1303.

[41] A Weyembergh, I Armada and C Brière, n 39 above, 50 onwards.

[42] *Aranyosi and Căldăraru*, AG's Opinion, EU:C:2016:140, paras 30–34.

[43] However, the case-law ECtHR has significantly improved over the years, and has lowered the threshold required especially with regard to the burden of proof. See on this V Moreno-Lax, 'Dismantling the Dublin System: *M.S.S. v. Belgium and Greece*' (2012) 14(1) *European Journal of Migration and Law* 1; P Mallia, 'Case of *M.S.S. v Belgium and Greece*: A Catalyst in the Re-thinking of the Dublin II Regulation' (2011) 30(3) *Refugee Survey Quarterly* 107.

in order to better protect individual rights. This anchor is the right to liberty. The ECtHR has stated that detention conditions can be a symptom of a possible violation of Article 5 ECHR.[44] The requirement that one shall be deprived of liberty according to the *procedures* established by the law means that, until deprivation of liberty is ongoing, the legal procedures are to be abided by. This concerns in particular the rules on enforcement. Poor detention conditions may not violate Article 3 ECHR, but may be unlawful and create a situation of arbitrariness all the same, so giving rise to breach of the right to liberty.

The *Căldăraru* judgment could have far-reaching consequences in this respect. Firstly, the CJEU established a link between Article 1(3) EAW FD and the obligation to respect fundamental rights in relation to the execution of an EAW. The Court explicitly opened up to the possibility of non-implementation of EU law, in case of the risk of a fundamental rights violation. Granted, what was at stake in *Căldăraru* was an absolute prohibition, such as that enshrined in Article 4 CFREU. Other fundamental rights can be balanced, as is the case of the right to a fair trial. One could not expect the application of the *Căldăraru* test to any fundamental rights violations. Probably, the Court will have the opportunity to clarify the actual reach of the principles stated in this judgment. Nonetheless, the Court acknowledged that Article 1(3) EAW FD can give the basis for limiting the implementation of mutual recognition. Furthermore, the conditions set out by the Court for the request of supplementary information (which may in turn lead to postponement and non-execution of the EAW) are not cumulative, as the deficiencies can be systemic *or* affect certain groups of people *or* places of detention.

The question arises as to what consequences this can have for the right to liberty. The *LM* case sets two conditions for the activation of the *exceptional circumstances* clause: the essence of the right must be threatened; and the right at stake must be connected to the EU values under Article 2 TEU.

The question as to whether the issues discussed here comply with those two factors comes with a reflection on the role of detention conditions in the right to liberty, on the one hand, and on the role of the right to liberty in a polity founded on the rule of law, on the other. Detention conditions reflect the way in which deprivation of liberty is enforced and the procedures whereby detention is carried out. If those conditions are not in line with what the law prescribes, they are in violation of an essential requirement of the right to liberty. Likewise, a situation of arbitrariness would occur where standards do not live up to those required by the law. This might be due to the source containing them, or the vacuous wording of the rules. While systemic deficiencies can contribute to the evidence of a real risk, the focus should be on the specific circumstances of the case – for the purposes of the present discussion, on the specific group of people or the particular place of detention.[45] The essence of the right is in jeopardy where one of its pillars is likely to be violated.

[44] *Chahal v United Kingdom*, Application no 22414/93, (1996) 23 EHRR 413, para 74.
[45] This approach was confirmed by the Court in Case C-220/18 PPU, *ML*, EU:C:2018:589, para 117.

This is the case with the independence of the tribunal in relation to the right to a fair trial. The same may hold true with regard to detention conditions (as part of the established procedures requirement) and the right to liberty.

Having shown that unlawful detention conditions (on paper or in action) undermine the essence of the right to liberty, the second step requires establishing a connection between the latter and Article 2 TEU. The right to liberty is probably the most basic stronghold protecting the individual against abuses of public powers. This statement is not only confirmed by its role and consistent understanding of it throughout the centuries. In this sense, the *LM* case finally revealed that the relative nature of a right does not downplay its centrality to the preservation of the rule of law. Though possibly subject to limitations, the right to liberty requires those limits to be strictly interpreted. Firstly, no grounds for detention beyond those laid down in Article 5 ECHR are allowed. Secondly, deprivation of liberty is not lawful merely due to the fact that it is carried out in one of the cases provided therein: it must also not be arbitrary, which would be the case if it took place contrary to procedures established by law. Accepting the possibility to effect an intra-EU transfer to a state where the person is likely to be placed in unlawful detention conditions would mean tolerating an attack against a centrepiece of the rule of law. Turning a blind eye to deprivation of liberty *in violation* or *in the absence* of clear and legally established procedures is opening the door to the systematic exercise of arbitrary powers over individuals within the EU, which hardly seems compatible with the values enshrined in Article 2 TEU.

II. The Procedural Rights Directives

A. The Legal and Policy Context

The increasing involvement of the EU in criminal law over the years came with a discussion on how to safeguard persons subject to investigation and EAW procedures. The Directives adopted so far stemmed from a long-lasting discussion about the appropriate level of protection of individual rights in criminal proceedings, especially after the adoption of the EAW.[46] Following the Tampere Programme, the Commission issued a communication stating that it must have been 'ensured that the treatment of suspects and the rights of the defence, would not only suffer from the implementation of the principle [of mutual recognition] but that the

[46] See for instance E Cape, Z Namoradze, R Smith and T Spronken, *Effective Criminal Defence in Europe* (Antwerpen/Oxford, Intersentia, 2010); and E Guild and L Marin (eds), *Still not resolved? Constitutional Issues of the European Arrest Warrant* (Nijmegen, Wolf Legal Publishers, 2009). KA Nicolaidis and G Shaffer, 'Transnational Mutual Recognition Regimes: Governance without Global Government' (2005) 68 *Law and Contemporary Problems* 263, 267–322.

safeguards would even be improved through the process'.[47] Shortly after the EAW, the Commission stated the need for a balanced protection of procedural rights across the EU,[48] and put forward a comprehensive proposal on individual rights in criminal proceedings.[49] While the instrument never saw the light of day, the Commission persevered in its endeavour and in 2005 decided to carry out a study on procedural rights in the EU.[50]

Policy and legal developments gave new stimulus to the discussion.[51] On the one hand, the Treaty of Lisbon redesigned the constitutional architecture of the Union and communitarised EU substantive and procedural criminal law. On the other, the start of the Swedish EU Presidency marked a shift from a holistic to a step-by-step approach. This materialised in the so-called 'roadmap' for improving protection of suspected and accused persons in criminal proceedings,[52] consisting of six initiatives: a measure on interpretation and translation; a measure on the provision of information about rights; a measure on the right of access to a lawyer and on the right to communicate upon arrest and a measure on legal aid;[53] a measure on communication with relatives, employers and consular authorities; a measure on special safeguards for vulnerable accused;[54] and a Green Paper to examine appropriate measures concerning the period of pre-trial detention, which was published in June 2011.[55] The EU legislature has also adopted a Directive on

[47] Communication to the Council and the European Parliament of 26 July 2000 on Mutual Recognition of Final Decisions in Criminal Matters (COM(2000)495 final, 29 July 2000).

[48] Procedural Safeguards for Suspects and Defendants in Criminal Proceedings throughout the European Union, Brussels, 19.2.2003, COM(2003) 75 final.

[49] Commission proposal for a Council Framework Decision on certain procedural rights in criminal proceedings throughout the European Union, COM(2004) 328 final, 28 April 2004.

[50] TNBM Spronken and M Attinger, 'Procedural Rights in criminal proceedings: Existing Level of Safeguards in the European Union', funded and published by the European Commission, 12 December 2005 <http://arno.unimaas.nl/show.cgi?fid=3891> See also the follow-up report to that study, focused on the right to information, the right to legal advice, the right to legal assistance free of charge, the right to translation and interpretation of documents. T Spronken, G Vermeulen, D De Vocht and L van Puyenbroeck, *EU Procedural Rights in Criminal Proceedings* (Universiteit Gent (Dept of Penal Law and Criminology), 2009).

[51] G Vermeulen and L van Puyenbroeck, 'Approximation and mutual recognition of procedural safeguards of suspects and defendants in criminal proceedings throughout the European Union' in M Cools and others, *EU and International Crime Control: Topical Issues* (Antwerp, Maklu, 2010) 43–62.

[52] Roadmap with a view to fostering protection of suspected and accused persons in criminal proceedings ('Roadmap'), Council Document 11457/09, 1 July 2009; and Draft Resolution 12116/09, 15 July 2009.

[53] Directive (EU) 2016/1919 of the European Parliament and of the Council of 26 October 2016 on legal aid for suspects and accused persons in criminal proceedings and for requested persons in European arrest warrant proceedings, [2016] OJ L297/1, 4.11.2016.

[54] Directive (EU) 2016/800 of the European Parliament and of the Council of 11 May 2016 on procedural safeguards for children who are suspects or accused persons in criminal proceedings, [2016] L132/1 21.5.2016.

[55] Green Paper on the application of EU criminal justice legislation in the field of detention, COM(2011) 327 final, 14 June 2011.

the strengthening of certain aspects of the presumption of innocence and of the right to be present at the trial in criminal proceedings.[56]

Article 82 TFEU empowers the EU to establish minimum rules to facilitate police and judicial cooperation in the following areas: mutual admissibility of evidence; the rights of individuals in criminal procedures; the rights of victims of crime; any other specific aspects of criminal procedure which the Council has identified in advance by a decision. Based on the presumption that fundamental rights are complied with by Member States, the procedural rights directives aim to strengthen trust within the Union.

The analysis below focuses on the Directives on interpretation and translation, information, and access to a lawyer in criminal proceedings and EAW procedures. In accordance with the wording of the legal basis under Article 82 TFEU, these instruments aim to strengthen mutual trust and to facilitate mutual recognition. Having their place in the balance between legal integration and fundamental rights protection, the instruments contribute towards shaping the EU right to liberty. They establish common rules in an area covered by Article 6 CFREU, which includes the right for arrested persons to be informed promptly, in a language which they understand, of the reasons for their arrest and of any charge brought against them.[57] While access to a lawyer seems not to be directly related to right to liberty, the relevant Directive features provisions involving deprivation of liberty. Furthermore, the possibility to have access to a lawyer is undeniably part and parcel of the effective enjoyment of the right to liberty. The analysis is important for the adoption of EU rules on detention conditions. The scope of application of these Directives could represent a starting point for the elaboration of a Union strategy on prisoner rights.

B. The Directives

The Directive on the right of accused and suspected persons to translation and interpretation in criminal proceedings was the first instrument adopted under the roadmap on procedural rights.[58] The provisions of the Directive that correspond to rights guaranteed by the ECHR or the Charter should be interpreted and implemented consistently with those rights, as interpreted in the relevant case-law of the ECtHR and the CJEU.

[56] Directive (EU) 2016/343 of the European Parliament and of the Council of 9 March 2016 on the strengthening of certain aspects of the presumption of innocence and of the right to be present at the trial in criminal proceedings [2016] OJ L65/1 11.3.2016.

[57] Art 5(3) ECHR.

[58] Directive 2010/64/EU of the European Parliament and of the Council of 20 October 2010 on the right to interpretation and translation in criminal proceedings, [2010] OJ L280/1, 26.10.2010. R Vogler, 'Lost in Translation: Language Rights for Defendants in European Criminal Proceedings' in S Ruggeri (ed), *Human Rights in European Criminal Law* (Berlin, Springer, 2014) 95–110.

The three Directives apply *from* the moment the person concerned is made aware by the competent authorities of a Member State that they are suspected or accused of having committed a criminal offence *until* the conclusion of the proceedings, understood as the final determination of whether the suspect or accused person has committed a criminal offence. This includes, where applicable, sentencing and the resolution of any appeal.[59] Suspected or accused persons who do not speak the language of the proceedings must be provided with an interpreter during criminal proceedings before investigative and judicial authorities, and during police questioning.

The persons concerned must have the opportunity to challenge a decision denying the need for an interpreter, or where the quality of the interpreter is not such as to ensure the fairness of the proceedings.[60]

Persons who do not understand the language of the proceedings must, within a reasonable period of time, be provided with a written translation of the documents essential to guarantee respect of the right to defence and a fair trial (including any decision depriving a person of his liberty, any charge or indictment, and any judgment).

The obligation of translation does not relate to parts which are not relevant for the purposes of enabling suspected or accused persons to have knowledge of the case against them. However, the person concerned must be provided with the right to challenge a decision finding that there is no need for translation, or when the translation is not of such a quality as to guarantee the fairness of the proceedings.

When a written version cannot be drawn up, and so long as the fairness of the proceeding is not jeopardised, an oral translation or oral summary of essential documents may be provided.[61] At a general level, Member States must take concrete measures to ensure that the interpretation and translation service provided meets the quality required.[62]

The second instrument adopted was the Directive on the right to information of suspects or accused persons in criminal proceedings and of persons subject to an EAW.[63] Where the law of a Member State provides for the imposition of a sanction regarding minor offences by an authority other than a court having jurisdiction in criminal matters, and the imposition of such a sanction may be appealed to such a court, the Directive shall apply only to the proceedings before that court, following such an appeal.

[59] Ibid, Art 1.
[60] Ibid, Art 2.
[61] Ibid, Art 3.
[62] Ibid, Art 5.
[63] Directive 2012/13/EU of the European Parliament and of the Council of 22 May 2012 on the right to information in criminal proceedings, [2012] OJ L142/1, 1.6.2012. For a comment see S Quattrocolo, 'The Right to Information in EU Legislation' in S Ruggeri (ed), n 58 above.

The person concerned must be provided with a Letter of Rights containing information on: the right of access to a lawyer; any entitlement to free legal advice and the conditions for obtaining such advice; the right to be informed of the accusation; the right to an interpreter and translation of documents; and the right to remain silent. The Directive also establishes that information must be included with regard to the following rights *as they apply under national law*: the right of access to the materials of the case; the right to have consular authorities and one person informed; the right of access to urgent medical assistance; and the maximum number of hours or days suspects or accused persons may be deprived of liberty before being brought before a judicial authority. Other information that shall be featured concerns the possibility, *under national law*, of challenging the lawfulness of the arrest; of obtaining a review of the detention; and of making a request for provisional release. Member States shall ensure that suspects or accused persons receive the Letter of Rights written in a language that they understand. The rights can be communicated orally when the former option is not available.

Along with this information, the person must be informed of the reasons for their arrest or detention, including the criminal act they are suspected or accused of having committed. On the other hand, information must be given – at the latest on submission of the merits of the accusation to a court – on the accusation, including the nature and the legal classification of the criminal offence, and the level of involvement of the person concerned. Changes in this respect must be given to the person where this is necessary to safeguard the fairness of the proceedings. Member States shall ensure that suspects or accused persons or their lawyers have the right to challenge, in accordance with procedures in national law, the possible failure or refusal of the competent authorities to provide information in accordance with this Directive. The Directive also clarifies that its provisions cannot result in lowering the level of protection as guaranteed by the Charter, the ECHR, other relevant provisions of international law or the law of any Member State.

The third instrument adopted is the Directive on the right to access to a lawyer.[64] Suspects or accused persons must have access to a lawyer from whichever of the following points in time is the earliest: before they are questioned by the police or by another law enforcement or judicial authority; or without undue delay after deprivation of liberty. This right can be limited only at the pre-trial stage, where the geographical remoteness of a suspect or accused person makes it impossible to ensure the right of access to a lawyer without undue delay after deprivation of liberty.

[64] Directive 2013/48/EU of the European Parliament and of the Council of 22 October 2013 on the right of access to a lawyer in criminal proceedings and in European arrest warrant proceedings, and on the right to have a third party informed upon deprivation of liberty and to communicate with third persons and with consular authorities while deprived of liberty, [2013] OJ L294/1, 6.11.2013. See L Bachmaier Winter, 'The EU Directive on the Right to Access to a Lawyer: A Critical Assessment' in S Ruggeri, n 58 above.

In exceptional circumstances and only at the pre-trial stage, Member States may temporarily derogate from the application of the rights provided for if justified in the particular circumstances of the case, on the basis of one of the following reasons: (a) where there is an urgent need to avert serious adverse consequences for the life, liberty or physical integrity of a person; (b) where immediate action by the investigating authorities is imperative to prevent substantial jeopardy to criminal proceedings.

Persons deprived of liberty must have the right to inform at least one third party and to communicate with them. The right may be temporarily limited or deferred where there is: an urgent need to avert serious adverse consequences for the life, liberty or physical integrity of a person; an imperative requirement or proportionate operational requirement; or an urgent need to prevent a situation where criminal proceedings could be substantially jeopardised.

These derogations must be: proportionate and not go beyond what is necessary; strictly limited in time; not based exclusively on the type or the seriousness of the alleged offence; in compliance with the overall fairness of the proceedings. However, these requirements do not also relate to the right to communicate with third parties. This is also true with regards to the requirement that decisions on derogations must be taken on a case-by-case basis, either by a judicial authority, or by another competent authority on the condition that the decision can be submitted to judicial review. The person concerned must be informed of the right to waiver and the consequences thereof in understandable language. The waiver is given voluntarily and unequivocally. Persons concerned must have the option to revoke it.

With regard to the person subject to the EAW, the Directive lays down a specific provision. The person concerned must be given the right to access to a lawyer upon arrest pursuant to the EAW in the executing Member State. Hereby, the requested person must have the right to promptly have *access to* and *communicate with* a lawyer, and the latter has the right to be present and participate during any hearing. The executing Member State must inform the requested person that they have the right to appoint a lawyer in the issuing Member State. The issuing Member State must assist the lawyer in the executing Member State by providing them with information and advice, so that the effective exercise of the rights of requested persons under the EAW FD is ensured. Where the requested person wishes to exercise the right to appoint a lawyer in the issuing Member State and does not already have such a lawyer, the issuing state must be informed and provide the requested person with information to facilitate their appointment of a lawyer there. The person concerned must be given a remedy in case of breach of such rights. Member States, in making use of evidence collected in derogation or breach of those rights, must respect the fairness of the proceeding.[65]

[65] Ibid, Art 10.

C. Arbitrariness and the Right to Liberty in EU Procedural Criminal Law

The Directives have been closely scrutinised by scholars from different points of view:[66] the relationship between the EU and the ECtHR's standards;[67] the level of protection offered by the Directives in terms of gathering of evidence;[68] the broader implications of these instruments for national systems of criminal justice.[69]

The instruments operate in two distinct – but connected – ambits: criminal proceedings and EAW procedures. This distinction is relevant for the scope of application of the Directives, and the nature of the EAW procedures. On the one hand, Article 82(1) TFEU states that instruments of minimum harmonisation can be adopted to strengthen individual rights in *criminal procedure*. On the other, the Directives approximate rights in *criminal proceedings* and apply *until the final judgment*. The outer boundary and applicative limit of the concept of *criminal proceedings* lies in the final judgment. Criminal procedure and criminal proceedings are then two concentric circles, the latter being entirely encompassed in the former. This distinction might prove decisive, for the purpose of finding an appropriate legal basis for EU legislation in the area of detention conditions.[70]

The distinction between criminal proceedings and EAW procedures is also important with regard to the safeguard provided during mutual recognition procedures. The fundamental rights reference usually resorted to when broadly dealing with the EAW and mutual recognition is Article 5(1)(f) ECHR, which refers to extradition. The ECtHR has explicitly stated that the protection offered by that provision is not the same as Article 5(1)(c), regarding pre-trial detention. The case-law of the Strasbourg Court is rather clear on this point: extradition procedures feature a lower level of protection. This has also affected the EAW, as the CJEU's interpretation heavily relied on the ECtHR's judgments. On the one hand,

[66] M Caianello, 'Dal terzo pilastro ai nuovi strumenti: diritti fondamentali, "Road Map" e l'impatto delle nuove direttive' (2015) *Diritto Penale Contemporaneo*.

[67] L van Puyenbroeck and G Vermeulen, 'Towards Minimum Procedural Guarantees for the Defense in Criminal Proceedings in the EU' (2011) 60 *International & Comparative Law Quarterly* 1017–38.

[68] Some other authors regret that the Directive has not taken into account the possibility to give national courts the power to exclude evidence obtained in circumstances where safeguards are provided for by the Directive. See JR Spencer, 'EU Fair Trial Rights – Progress at Last' (2010) 1(4) *New Journal of European Criminal Law* 457.

[69] S Ruggeri, 'Procedimento penale, diritto di difesa e garanzie partecipative nel diritto dell'Unione Europea' (2015) *Diritto Penale Contemporaneo*. It is argued that the Directives, with the added contribution of the legally-binding value of the Charter, will create a network of individual rights which will enrich the national system. The standard of protection will not be a problem, as the principle of loyal cooperation requires both the EU and the Member State to act in such a way as to meet the objectives established at Union level.

[70] For an analysis on possible EU competences in the area of pre-trial detention, see Thea Coventry, 'Pretrial detention: Assessing European Union Competence under Article 82(2) TFEU' (2017) 8 *New Journal of European Criminal Law* 43.

the Luxembourg Court has claimed the autonomy of the EAW from extradition; on the other, it has extended a test conceived for the latter to the EAW.

Firstly, the Court seems to be increasingly aware of the need to develop a proper interpretation, more suitable to the EAW system. Secondly, the Directives approximate the standard of protection of criminal proceedings and EAW procedures. The Directives clarify that their provisions cannot result in lowering the level of protection as guaranteed by the Charter, the ECHR, other relevant provisions of international law or the law of any Member State. Whether or not this non-regression clause implicitly gives way to the primacy, unity and effectiveness of EU law, remains to be seen.

The Directives aim to approximate rights in an area covered by the right to liberty as defined by Article 5 ECHR. In the years following the introduction of the EAW, individual rights seemed to be granted inasmuch as they did not frustrate the enforcement aim of the EAW FD. The effectiveness of that measure shall now be balanced out against that of the Directives. The suitability of the Directive for actually improving protection has been questioned. The legislation establishes a more detailed regime, at EU secondary law level, regarding the essential aspect of the right to liberty. However, the piecemeal nature of the EU legislation in this area has drawn criticisms by those who see the Directives as not demonstrating a 'holistic understanding of the criminal justice process and this is exposed in an incremental methodology which articulates defence rights individually, arbitrarily compartmentalising them'.[71]

Secondly, the Directives provide no consequences for violations of the rights enshrined therein.[72] Thirdly, and relatedly, questions arise from the discretion left by the Directives with regards to limitations of the rights foreseen therein.[73] Various provisions laid down in the instruments stipulate that the rights granted may be limited to the extent that *the fairness of the proceedings* is not jeopardised. A particularly thorny area is the limitation of application of the Directives – and especially the right to interpretation and translation – to essential documents. The issue naturally arises as to how rigorously the essentiality of documents will be defined and assessed at the investigation stage. Scholars have highlighted that procedural safeguards can be perceived by the competent authorities across the

[71] D Sayers, 'Protecting Fair Trial Rights in Criminal Cases in the European Union: Where does the Roadmap take Us?' (2014) *Human Rights Law Review* 14, 760.

[72] Michele Caianiello, 'To Sanction (or not to Sanction) Procedural Flaws at Level?' (2014) 22 *European Journal of Crime, Criminal Law and Criminal Justice* 317 The author, however, recognises that introduction of sanction might be problematic in terms of EU competences. On the implementation of the Directive on access to a lawyer and its system of remedies, see Anneli Soo, 'How are the member states progressing on transposition of Directive 2013/48/EU on the right of access to a lawyer?: An inquiry conducted among the member states with the special focus on how Article 12 is transposed' (2017) 8(1) *New Journal of European Criminal Law* 64.

[73] Authors point to the practical difficulties that lawyers encounter in protecting suspects' rights across the EU. See Violet Mols, 'Bringing directives on procedural rights of the EU to police stations: Practical training for criminal defence lawyers' (2017) 8 *New Journal of European Criminal Law* 300.

EU as potentially jeopardising the purposes of their investigations.[74] Furthermore, national practices and bureaucratic considerations can contribute to undermine the effectiveness of procedural rights in criminal proceedings.[75]

The importance of a balance between common rules and national discretion emerges from the Court's interpretation of the Directives. On the one hand, a measure imposing sanctions in relation to minor offences and delivered by a judge following a simplified unilateral procedure, constitutes a 'document which is essential', of which a written translation must be provided to persons who do not understand the language of the proceedings.[76] On the other hand, national legislation may prevent the individual against whom a penalty order has been made from lodging an objection in writing against that order in a language other than that of the proceedings, even though that individual does not have a command of the language of the proceedings, provided that the competent authorities do not consider that that objection constitutes an essential document under Article 3(3).[77]

Two further instances of restriction are worth mentioning. The access to a lawyer can be limited in the case of geographical remoteness of the person concerned, but that must: be proportionate and not go beyond what is necessary; be strictly limited in time; not be based exclusively on the type or the seriousness of the alleged offence; and be in compliance with the overall fairness of the proceedings. The meaning of remoteness and the reasons why that would justify a restriction are not entirely clear. The right to communicate, while deprived of liberty, with third parties may be subject to derogation in view of imperative requirements or proportionate operational requirements, and without further guarantees for the person concerned. The absence of guarantees with regard to communication with third parties may give rise to issues in terms of proportionality.

These controversial aspects notwithstanding, these Directives have the merit of having reduced the distance between the protection in terms of the right to liberty under criminal proceedings, and that provided for in procedures pending an EAW. The next chapter shows that, unfortunately, the other instruments of mutual recognition involving detention have not benefitted from this development.

III. Conclusions

Free movement of judicial decisions is key to ensuring the effectiveness of EU law and the safe exercise of free movement. The Directives on procedural safeguards

[74] J Blackstock and others, *Inside Police Custody: An Empirical Account of Suspects' Rights in Four Jurisdictions* (Cambridge, Intersentia, 2014).

[75] J Hodgson, 'Criminal procedure in Europe's Area of Freedom, Security and Justice: the rights of the suspect' in V Mitsilegas, M Bergstrom and T Konstadinides, *Research Handbook in EU Criminal Law* (Cheltenham, Edward Elgar, 2015) 184.

[76] C-278/16, *Criminal proceedings against Franck Sleutjes*, EU:C:2017:757.

[77] C-216/14, *Criminal proceedings against Gavril Covaci*, EU:C:2015:686.

aim to make mutual trust – a foundation of mutual recognition – real. Those measures balance the relationship between integration and fundamental rights protection, although concerns must not be overlooked in terms of fragmentation of procedural safeguards and the margin for restricting rights with a direct impact on the right to liberty. What the Directives prominently bring to the fore, however, is the cleavage between protection in criminal proceedings and mutual recognition procedures. The peculiar nature of the latter – not just a variant of extradition – casts doubt on the suitability of the ECtHR's arbitrariness test on Article 5(1)(f) *sic et simpliciter* for these procedures.

If anything, the analysis of the EAW FD and relevant case-law consolidates the argument that increasing the EU's involvement in deprivation of liberty requires adjustment of traditional guarantees in a fashion that is Union-specific. Since the devil is in the detail, grey areas in a multi-level system of coercive movement of persons are very likely to arise. This may hold true for the – interrelated – issues of legal certainty and proportionality, as well as the role of detention conditions for the right to liberty. While the former suffers from possible 'hiccups' in the EAW system, with the requested person continuously deprived of liberty for circumstances beyond their responsibility, the latter makes even clearer the need for a re-conceptualisation of the right to liberty in EU law. As implicitly hinted at in the ECtHR's test, detention conditions are an aspect of the right of liberty: ongoing deprivation of liberty must comply with the procedures established by law. These themes imbue the next chapter as well. The arguments on proportionality, legal certainty and detention conditions are broadened, and converge towards a case for harmonisation of detention conditions within the Union.

8

Mutual Recognition of Custodial Penalties, Probation Measures and the European Supervision Order

I. Introduction

Further to Chapter 7, the instruments discussed below see free movement as their trigger, backbone and horizon of the Union's action.

The creation of a borderless area increases the possibility for persons to be investigated, tried and convicted in Member States other than those of their nationality. Research has consistently shown that judicial authorities are not inclined to grant pre- and post-conviction measures alternative to the deprivation of liberty to people not residing within their jurisdiction, as they cannot be monitored properly.[1] Furthermore, people sentenced to custodial penalties in other Member States might have reduced chances of reintegration than they would have in their countries of nationality or residence. The three FDs aim to overcome these problems through a system of mutual recognition (free movement) of custodial penalties, probation measures and pre-trial measures alternative to detention. However, the analysis shows that the persons concerned are treated as the object of mutual recognition, the main objective being public safety, or – in the words of the Tampere Programme – citizens' and businesses' safe exercise of free movement.

The three FDs are particularly relevant to the right to liberty. They all result in the deprivation of liberty (the coercive transfer) of the person concerned, once the judicial decision at stake has been recognised. After the transfer is completed, the individual will be subject to a new legal regime, which will differ from that of the issuing state, with the possibility of different rules concerning the substantive

[1] E Cape, J Hodgson, T Prakken and T Spronken (eds), *Suspects in Europe. Procedural Rights at the Investigative Stage of the Criminal Process in the European Union* (Antwerp/Oxford, Intersentia, 2007); AM van Kalmthout, MM Knapen, C Morgenstern and Z Bahtiyar (eds), *Pre-trial Detention in the European Union. An Analysis of Minimum Standards in Pre-trial Detention and the Grounds for Regular Review in the Member States of the EU* (Tilburg, Wolf Legal Publishers, 2009).

basis for detention and the procedural measures for deprivation of liberty. For example, the breach of a *pre-* or *post*-trial measure alternative to detention may have differing penalties in each Member State. Procedures for the deprivation of liberty, concerning the enforcement of detention, the penitentiary regime and detention conditions, may also vary significantly. The FDs lay down no guarantees to ensure that each individual is adequately informed of the potential alteration to the content of their right to liberty.

Similarly to the previous chapter, the discussion focuses on three issues: legal certainty, proportionality and the role of detention conditions. The analysis differs from that of the EAW in a fundamental respect. The procedural rights Directives have heightened the level of individual protection in EAW procedures but not with regard to the other FDs, so leaving the latter with a lower standard of safeguards. In conclusion, the assessment highlights the need for a new right to liberty in EU law adjusted to the peculiarities of the Union legal order.

II. The FD on Transfer of Prisoners, Probation Measures and the ESO

The FD on the transfer of prisoners creates a mechanism of mutual recognition of custodial sentences and judgments involving deprivation of liberty between Member States. When the judgment is recognised by the executing Member State, the prisoner is consequently transferred thereto. The purpose of the FD is to increase prisoners' chances of rehabilitation. However, in the preamble it is stated that the consent of the person concerned should no longer be dominant, for the purposes of recognition and enforcement of the sentence imposed.[2] This approach seems to permeate the other FDs as well, though to a lesser extent.

The FD does not have the effect of modifying the obligation to respect fundamental rights and fundamental legal principles as enshrined in Article 6 TEU.[3] The person can be transferred even where s/he has not provided consent, where: the executing Member State is the Member State of nationality in which the sentenced person lives; the sentenced person will be deported, once s/he is released from the enforcement of the sentence on the basis of an expulsion or deportation consequential to the judgment; or the sentenced person has fled or otherwise returned in view of the criminal proceedings pending against him or her in the issuing Member State or following the conviction in that issuing Member State. In the absence of the possibility to give his/her consent, the person concerned is provided

[2] Council Framework Decision 2008/909/JHA of 27 November 2008 on the application of the principle of mutual recognition to judgments in criminal matters imposing custodial sentences or measures involving deprivation of liberty for the purposes of their enforcement, recital 5, Art 4.

[3] Ibid, Art 3.

with a generic 'opportunity' to express his/her opinion, which in turn must be taken into account.[4] However, the FD lays down no rules to ensure an appropriate level of participation by the person concerned in the procedures of recognition and execution.

The FD on probation measures provides for the application of mutual recognition to judgments and probation decisions with a view to the supervision of probation measures and sanctions alternative to the deprivation of liberty.[5] The aim of the FD is enhancing the prospects of the sentenced person being reintegrated into society and improving protection of the general public.[6] The FD involves the recognition of judgments and probation measures, and the consequent transfer of responsibility for the supervision of probation measures and alternative sanctions from the issuing to the executing Member State. The issuing state may forward a decision to the state where the sentenced person is lawfully and ordinarily residing, when the sentenced person has returned or wants to return to that state. The law applicable is that of the executing Member State, which has the jurisdiction to decide on: modification of the measure; revocation of the suspension of the execution of the judgment or revocation of conditional release; the imposition of a measure involving deprivation of liberty.[7] If so requested, the executing state shall inform the issuing state of the maximum duration of deprivation of liberty foreseen in the executing state that could be imposed in case of breach of the probation measure or alternative sanction.[8] The executing state shall immediately notify the issuing one of any finding which may bring about the revocation of the alternative measure, or the imposition of a measure involving deprivation of liberty. Also in this case, the FD provides no rights or rules on the participation of the person concerned in the procedures of recognition and transfer.

The ESO FD establishes a system of recognition of supervision measures alternative to detention. To address this thorny issue, the EU has adopted an FD on the mutual recognition of decisions on supervision measures alternative to provisional detention. The ESO FD has a twofold aim: monitoring the defendants' movements; enhancing the right to liberty and the presumption of innocence of the persons concerned.[9] Should the person concerned not return to the issuing

[4] Ibid, Art 6.

[5] For an historical analysis, see S Neveu, 'Probation Measures and Alternative Sanctions in Europe: From the 1964 Convention to the 2008 Framework Decision' (2013) 4 (1)–(2) *New Journal of European Criminal Law* 134.

[6] Council Framework Decision 2008/947/JHA of 27 November 2008 on the application of the principle of mutual recognition to judgments and probation decisions with a view to the supervision of probation measures and alternative sanctions, [2008] OJ L337/102, 16.12.2008, recital 8.

[7] For consideration on probation in Europe, see I Durnescu, 'The future of probation in Europe: Common in the middle and diverse at the edge' (2013) 60 (3) *Probation Journal* 316; I Durnescu and B Stout, 'A European approach to probation training: An investigation into the competencies required' (2011) 58 (4) *Probation Journal* 395.

[8] See FD 2008/947/JHA, Arts 13–16.

[9] Council Framework Decision 2009/829/JHA of 23 October 2009 on the application, between Member States of the European Union, of the principle of mutual recognition to decisions on supervision measures as an alternative to provisional detention, [2009] OJ L294/20, 11.11.2009, recital 3.

state voluntarily, he or she may be surrendered to the issuing state in accordance with the EAW FD, so that the latter provisions apply.

The FD does not confer any right on the person to the use, in the course of criminal proceedings, of a non-custodial measure. A decision on supervision measures may be forwarded to the Member State where the person is lawfully and ordinarily residing, so long as s/he consents to return to that state. The law applicable is the law of the executing Member State.[10] The issuing state has the competence on all subsequent decisions relating to a decision on supervision measures, and in particular: the renewal, review, withdrawal, or modification of the supervision of the measures; the issuing of an arrest warrant or any other enforceable judicial decision having the same effect.[11] The issuing Member State must be immediately informed of any finding which can lead to the adoption of any of those measures. If the competent authority of the issuing State has issued a EAW or any other enforceable judicial decision having the same effect, the person shall be surrendered in accordance with the EAW FD.

The relevance of these instruments to the right to liberty is twofold. Firstly, they all entail deprivation of liberty of the person concerned, due to the transfer from the issuing to the executing Member State. Secondly, the lack of clear rules concerning the participation of the individual in the procedures of recognition emerges. This is highly relevant to the right to liberty not just because the individual can be subject to the coercive transfer. The transfer to another state results in the application of rules possibly different from those of the issuing state, with regard to *cases* and *procedures* for deprivation of liberty. In the following, it is argued that the minor involvement of the individual in procedures of recognition can significantly affect the awareness of how his/her right to liberty can be limited in the executing state.

III. The Right to Liberty and Coercive Movement of Persons within the EU

The discussion in the previous chapter threw into relief the importance of proportionality and poor detention conditions to the right to liberty in the context of mutual recognition. The three FDs bring to the fore other significant – and related – aspects concerning the relationship between the right to liberty, and the higher level of automaticity in inter-state cooperation in criminal matters introduced by mutual recognition. The analysis focuses on three points: the inadequate level of individual rights in procedures resulting in deprivation of liberty in terms of proportionality; the lack of legal certainty concerning possible grounds and

[10] Ibid, Art 16.
[11] Ibid, Art 18.

procedures for deprivation of liberty; the role for detention conditions and the case for approximation of rights of detainees within the EU.

A. Proportionality and Procedural Rights of the Individuals

The FDs are relevant to proportionality under Articles 49 and 52 CFREU. As to the former, the FDs state that the adapted sentence shall not aggravate the penalty in terms of nature and duration (in the case of the ESO the measure shall not be more severe). The question arises as to what factors may result in aggravating the penalty, such as for example rules on the enforcement of the sentence (eg custodial penalty in isolation, special security regimes and the like). The problem also concerns the FD on probation measures: the law of the executing Member State can be much stricter, eg concerning the consequences of a breach of the measure in question. The FD on probation measures states that

> Where the probation measure, the alternative sanction or the probation period has been adapted because its duration exceeds the maximum duration provided for under the law of the executing State, the duration of the adapted probation measure, alternative sanction or probation period shall not be below the maximum duration provided for equivalent offences under the law of the executing State.[12]

The adaptation takes place because there is a difference between the two states with regard to the penalty generally imposed in relation to that particular offence. With that in mind, it would be fairer granting the executing state with a margin of discretion in this respect. So far, the CJEU has been inclined to allow national judges much more discretion in terms of adaption of the sentence. It found that the executing state was to grant to the sentenced person a reduction in sentence by reasons of work he carried out during the period of his detention in the issuing state, although no such reduction in sentence was granted by the competent authorities of the issuing state, in accordance with the law of the issuing state.[13]

Issues of Article 52 CFREU stem from the absence of procedural guarantees, with the requirement that deprivation of liberty be carried out according to clear and legal procedures being under pressure. The FDs are completely silent as to the procedures to be followed when adopting the decision on the transfer: no individual rights are provided for in this respect. The FD on probation measures and the ESO FD are 'triggered' at the request of the person concerned. Also, in these cases the individual will be subject to deprivation of liberty, as s/he will be

[12] FD 2008/947/JHA, n 6 above, Art 9(2).

[13] Case C-25/15, *Criminal proceedings against Ognyanov*, EU:C:2016:835, para 51. Jamil Ddamulira Mujuzi, 'The Transfer of Offenders between European Countries and Remission of Sentences: A Comment on the Grand Chamber of the Court of Justice of the European Union's Judgment in Criminal Proceedings against Atanas Ognyanov of 8 November 2016 Dealing with Article 17 of Council Framework Decision 2008/909/JHA' (2017) 7 *European Criminal Law Review* 289.

transferred to the executing Member State. However, these instruments do not ensure an adequate level of participation by the person concerned in the procedures of recognition, nor do they ensure that the person is aware of differences between the two legal systems.[14] The FD on the transfer of prisoners removes the need for consent of the person concerned for the purposes of the transfer, in particular where the executing state is where the person lives or where s/he should be returned on the basis of an expulsion order.[15] The instrument establishes only that the opinion of the person concerned must be taken into account.

As counter-objections, it might be argued that Member States would be individually responsible for establishing the relevant procedures, and that the FD on transfer of prisoners would operate in a situation where the persons concerned are already deprived of liberty. The division of labour between EU and state law may not be justification for situations of legal vacuum or uncertainty, nor for discharging the fundamental rights obligation on the part of the Union.[16] Secondly, and relatedly, the *established procedures* requirement should logically apply to the enforcement phase as well.

Can that measure be seen as proportionate? Depriving the person of the power of consent, against a poor system of procedural guarantees, casts serious doubt on its compatibility with the rehabilitation purposes declared by the FD. The preamble takes a clear stance in stating that the consent of the prisoner should no longer be an overriding requirement. The prisoner is considered an object in the hands of Member States for judicial cooperation. Furthermore, critical remarks could be addressed to the specific grounds on which the need for consent is removed, eg the circumstance that the person has been subject to an expulsion measure from the sending state. There are Member State laws providing for automatic liability to expulsion once a certain kind/threshold of penalty is met, which the CJEU has found potentially incompatible with EU law.

What emerges from the analysis of the three FDs is a sharp contrast in individual rights protection between criminal proceedings, on the one hand, and mutual recognition procedures, on the other. Mutual recognition procedures have an uncertain nature: they cannot be considered part of criminal proceedings, but have a significant impact on personal liberty all the same. The EU has adopted three Directives on (1) translation and interpretation, (2) information and (3) the access to a lawyer in criminal proceedings. In terms of their scope of

[14] Wendy De Bondt and Annika Suominen, 'State Responsibility When Transferring Non-consenting Prisoners to Further their Social Rehabilitation – Lessons Learnt from the Asylum Case Law' (2015) 5 *European Criminal Law Review* 347.

[15] For critical considerations on this aspect, see V Mitsilegas, 'The third wave of third pillar' (2009) 34 (4) *European Law Review* 523, 541 onwards.

[16] For an argument supporting the idea that the EU's engagement in an area of law implies a corresponding obligation to minimise the risk that fundamental rights violations occur, see Nina Marlene Schallmoser, 'The European Arrest Warrant and Fundamental Rights' (2014) 22 *European Journal of Crime, Criminal Law and Criminal Justice* 135.

application, the Directives lay down rules concerning these rights (1) *in criminal proceedings* and (2) *in proceedings for the execution of an EAW*.[17] Therefore, the EU legislature acknowledges the difference between these two kinds of procedures. The Directives reduce the existing distance between the standard of protection in criminal proceedings, on the one hand, and in the execution of an EAW, on the other.

Unfortunately, this improvement has not involved the other three FDs. However, they have significant implications in terms of the right to liberty as well, so that there is no good reason for this discrepancy in terms of individual guarantees. The cleavage is confirmed by the Court's finding that, in the context of the European Criminal Records Information System (ECRIS), the Directive on the right to interpretation and translation

> is not applicable to a national special procedure for the recognition by the court of a Member State of a final judicial decision handed down by a court of another Member State convicting a person for the commission of an offence.[18]

While the legal framework set out by the FDs challenges the *established procedures* requirement inherent in the right to liberty, serious concerns can be voiced about the proportionality of these measures with the objectives of the instrument, be they reintegration or public safety.

B. Legal Certainty

In terms of legal certainty and the right to liberty, the FDs leave much to be desired. The FDs on probation measures and pre-trial measures alternative to detention stipulate that the decision on the recognition is to be taken within 60 days. However, they also provide that this time-limit need not be complied with, where *exceptional circumstances* occur.[19] No further deadlines are laid down, so that the transfer of the person concerned can be suspended *sine die*.[20] As shown, the ESO FD usually applies where the person concerned is in pre-trial detention just for not being in his/her country of residence. The transfer to the executing state would be conducive to setting him/her free. The same logic underlies the FD on probation measures. Allowing for continuing detention of the individual on a very broadly worded legal basis (*exceptional circumstances*), without a term for a decision being set, could be highly detrimental to the right to liberty.

[17] See T Spronken, G Vermeulen, D de Vocht and L van Puyenbroeck, *EU Procedural Rights in Criminal Proceedings* (Antwerp, Maklu, 2009); E Guild and L Marin (eds), *Still not resolved? Constitutional Issues of the European Arrest Warrant* (Tilburg, Wolf Legal Publishers, 2009).

[18] Case C-25/15, *Proceedings brought by István Balogh*, EU:C:2016:423, para 56.

[19] See FD 2008/947/JHA and FD 2009/829/JHA nn 7 and 10 above, Arts 12(2) and 12(3).

[20] However, the FD on probation measures states that a new time-limit should be established by the authority of the executing state (Art 12(2)).

The impact of these instruments on the right to liberty also involves the lack of legal certainty with regard to *cases* and *procedures* for deprivation of liberty. To this end, the ECtHR has clarified that the right to liberty presupposes legal certainty: the law *authorising* and *regulating* deprivation of liberty is to be of sufficient quality. The automaticity introduced by mutual recognition in inter-state cooperation in criminal matters calls for reconsidering the requirement that deprivation of liberty take place in the *cases* and according to the *procedures* established by the law. On the one hand, the FDs confer upon the Member States the power to deprive a person of liberty; on the other, the procedures on the basis of which deprivation should be carried out, as well the participation of the individual in these procedures, are not regulated at all.

The phase that follows the transfer to the executing state is no less problematic. Once the transfer is completed, the person will be subject to a different legal regime. This regards both the *cases* and the *procedures* for detention. The 'cases' of deprivation of liberty are understood as situations that can lawfully give rise to deprivation of liberty. For instance, the executing state can feature stricter rules than the issuing state in case of a breach of a *pre*- or *post*-trial measure alternative to detention, and sanction these infringements with deprivation of liberty (as a punishment or more severe pre-trial measure). The lack of involvement of the person in the procedures of recognition can seriously affect awareness of these aspects, capable of resulting in deprivation of liberty. Such uncertainty also involves the *procedures* of detention, and in particular the phase of enforcement. The requirement that deprivation of liberty be carried out according to the procedures established by the law logically includes the phase that follows the apprehension of the person concerned. So long as deprivation of liberty is ongoing, clear legal procedures are to be established and abided by.

In this context, significant difference in procedures can relate particularly to the penitentiary regime in the executing Member State. This is particularly problematic as far as the FD on the transfer of prisoners is concerned, since this instrument provides for the transfer of the person even without their consent. The FDs allow for and regulate – to very little extent – deprivation of liberty and transfer of the person concerned, on the one hand. On the other hand, they provide no guarantees that the individual is made aware of his/her rights with regard to transfer procedures, as well as the difference in legal regimes that can affect his/her right to liberty. This has to do with those situations that can give rise to deprivation of liberty, and the way in which deprivation of liberty is enforced in the executing state.

One could object that the rules are still provided at national level, so that EU law would not be involved in such considerations. It is for national laws to determine the rules regarding prison regimes, or the consequences of breach of probation measures.[21] However, the person concerned is subject to a different legal

[21] On the state of play of implementation of these FDs at national level, see the Report from the Commission to the European Parliament and the Council on the implementation by the Member States

framework after s/he has been forcibly transferred to another Member State. That transfer is based on a procedure regulated by EU law; a procedure in which the person concerned has no specific rights or guarantees. Either by directly providing for deprivation of liberty (eg the coercive transfer), or giving the basis for further and different deprivation (rules on *pre*- and *post*-trial measures), these EU law instruments are undeniably relevant to the right to liberty, and create an unbalanced legal framework at the expense of individual rights.

Issues of legal certainty emerge from the relationship between the FDs and the EAW. The FD on transfer of prisoners provides that a Member State requested to permit transit of the prisoner (en route to the issuing state) must inform the issuing state if it cannot guarantee that the sentenced person will not be prosecuted or detained there. In such a case, the issuing state may withdraw its request.[22] What if the state decides not to withdraw the request, that 'warning' notwithstanding? The risk that the state of transit resorts to that provision for circumventing the EAW procedures should not be underestimated.

The FD on probation measures states that, in case of new criminal proceedings against the person concerned in the issuing state, the latter may ask the executing Member State to transfer back to it the jurisdiction on the supervision and all further decisions relating to the judgment.[23] Also in this case there are no references to the EAW FD, but the mechanism seems to be pretty similar. Are there, if any, grounds for refusal of such a request? According to which procedures should the decision on the surrender be taken? What is the position of individuals?

Doubt is engendered also by the ESO FD, which provides that if the competent authority of the issuing state has issued an EAW or *any other enforceable judicial decision having the same effect*, the person shall be surrendered in accordance with the Framework Decision on the EAW.[24] The reference to other decisions having the same effect is not straightforward. Quite the contrary, it seems to legitimate the logic of uncertainty which surrounds the reach of state discretion within the EU, when the forced movement of the detainee is at stake.

C. Detention Conditions. The Case for Harmonisation

We have seen that detention conditions in EU law become particularly relevant in the context of intra-EU transfer of people, in turn based on the interaction between the static and dynamic dimensions.

of the Framework Decisions 2008/909/JHA, 2008/947/JHA and 2009/829/JHA on the mutual recognition of judicial decisions on custodial sentences or measures involving deprivation of liberty, on probation decisions and alternative sanctions and on supervision measures as an alternative to provisional detention, Brussels, 5.2.2014 COM(2014) 57 final.

[22] FD 2008/909/JHA, Art 16.

[23] FD 2008/947/JHA, Art 20.

[24] FD 2009/829/JHA, Art 21.

The case for approximation of detention conditions in EU law is both principled and functional. The right to liberty heavily relies on legal certainty, which materialises in the cases and the procedures requirements especially. The (quasi-) automatic system of forced movement of persons within the EU requires a broader and deeper application of that requirement. Building on the understanding of Article 6 CFREU stated here, it is argued that common standards should be established throughout the Union, for detention conditions are part of a centrepiece of the right to liberty. Bringing detention conditions under the umbrella of the EU would also entail an additional layer of monitoring, constituted by the CJEU's oversight and the Commission's power under Article 258 TFEU for non-compliant Member States. There are, however, also pragmatic reasons to support action from the EU legislature. The procedural rights Directives were explicitly adopted with the view to increasing mutual trust as between Member States, which in turn is key to fostering the smooth operation of mutual recognition – and the intra-EU transfer of persons broadly. The argument stated in the previous sub-section and the CJEU's case-law highlight that flaws in the static dimension can compromise the proper functioning of forced movement.

Approximation of detention in criminal law is more problematic. A possible objection to an EU competence is that the legal basis does not empower the Union to adopt measures in this area. To this end, Article 82(1) TFEU refers to the possibility of minimum harmonisation with regard to individual rights in *criminal procedure*. Such a concept should not be used interchangeably with that of criminal proceedings. A systematic interpretation rests on the understanding of criminal procedure and criminal proceedings as two concentric circles, with the latter being entirely contained in the – broader – former one. The procedural rights Directives state the objective of establishing rights in criminal proceedings. They define their scope of application as *until the final judgment*.

The coincidence between criminal proceedings and final judgment implies a broader scope for criminal procedure, which naturally includes enforcement as well. Such a finding must be read in combination with the legal basis in EU procedural criminal law as laid down in Article 82(2)(b) TFEU. That provision confers upon the EU the power to adopt minimum rules on the rights of individuals in criminal procedure. As the Treaty refers to individual rights, this article argues for the *proceduralisation* of detention conditions. By turning upside down the existing perspective, a possible Directive should understand those conditions as individual rights rather than as impersonal standards. The European Prison Rules should constitute the main source of the EU legislative initiative. Where these refer to the required characteristics of, for example, accommodation, hygiene, nutrition, clothing and bedding,[25] a Directive should lay down those provisions as detainees' entitlement. This should be supported by the inclusion of a system of remedies for

[25] European Prison Rules, sections 16 onward.

their violation. It is true that, on looking at the Travaux préparatoires for Article 82 TFEU, that its legal basis seems meant to cover situations under Article 6 ECHR and not Article 5 ECHR. That objection can be overcome by reasons of effectiveness of EU law, first. The establishment of common standards would facilitate mutual recognition as required by the legal basis under examination. Secondly, the original intention of the Treaty-makers would be adjusted and aligned with the EU-specific understanding of the right to liberty proposed here.

The present argument does not overlook the political and legal difficulties that would emerge, such as the definition of the concept of minimum rules, objections about proportionality and subsidiarity, or recourse to the so-called emergency brake under Article 82(3) TFEU. However, the foregoing argument aims to establish the first step toward a legal debate concerning approximation of detention conditions at EU law level.

IV. Conclusions

This chapter completes the discussion on deprivation of liberty in judicial cooperation and EU procedural criminal law. The analysis focused on three FDs forming part of a system of transfer of convicted or suspected persons within the Union. These measures are relevant to the right to liberty, as they set up a framework of coercive movement of the persons concerned, with a significant impact in terms of *cases* and *procedures* requirements both before and after the transfer has occurred.

While they are formally concerned with rehabilitation or presumption of innocence, the structure of the instruments seems to be conceived with public safety and states' interests in mind.

Integration in the specific areas is founded on mutual recognition and trust as well. The tensions with fundamental rights protection are rather evident. These instruments worsen the criminal proceedings–mutual recognition procedure divide, and introduce a mechanism of forced transfer of persons with a particularly low standard of individual safeguards. The immaterial involvement of the transferees clashes with the established procedures requirement under the right to liberty, and seems to be disproportionate to the objectives of the FDs. The FD on recognition of custodial penalties is paradigmatic, where the need for consent of the prisoner is removed for the purposes of the smooth operation of mutual recognition.

The understanding of detainees as an object of mutual recognition is confirmed by the provisions of the FDs allowing for suspension of transfer procedures – and of the consequent release of the person – *sine die* and on extremely broadly worded grounds. Aside from its impact in terms of established procedures, the removal of the person from the transfer procedures impacts on the *cases* requirement of the right to liberty, as the law of the issuing state might be very different. These being some of the unprecedented challenges posed by mutual recognition to the right to liberty, it is submitted that a partial solution would be provided by the adoption of an instrument establishing a level playing-field of detainees' rights within the EU. Other than being compliant with the limits posed by the Treaties in terms of the Union's competence, the instrument would strengthen mutual trust on what has emerged as the most burning issue concerning judicial cooperation within the EU, and facilitate cooperation as between Member States when a coercive transfer of persons is involved.

Concluding Remarks on Deprivation of Liberty in Mutual Recognition and EU Criminal Procedure

The analysis of the EU approach to deprivation of liberty in judicial cooperation and EU criminal procedures consolidates and broadens the findings emerging from previous Parts of the story. Similarly to – and in conjunction with – what happened in EU substantive criminal law, the Union's involvement in the inter-state fight against crime has grown out of the core project of the EU as a borderless area. The threefold dimension of free movement as trigger, laboratory and horizon shines brightly: free movement is sustainable *provided that* it can be *safely* exercised.

This condition – amounting to *higher effectiveness of* (EU) law – is pursued through further legal integration. The dialectic with fundamental rights protection becomes even tenser since a closer Union in this case implies free movement of judicial decisions (mutual recognition), which in turn rests on the presumption that fundamental rights are complied with across the EU.

With a view to preserving free movement and the Union as a borderless area, the EU has set up a system of forced movement of persons – having, as seen above, a key ally in static rules approximating substantive criminal law and levels of penalty – that introduces automaticity in inter-state cooperation in criminal matters, and is premised on the presumption that fundamental rights are respected throughout the Union. Those being the background and horizon of the EU action, the episode narrated in this Part highlighted once again the unsuitability of the current understanding, at EU law level, of traditional strongholds of personal liberty. Mutual recognition poses unprecedented challenges to the right to liberty in three main respects: proportionality, legal certainty, and scope of application – which concern, inter alia, the role of detention conditions for the EU law right to liberty. The construction of a new habeas corpus that is Union-specific must start from the following premises. Firstly, the right to liberty is built on two main pillars, constituted by the requirement that deprivation of liberty occurs on the basis of clear and accessible rules concerning *cases* and *procedures established by the law*. On the one hand, cases are situations that can lawfully result in deprivation of liberty; on the other, the procedures logically concern the enforcement of detention. The argument naturally flows from the dynamic requirement that deprivation of liberty be carried out according to established procedures. Secondly, proportionality and certainty are inherent requirements of the right to liberty: the more uncertain the rule, the less clear the boundaries for the exercise of public powers, with a higher likelihood that disproportionate use of force will occur.

In this context, proportionality places the competent authorities under the spotlight. Much debate on the EAW especially arose as to the obligation for the issuing judge to apply a proportionality test before issuing an EAW. Though acknowledging the importance of the argument, judgments like *Lanigan* and *Vilkas* bring to the fore the prominent role of the executing judge when it comes to deciding on the continuing detention of the person concerned. When hiccups and delays occur in transferring the person, the latter can be detained beyond the deadline stated in the EAW FD and for reasons for which the person is not responsible. While stating the obligation to interpret the FD in light of Articles 6 and 52 CFREU, the CJEU seems willing to leave the national judge a wide margin to keep the person in detention after the expiry of the terms laid down in the FD.

Judicial cooperation may aim to improve individual rights as well. The FDs on transfer of prisoners, probation measures and the ESO form part of the system of forced transfer with the view to promoting public safety, reintegration and the right to liberty. Free movement facilitates the emergence of scenarios where people are investigated in a state where they are not resident, and are not released on bail as they cannot be monitored properly; or else, they are convicted and serve the sentence in a state where the chance of reintegration is reduced due to the absence of a social, personal and employment connection. The FDs, however, lay down neither clear procedures governing recognition and transfer, nor safeguards for the persons concerned. In the case embodied by the FD on the transfer of prisoners, the transfer may take place even without the consent of the person concerned. Serious doubts arise as to the proportionality of these constraints on the established procedures requirement with the objectives stated in the FDs. This is even more so in consideration of possible great differences between issuing and executing states in terms of cases and procedures of deprivation of liberty of which the person might not be aware. The issue here is one of proportionality *and* legal certainty.

Issues of legal certainty arise from the very nature of the system of judicial cooperation. Firstly, there is the overarching question concerning the threshold to overcome the presumption of mutual trust. While *Căldăraru* made clear that no systematic violations are required when absolute prohibitions are involved, *LM* has opened the door to non-execution where relative rights are at stake, as long as exceptional circumstances can be envisaged. Whether this could be the case with the right to liberty remains to be seen. Secondly, the FDs leave considerable margin to Member States. The FD on probation measures and the ESO allow for suspending *sine die* the transfer – and therefore the release of the person – in case of unforeseen circumstances. This has great implications in terms of the right to liberty. Thirdly, the very nature of mutual recognition creates uncertainty and imbalance. While the procedural rights Directives can certainly contribute to strengthening trust – and, therefore, mutual recognition – within the EU, they worsen the divide between mutual recognition procedures and criminal proceedings. They only apply to criminal proceedings and EAW procedures, so that the other FDs do not benefit from the rights stated and approximated with regard to the right to information, interpretation and translation, and access to a lawyer. EU law currently features an unacceptable double standard of protection of the right to liberty.

In that context, detention conditions are in the background of all the issues discussed so far. They form part of the established procedures requirement. This was referred to by the ECtHR, which indicated detention conditions as one of the possible signifiers of arbitrariness of detention. On that ground, they should be relevant not only for reasons of degrading and inhuman treatment, but also – and mostly, at least quantitatively speaking – where situations of non-compliance with standards of detention conditions established by law occur; or, to reiterate the formula used above, for all those scenarios where detention conditions are not *poor enough* to meet the threshold of Article 4 CFREU, but they do violate the law and result in a situation of arbitrariness. A case has been made that unlawful detention conditions result in situations of arbitrary detention, so that the activation of the exceptional circumstances clause should be considered.

To overcome the flaws of the existing legal framework, and in continuity to what was argued with regard to EU substantive criminal law, Union-specific re-conceptualisation is needed. The EU's new right to liberty could materialise in a code of safeguards in mutual recognition procedures which should place at its core detention conditions. The proceduralisation of detention conditions and the overall coordination of a person's prerogative in mutual recognition would be compliant with Article 82 TFEU, which empowers the EU to approximate (1) individual rights (2) in criminal procedure (3) to facilitate mutual recognition. The first and third conditions are self-evidently complied with, as well as the second, since criminal procedure clearly envisages a broader concept than criminal proceedings, with only the latter overlapping with the outer boundaries of the final judgment.

The next Part takes the story out of the realm of criminal law, and addresses the problem of immigration detention and the right to liberty. It will be shown, however, that the discussion in that area also falls within the overarching framework of the book, and offers possible solutions for overcoming a common legal dilemma emerging across the spectrum of Union law.

PART IV

Asylum and Immigration Detention

9

Deprivation of Liberty in the Context of Immigration Control. Overview

I. Introduction

This Part takes the story of the book outside the realm of criminal law over to asylum and immigration detention, understood as administrative deprivation of liberty of Third Country Nationals (TCNs) in a Member State.[1] Historically, detention of TCNs has been a key tool used by states for the purposes of migration control, and has now become part and parcel of the Union's policy.[2]

While detention in criminal law, and immigration law, are different, they are both an expression of the narrative concerning EU law and deprivation of liberty.[3] That story started in the context of the internal market, with the CJEU posing limits to states' use of custodial penalties to protect freedom of movement. The pursuit of the Union as a borderless area resulted in the creation of a body of law that, with that objective in mind, would require or allow Member States to adopt coercive measures. The analysis of EU substantive and procedural EU criminal law brought to the fore the clear connection between the coming into being of those areas, on the one hand, and the integration–fundamental rights protection dynamic on the other.

EU asylum and immigration law are part of the broader project of creating an area of freedom, security and justice, where (negative and positive) legal integration rests on the presumption that fundamental rights are respected throughout the EU. As is well known, the abolition of internal frontiers was linked from the very start to the strengthening of the Union's external borders. The embryos of

[1] For the purpose of the present work, 'immigration detention' refers to that type of administrative deprivation of liberty (not necessarily linked to a criminal offence) carried out during a removal procedure or when the determination of an asylum claim is under way. Likewise, terms such as 'immigrant', 'migrant', 'third-country national' or 'non-EU citizen' are interchangeably used.

[2] For the origin of use of immigration detention, see D Wilsher, *Immigration Detention: Law, History, Politics* (Cambridge, Cambridge University Press, 2011) 1 onwards.

[3] Authors have argued that immigration detention might be used for purposes similar to those of custodial penalties. See A Leekers and D Broeders, 'A case of mixed motives? Formal and informal functions of Administrative Immigration Detention' (2010) 50 *British Journal of Criminology* 830–50.

the Union commitment to asylum and immigration law materialised shortly after the infamous Commission white paper on the completion of the internal market.[4]

On the one hand, the Dublin Convention was adopted in 1990, establishing a first system of allocation of responsibility on asylum claims amongst (some) Member States. On the other, the 1992 Maastricht Treaty introduced EU competences in certain areas of Justice and Home Affairs for achieving the free movement of persons, including asylum and immigration policy.[5]

The Dublin Convention itself was conceived as a system for resolving 'conflicts of jurisdiction' over the examination of asylum claims and for containing a massive influx of asylum-seekers.[6] EU asylum and migration law was born with the need to compensate for the opening of internal frontiers in mind, and built upon an approach where 'the movement of asylum seekers and legal and illegal immigrants, on the one hand, and of terrorists and criminals, on the other, were conceptually blurred as negative consequences of the abolition of borders'.[7]

Since that first step, many more have been taken in policy and legal terms. The Union now has a Common European and Asylum System (CEAS), which aims to establish a common legal framework on reception conditions, procedures of asylum and recognition of the status of refugee. Under Title V TFEU, the EU is currently empowered to adopt measures on border checks, asylum and immigration.[8] The objective of building an Area of Freedom, Security and Justice 'without internal frontiers, *and* with full respect for fundamental rights'[9] signals that the two centrepieces, while not incompatible a priori at all, do not necessarily overlap. Policy documents confirm the dual soul of the Union approach, with the objective of a high standard of protection going hand in hand with the prevention or reduction of secondary movement within the EU, and an increase in mutual trust between Member States.[10]

The Union aims for an efficient and well-managed migration, asylum and border policy, which rests on the implementation of the CEAS and the fight against irregular migration. Action on those ambits contemplates measures covering a very broad spectrum of situations, including: decisions on short- and long-term visas, entering alerts in the Schengen Information System on persons not allowed

[4] For an historical analysis of the path preceding the Dublin Convention and the Maastricht Treaty, see A Hurwitz, *The Collective Responsibility of States to Protect Refugees* (Oxford, Oxford University Press, 2009) 30 onwards.

[5] [1992] OJ C191/4, 29.7.1992, Title VI.

[6] S Peers, *EU Justice and Home Affairs Law*, 3rd edn (Oxford, Oxford University Press, 2011) 295.

[7] A Hurwitz, *The Collective Responsibility of States to Protect Refugees*, n 4 above, 33.

[8] For an analysis of the institutional framework under the Amsterdam Treaty, see S Peers, 'From Black Market to Constitution: The Development of the Institutional Framework for EC Immigration and Asylum Law' in S Peers and N Rogers (eds), *EU Immigration and Asylum Law* (Leiden, Martinus Nijhoff, 2006) 19.

[9] Conclusions of the European Council (26/27 June 2014). EUCO 79/14, 1.

[10] The Stockholm Programme – An open and secure Europe serving and protecting citizens, [2010] OJ C115/124, 69.

to stay in the EU territory, and interception operations at the maritime borders of the Union.[11]

In that context, a major role is played by the allocation of responsibility for the examination of asylum claims and the pursuit of a common return policy. Administrative detention is key to the EU endeavour, and can take place in asylum law and irregular migration management. The former scenario sees detention used pending: the examination of an asylum claim, determination of the state responsible for that purpose, or removal to the third country of origin. In the latter case, detention serves to secure the completion of procedures for return of irregular migrants from a Member State to outside the Union. While governed by different rationales, the two types of deprivation of liberty are highly interconnected and share key features. Once the person is refused asylum, and is given no other qualification to stay in the territory, s/he will most probably be subject to EU rules on returns, including those concerning pre-removal detention.[12]

What is more, asylum and immigration detention present similarities with the analysis carried out in Part III. Detention of TCNs is linked to a system of forced transfer of persons within or outside the EU. Similarly to what was discussed in the case of mutual recognition, the right to liberty – which applies regardless of the nature of the detention at stake – comes into play primarily under Article 5(1)(f): the lawful arrest or detention of a person to prevent him effecting an unauthorised entry into the country, or of a person against whom action is being taken with a view to deportation or extradition. Administrative detention is also a key step toward criminalisation of migration in Europe: namely, the use of tools typical of criminal law for the purposes of migration control.[13]

Administrative and criminal deprivation of liberty should firmly be kept separate, since the former group of persons concerned are not suspected of or convicted for having committed a crime. However, both express the most serious form of interference with personal liberty exercised by public powers over an individual. Coercive measures have a precise meaning: through them, a polity states a situation of risk posed by the person concerned to a very important and usually

[11] On the Commission agenda on interoperability of databases for the purposes of migration control, see: http://eur-lex.europa.eu/legal-content/EN/TXT/PDF/?uri=CELEX:52005DC0597&from=EN. On surveillance, see Baldaccini, 'Counter-terrorism and the EU strategy for border security: Framing suspects with biometric documents and databases' (2008) 10(1) *European Journal of Migration and Law* 31; F Aas, '"Crimmigrant" bodies and bona fide travelers: Surveillance. Citizenship and global governance' (2011) 15(3) *Theoretical Criminology* 331. A key role in the context of border control and prevention is played by specialised EU agencies. See on this Rijpma and Vermeulen, 'EUROSUR: saving lives or building borders?' (2015) 24(3) *European Security* 454.

[12] For an overview on the use of asylum detention and interaction with pre-removal deprivation of liberty, see M Walter-Franke, 'Asylum Detention in Europe: State of Play and Ways Forward' (Jacques Delors Institut, Policy Paper No 195 (Berlin) May 2017).

[13] V Mitsilegas, *The Criminalisation of Migration in Europe. Challenges for Human Rights and the Rule of Law* (Berlin, Springer, 2015) 77 onward; R Cholewinski, 'The Criminalisation of Migration in EU Law and Policy' in H Toner, E Guild and A Baldaccini, *Whose Freedom, Security and Justice?* (Oxford, Hart Publishing, 2007) 301–36.

supra-individual interest. The analysis of the ambit of immigration detention (asylum and irregular migration law) brings to the fore security and effectiveness as the main protagonists. Once again, the quest for balance in EU law and policy is all internal to the sustainability of the area without internal frontiers, rather than between that objective and fundamental rights protection. Once again, the significant absence is a stronghold of personal liberty (the right to liberty) aptly conceived of, interpreted and protected to suit the peculiarities of the EU legal order.

That being the place of immigration detention in the broader context of the book, the following section focuses on the structure and materials discussed in Part IV, and the specificities of the right to liberty in the context of EU asylum and immigration law.

II. EU Law and Migration Issues

The EU's involvement in migration issues is a relatively recent phenomenon. Migration and border control are traditionally regarded as a stronghold of national sovereignty. The first 'common' step in the field – though initially taken by a small group of Member States – was the Schengen agreement, signed with a view to abolishing 'checks on persons at the common borders of the Member States and [transferring] those checks to their external borders'.[14] However, the Schengen *acquis* would be built into Union law only with the Treaty of Amsterdam,[15] to support the stated objective to create an Area of Freedom, Security and Justice (AFSJ).[16] Alongside that, competences in migration and asylum were transferred from the third pillar (as provided in the Maastricht Treaty) to the Community pillar (Title IV of the Amsterdam Treaty), with Justice and Home Affairs law remaining relevant for measures related to judicial cooperation in criminal matters (Title VI). The Treaty of Lisbon has carried out the 'pillars collapse', with the AFSJ corresponding to Title V of the TFEU. Therein, Articles 77 to 80 confer upon the Union the power to adopt measures to establish a common policy related to asylum, visas, borders and irregular migration in compliance with principles of solidarity and the fair sharing of responsibilities.[17]

[14] Case C-77/05, *United Kingdom v Council*, [2007] ECR I-11459, para 83.

[15] [1997] OJ C340, 10.11.1997.

[16] See Protocol (No 2) of the EU Treaty and the EC Treaty integrating the Schengen *acquis* into the framework of the European Union of 2 October 1997, [1997] OJ C340/93, 10.11.1997; see, for the definition of the Schengen *acquis*, the Council Decision 1999/435/EC of 29 May 1999, [1999] OJ L176/1, 10.7.1999, corrected by the Council Decision 2000/645/EC of 17 October 2000, [2001] OJ L9/24, 13.01.2001. As with the Treaty of Lisbon, see Protocol No 19. See on it V Mitsilegas, *EU Criminal Law* (Oxford, Hart Publishing, 2009) 13 onwards. See also V Mitsilegas, J Monar and W Rees, *The European Union and Internal Security. Guardian of the People?* (Basingstoke, Palgrave Macmillan, 2003) 84 onwards.

[17] On the institutional framework, see Steve Peers and others, *EU immigration and asylum law: text and commentary*, 2nd revised edn (Leiden/Boston MA, Brill Nijhoff, 2012) 7 onwards.

The rules providing for detention of migrants can be grouped into two main categories: detention pending the examination of an asylum claim or the procedures laid down in the Dublin Regulation; and detention related to prevention of an unauthorised entry or preparation and completion of return procedures. The European legislature has partly provided the requirements, duration and intent of the detention, while leaving many questions unanswered. This Part discusses administrative deprivation of liberty of TCNs in EU law in light of the right to liberty. Consistent with the framework of this story, it does so by highlighting the tension between legal integration for preserving the borderless area, on the one hand, and issues of fundamental rights protection, on the other. It emphasises the need for an EU right to liberty suitable for the challenges posed by the system of migration management set up by the Union. In a similar vein to Part III, this Part features a 'default' right to liberty, and an evolutionary right to liberty. The former constitutes the starting point for defining the content of that right in the context of EU asylum and immigration law, and relies on what is established in the CFREU, the ECHR and the ECtHR's interpretation. The evolutionary right to liberty ensues from the interaction between the default right to liberty, and specific sources of EU law: instruments of asylum and immigration law, and the interpretation of the CJEU.

The analysis is structured into three chapters. The present chapter serves to place the discussion in the broader setting of the book and – in the next section – outlines the ECtHR's approach to Article 5(1)(f) in the context of immigration detention. Chapter ten focuses on immigration detention in the context of EU asylum law, by presenting the relevant legal rules featured in the CEAS, and the CJEU's interpretation thereof. Chapter eleven homes in on law and interpretation of Directive 2008/115/EC ('the Return Directive').[18] In both chapters, the focus is on the content of the EU right to liberty in asylum and migration law. In the same fashion as the Part on mutual recognition, the book highlights the controversial relationship between effectiveness of EU law and adequate protection of the right to liberty. More specifically, the emphasis is on the challenges posed by the existing EU legal framework to the *cases* and *established procedures* requirements.

On the one hand, the discretion left to Member States may lead to the use of one-size-fits-all grounds for deprivation of liberty. On the other, the legal opacity surrounding the functioning of detention centres and migrants' rights therein raises serious concerns in respect of the right to liberty. The CJEU and the ECtHR have been faced with legal questions on detention conditions as an issue of inhumane and degrading treatment. Consistently with what was argued in Part III, a broader understanding of the right to liberty is upheld, whereby detention conditions should be considered mainly from the perspective of Article 6 CFREU.

[18] Directive 2008/115/EC of the European Parliament and of the Council of 16 December 2008 on common standards and procedures in Member States for returning illegally staying third-country nationals, [2008] OJ L348/98 24.12.2008.

The book sets out possible solutions to address these problematic aspects: an interpretation of the right to liberty solidly anchored to the principles of proportionality and legal certainty; establishment of a level playing-field with regard to the functioning of detention centres within the EU.

III. The Right to Liberty in EU Asylum and Immigration Law

Article 5(1)(f) ECHR features two limbs: detention (1) to prevent unauthorised entry or (2) when action is being taken with a view to deportation. The ECtHR has recognised Article 5 as enshrining the protection of an individual's right to liberty against arbitrary interferences by the state.[19] The Strasbourg Court has shaped its stance on the application of the right to liberty to immigration detention in three main rulings: *Amuur v France*, *Chahal v United Kingdom*[20] and *Saadi v United Kingdom*.[21]

Amuur drew a distinction between the right to liberty as applicable to asylum-seekers, on the one hand, and to other categories of migrants, on the other. The case concerned a group of Somali nationals who flew from Syria to France. They were held in the airport's transit zone (and its extension, a secure hotel) for 20 days, and they were eventually returned to Syria without their asylum claims being determined. The Court stated that 'such holding should not be prolonged excessively, otherwise there would be a risk of it turning a mere restriction of liberty … into a deprivation of liberty'.[22] The French government stated that there had been no restriction, for the applicants were free to decide to come back to Syria at any time. The ECtHR denied the existence of freedom of choice, since no other country could have offered the applicants the same protection as they expected to find in the country where they were seeking asylum.[23] However, and whilst eventually finding a breach of Article 5 in the instant case, the ECtHR drew a worrying distinction between asylum-seekers and other migrants. As stated, by anchoring the coercion to the asylum claim it seems that

[19] ECtHR *Winterwerp v Netherlands*, 24 October 1979, para 37; ECtHR *Brogan and Others v United Kingdom*, Application no 11209/84; 11234/84; 11266/84; 11386/85, 29 October 1988, para 58.

[20] ECtHR *Chahal v United Kingdom*, Application no 22414/93, 15 November 1996.

[21] ECtHR *Saadi v United Kingdom*, Application no 13229/03, 29 January 2008. The Court's case-law on the topic is extensive. In *Kolompar v Belgium*, for instance, the ECtHR found that a detention pending extradition of two years and eight months did not amount to a violation of Article 5, because it was not ascribable to the detaining State, owing to the attempts by the migrant to set aside the extradition order.

[22] ECtHR *Amuur v France*, Application no 19776/92, 25 June 1996, para 43. The Court here confirms that the difference between restrictions and deprivation of liberty is one of degree or intensity, and not of nature and substance. See ECtHR *Guzzardi v. Italia*, Application no 7367/76, 6 November 1980, para 92, as well as Art 2 of Protocol No 4.

[23] *Amuur v France*, n 22 above, para 48.

> other categories of migrants held at airports would not be detained. This appears to endorse the idea that immigrants were held in prison with only *three walls*, from which they could choose to leave by withdrawing their application to enter.[24]

Chahal involved an Indian national who had been lawfully residing in the UK, when a deportation order was issued against him on grounds of national security. He tried to get his detention reviewed, but these attempts were always rejected by the national court. The Strasbourg Court stated that Article 5(1)(f) provides a different level of protection from that of Article 5(1)(c) (detention on remand). Article 5(1)(f) imposes no requirement in terms of necessity of detention, but only that deportation proceedings be carried out with due diligence.[25] The ECtHR recognised that the length of detention to which the applicant had been subject gave rise to serious concerns. However, no violations of Article 5(1)(f) could be found, in consideration of the exceptional circumstances of the case and the due diligence used by the Member State. Detention conformed to the substantive and procedural rules of national law, and such procedures provided an important safeguard against arbitrariness. To be thorough, such a procedure rests on an advisory panel which neither discussed the case nor deliberated publicly, with Mr Chahal having no chance to be in contact with his 'representatives' before the panel.

The Strasbourg Court found that that procedure was in breach of Article 5(4) ECHR, according to which

> Everyone who is deprived of his liberty by arrest or detention shall be entitled to take proceedings by which the lawfulness of his detention shall be decided speedily by a court and his release ordered if the detention is not lawful.

The Court ruled that neither the proceedings for habeas corpus, nor the judicial review of the decision to detain Mr Chahal before the domestic courts had satisfied the condition of Article 5(4).[26] However, the two statements concerning Article 5(1) and (4) are hard to reconcile.

In *Saadi v United Kingdom*, the ECtHR was 'called upon for the first time to interpret the meaning of the words in the first limb of Article 5(1)(f)':[27] namely, the lawful arrest or detention of a person to prevent his effecting an unauthorised entry into the country. The second limb, concerning the person against whom action is being taken with a view to deportation or extradition, was significantly discussed in *Chahal*. The applicant in *Saadi* was an Iraqi national who, as soon as he arrived in the UK's territory, surrendered himself to the authorities seeking leave to stay. The applicant was conferred a day-by-day permit, and complied

[24] Wilsher, *Immigration Detention*, n 1 above, 148.

[25] *Chahal*, n 20 above, paras 112–113.

[26] Indeed, in the national procedure the internal court could not review the decision to detain Mr Chahal, with the latter not being entitled to legal representation before the advisory panel. Such a body, in turn, had no power of decision, but gave advice to the Home Secretary which was neither binding, nor disclosed.

[27] *Saadi v United Kingdom*, n 21 above, para 61.

with every reporting condition imposed on him while he was held in detention (despite not being considered to be at risk of absconding). The ECtHR preliminarily maintained that states have an undeniable right to control alien entry into, and the taking up of residence in, their country. The power to detain immigrants who have applied for permission to enter, whether by way of asylum of not, is a necessary adjunct to that right.[28] Furthermore, since the interpretation of 'prevent his effecting an unauthorised entry' was at issue, the Court clarified that until a state has authorised entry to the country, any entry is to be regarded as unauthorised. That being so, the detention of any entry-seeking non-national is lawful under Article 5(1)(f).

By extending the *Chahal* rule to the first limb of Article 5(1)(f), the judges found that immigration detention must not be necessary. Also, the proportionality principle applies to such detention only to the extent that deprivation of liberty 'should not continue for an unreasonable length of time'.[29] According to the non-arbitrariness test elaborated by the Court, detention can be held to be in compliance with Article 5 when it: is carried out in good faith; is closely connected to the purpose of preventing unauthorised entry; is in appropriate places and conditions; and is of a duration reasonably required for the purpose pursued.[30] The ECtHR regarded the respondent state as satisfying the test, so that the applicant's detention was not arbitrary. This was so also in light of the difficult administrative problems that the UK was confronted with during the period in question.[31] However, the Court found that Mr Saadi had not been made sufficiently aware of the reasons for his detention, which had led to a violation of Article 5(2) ECHR. The latter provision states that 'Everyone who is arrested shall be informed promptly, in a language which he understands, of the reasons for his arrest and of any charge against him'.

What happens when pre-removal detention interacts with an application for international protection? In a case where the submission of the asylum application followed the illegal entry and detention under the second limb of Article 5(1)(f), the ECtHR found that the existence of a claim does not imply that detention is no longer with a view to deportation, as long as the conditions established in the judgments presented above are fulfilled.[32] Indeed, the ECtHR has confirmed *Saadi*, in that the applicant's detention pending the asylum claim falls under the first limb of Article 5(1)(f), namely to prevent his effecting an unauthorised entry into the country. In the context of detention of an asylum-seeker for the purpose of establishing identity, the Court stated that where a state which has gone beyond

[28] *Saadi*, n 21 above, para 64, reiterating the assumption predicated in *Amuur*, n 22 above, para 41; *Abdulaziz, Cabales and Balkandali v United Kingdom*, 28 May 1985, paras 67–68.

[29] *Saadi*, n 21 above, para 72; *Chahal*, n 20 above, para 112; *A v United Kingdom*, 100/1997/884/1096, 23 September 1998, para 164; *Gebremedhin [Gaberamadhien] v France*, Application no 25389/05, 26 July 2007, para 74; *Milolenko v Estonia*, Application no 10664/05, 8 August 2010, para 59.

[30] *Saadi*, n 21 above, para 74.

[31] *Saadi*, n 21 above, para 80.

[32] See ECtHR *Nabil and Others v Hungary*, Application no 62116/12, para 38.

its obligations in creating further rights or a more favourable position, enacts legislation explicitly authorising the entry or stay of immigrants pending examination of an asylum claim, an ensuing detention for the purpose of preventing an unauthorised entry may raise an issue as to the lawfulness of the detention under Article 5(1)(f).[33] In that case, it would be hard to connect the measure and the purposes of Article 5(1)(f). However, it is mainly for the national law to establish when the person is authorised to enter and stay, with the consequence that the first limb of Article 5 will no longer apply.[34]

The ECtHR's case-law has sparked a heated debate over the years. The connection between the definition of detention and status of asylum-seeker, coupled with the exclusion of a free choice only on the basis of the concrete circumstances of the case, seems to implicitly leave room for free will concerning deprivation of liberty. Conversely, 'detention by the State should *never* be considered consensual, because to do so introduces an unwelcome and unworkable subjective element into the protection of liberty of detainees' (emphasis added).[35] In this regard, the case-law has been criticised for having 'shied away from insisting that, as a matter of ECHR law, asylum seekers are not in pre-deportation detention, as they are temporarily authorised entrants'.[36] The outcome of the ECtHR's approach is that, by according an asymmetrical protection against arbitrary detention, the enjoyment of the right to liberty might become a dispensation dependent on the state's authorisation.[37] However, the Strasbourg Court has afterwards attempted to pose limits on Member States' power to detain aliens, especially in terms of length of deprivation of liberty.[38] Furthermore, the inclusion of 'detention conditions' into the 'arbitrariness test' may prove particularly helpful for better protecting migrants' right to liberty.[39]

[33] *OM v Hungary*, Application no 9912/15, 5 July 2016, para 47.

[34] ECtHR *Suso Muso v Malta*, Application no 42337/12, 9 December 2013, para 97.

[35] D Wilsher, 'The Administrative Detention of Non-Nationals Pursuant to Immigration control: International and Constitutional Law Perspectives' (2005) 53(4) *International and Comparative Law Quarterly* 905.

[36] C Costello, 'Human Rights and the Elusive Universal Subject: Immigration Detention Under International Human Rights and EU Law' (2012) 19(1) *Indiana Journal of Global Legal Studies* 282. The author also analyses the more recent ECtHR case-law on the subject.

[37] I Bryan and P Langford, 'The Lawful Detention of Unauthorised Aliens under the European System for the Protection of Human Rights' (2011) 80(2) *Nordic Journal of International Law* 193–218, wherein criticisms are also voiced as to the Court's inattention to relevant international sources, such as the Geneva Convention Relating to the Status of Refugees, the ICCPR and the Vienna Convention on the Law of the Treaties (201 onwards). See also, in this respect, the partly dissenting opinion of judge Pettiti in *Chahal*, n 20 above.

[38] ECtHR *Amie and Others v Bulgaria*, 12 February 2013, Application no 58149/08.

[39] H O'Nions, 'No Right to Liberty: The Detention of Asylum Seekers for Administrative Convenience' (2008) 10 *European Journal of Migration and Law* 173. The author also includes a necessary assessment of proportionality in the requirement of non-arbitrariness. Indeed, 'a deprivation of liberty in the absence of an individual assessment of its appropriateness or need, does not satisfy these requirements'. Furthermore, see in *Saadi* the joint partly dissenting opinion of judges Rozakis, Tulkes, Kovler, Bajiyev, Spielmann and Hirvelä. The judges also highlighted an alternative to detention, on the one hand; on the other, to the inadequate consideration of other international instruments.

A good deal of the ECtHR's interpretation – especially as far as asylum detention is concerned – has been incorporated into and improved in EU law. However, the following chapters show that the common system of returns and examination of asylum claims set up within the EU requires ad hoc legal solutions for the peculiarities of the Union legal order.

10

Asylum Law

I. The EU Rules on Detention

The Common European Asylum System (CEAS)[1] includes two instruments relevant to the detention of TCNs pending examination of an asylum claim: Directive 2013/33/EU (or 'the Reception Conditions Directive');[2] and Regulation (EU) No 604/2013 (or 'the Dublin III Regulation').[3] The former might be seen as a 'static' instrument, as opposed to the 'dynamic' nature of the Dublin III Regulation. The Reception Conditions Directive, indeed, aims to establish a level playing-field for the treatment of TCNs during examination of their asylum claims. Therefore, the Directive presents no significant cross-border element. Conversely, the Dublin Regulation is concerned with the allocation of responsibility for the examination of the asylum claim on the best-placed Member State. As observed, the Dublin Regulation sets out a system of mutual recognition

> in that the occurrence of one of the Dublin criteria creates a duty for one Member State to take charge of an asylum seeker and thus recognize the refusal of another Member State (which transfers the asylum seeker in question) to examine the asylum claim.[4]

The two dimensions are highly intertwined. Similarly to what was discussed in the context of judicial cooperation, issues of fundamental rights protection and poor

[1] The CEAS, which consists of the instruments I refer to in this chapter, has been recently recast by a comprehensive reform. See on this F Ippolito and S Velluti, 'The Recast Process of the EU Asylum System: A Balancing Act Between Efficiency and Fairness' (2011) 30(3) *Refugee Survey Quarterly* 24–62.

[2] Directive 2013/33/EU of the European Parliament and the Council of 26 June 2013 laying down standards for the reception of applicants for international protection (recast), [2013] OJ L180/96, 29.6.2013.

[3] Regulation (EU) No 604/2013 of the European Parliament and the Council of 26 June 2013 establishing the criteria and mechanisms for determining the Member State responsible for examining an application for international protection lodged in one of the Member States by a TCN or a stateless person (recast), [2013] OJ L180/31, 29.6.2013. See for an analysis R Cholewinski, 'The Criminalisation of Migration in EU Law and Policy' in H Toner, E Guild and A Baldaccini, *Whose Freedom, Security and Justice?* (Oxford, Hart Publishing, 2007) 301–36. Other instruments forming part of the CEAS, such as Directive 2013/32/EU or Directive 2005/85/EC, limit themselves to referring or reaffirming the principles established in the Reception Conditions Directive.

[4] V Mitsilegas, 'The Limits of Mutual Trust in Europe's Area of Freedom, Security and Justice: From Automatic Inter-State Cooperation to the Slow Emergence of the Individual' (2012) 31(1) *Yearbook of European Law* 319, 334.

conditions in the receiving state might limit the operation of the Dublin system and prevent the transfer. Interaction emerges between the CEAS and the Return Directive as well. Specific circumstances may determine a shift in status from asylum-seeker to irregular migrant waiting for removal, which in turn is likely to cause an extended period of detention under various legal regimes.

This chapter tests EU asylum law on immigration detention against the right to liberty. It highlights the tension between the pursuit of integration engendered by the need to protect the borderless area, on the one hand, and ensuring compliance with individual rights, on the other. It reaffirms the idea that the specifics of the Union legal order – and the system set up by the CEAS specifically – call for conceptualising a right to liberty more suitable for the EU.

II. Immigration Detention in the Common European Asylum System

A. The Reception Conditions Directive

The Reception Conditions Directive establishes common standards of living conditions of asylum-seekers within the Union. Detention is defined as the 'confinement of an applicant by a Member State within a particular place, where the applicant is deprived of his freedom of movement'.[5] An applicant cannot be deprived of liberty 'for the sole reason that he or she is seeking international protection'.[6] More specifically, the Directive lays down the following safeguards: the grounds for detention established in the Directive are exhaustive; detention is a measure of last resort (to apply only after all alternative measures have been examined); deprivation of liberty is governed by the principles of proportionality and necessity, with regard to its manner and purpose; and detainees should have effective access to the necessary procedural guarantees, such as judicial remedies before a national judicial authority.[7]

In terms of grounds for detention, an applicant may be deprived of his/her liberty only:

(a) in order to determine his or her identity or nationality;
(b) in order to determine those elements on which the application for international protection is based which could not be obtained in the absence of detention, *in particular* when there is a risk of absconding of the applicant (emphasis added);
(c) in order to decide, in the context of the procedure, on the applicant's right to enter the territory;
(d) when he or she is detained [by virtue of the Return Directive, and when the Member State can substantiate that the application for international protection

[5] Directive 2013/33/EU, n 2 above, Art 2(1)(h).
[6] Ibid, recital 15.
[7] Ibid and recital 20.

has been made only] in order to delay or frustrate the enforcement of a return decision;

(e) when protection of national security or public order so requires; [or]

(f) in accordance with Article 28 of [the Dublin III Regulation].[8]

When such requirements are no longer applicable, detention must cease. Furthermore, delays occurring in the course of the procedure under the Directive may not justify detention, unless they are ascribable to the applicant. The lawfulness of detention, whose order must be motivated in fact and in law, is to be reviewed shortly after the internment has taken place, as well as at reasonable intervals afterwards. The migrant, for his part, must be informed of the reasons for detention, of any circumstance which may affect its legality, and of their rights to free legal assistance and representation.[9]

The Directive distinguishes the detention of asylum-seekers from that 'within the framework of criminal proceedings … which is unrelated to the third country national's or stateless person's application for international protection'.[10] Firstly, Member States are required to detain the applicants in specialist detention facilities. When Member States have no option but to resort to prison accommodation, the applicants must be kept separately from ordinary prisoners. Migrants in detention 'should be treated with full respect for human dignity'.[11] As for communication with applicants in detention, only representatives of the United Nation High Commissioner for Refugees (UNHCR) (or organisations working on behalf of it, upon previous agreement with the Member State concerned), family members, legal advisers and persons representing relevant Non-Governmental Organisations (NGOs) recognised by the Member State are entitled to access the centres in this respect. Access may be limited by national law on grounds of security, public order or administrative management of the detention facility.

Applicants must be provided with information regarding the rules operating in the centres and their rights in an understandable language. However, Member State may derogate from this obligation in duly justified cases and for a reasonable period of time, where detention takes place at a border post or in a transit zone, barring the cases established by Article 43 Directive 2013/32/EU ('the Procedures Directive').[12]

B. The Dublin III Regulation

The Dublin III Regulation replaced earlier instruments, namely the Dublin Convention and the Dublin II Regulation. The Regulation establishes a number of criteria to determine the Member State responsible for the asylum application,

[8] Ibid, Art 8(3).
[9] Ibid, Art 9(1).
[10] Ibid, recital 17.
[11] Ibid, recital 18.
[12] Ibid, Art 10.

among which one of the most prominent is the first entry rule provided for in Article 3(1): the first Member State which the person concerned has illegally entered from a third-country will be responsible for the examination. An exception to the criterion was stated in Article 3(2):

> each Member State may examine an application for asylum lodged with it by a third-country national, even if such examination is not its responsibility under the criteria laid down in this Regulation. In such an event, that Member State shall become the Member State responsible within the meaning of this Regulation and shall assume the obligations associated with that responsibility. Where appropriate, it shall inform the Member State previously responsible, the Member State conducting a procedure for determining the Member State responsible or the Member State which has been requested to take charge of or take back the applicant.

The Dublin III Regulation adds specific rules on detention to its predecessor version, and addresses deprivation of liberty pending transfer procedures. As for individual guarantees and detention conditions, the Regulation refers to the rules established in Directive 2013/33/EU. Furthermore, when deficiencies occur in the asylum system of a Member State, the Commission may require the latter to draw up a crisis management action plan, with the intention of ensuring respect of applicants' human rights in the Member State concerned. Afterwards, the Member State is to report on the implementation of the crisis management action plan, including with respect to the detention conditions.[13]

Important to detention pending transfer is the system of remedies established by the Regulation. The applicant has the right to appeal or request a review of a transfer decision. Pending appeal or review, states have two alternative options. They may automatically suspend the transfer for a reasonable period of time, after which the authority shall decide on whether or not to grant the suspension of the appeal or review. Alternatively, they can give the applicant the possibility to request suspension of the transfer until the Member State judge has decided on the appeal or review.[14]

The applicant cannot be detained for the sole reason that s/he is subject to the procedures established in the Regulation. Following an individual assessment and subject to the principles of last resort and proportionality, an applicant can be detained where there is a significant risk of absconding. Detention shall last for no longer than the time reasonably necessary to fulfil the required administrative procedures with due diligence until the transfer is carried out. When a person is deprived of liberty, the state must submit the request to take charge of an applicant within one month from the asylum application. The answer shall be given within two weeks, failing which the state is presumed to have accepted the request and is then obliged to take charge of him/her. When a person is in detention, the transfer

[13] Regulation (EU) No 604/2013, Art 33(3).
[14] Ibid, Art 27.

must be carried out within six weeks of the explicit or tacit acceptance, or of the expiry of the suspension of the appeal or review. If the state fails to submit the request within two weeks, or the transfer does not take place within six weeks, the applicant shall be released.[15]

III. Deprivation of Liberty in EU Asylum Law and the Presumption of Mutual Trust

Detention of asylum-seekers lives within the broader context of the CEAS, a system based on the presumption that fundamental rights are respected by all Member States. Deprivation of liberty is key to the functioning of the CEAS, which has its centre of gravity in the system of mutual recognition embodied by the Dublin Regulation. Detention is the backbone of that system in all phases of its operation. Applicants are deprived of liberty *pending* allocation of responsibility and transfer procedures in the sending state, *during* the transfer and will probably also be detained *in* the receiving state.[16] Rules and practices governing *grounds for* and *procedures of* detention (understood also as standards of detention conditions) are therefore key, and can have a significant impact on the CEAS.

Similarly to mutual recognition in the context of criminal justice, the importance of detention emerges first and foremost in relation to its foundation, namely the principle of mutual trust. Unlike issues of migrants' rights in asylum procedures or the thoroughness of the examination of asylum claims,[17] questions of detention in EU asylum law constitute a fairly recent phenomenon.[18] Furthermore, detention of asylum-seekers has been one of the most prolific areas of dialogue between the ECtHR and the CJEU, with the latter being very receptive to input by the Strasbourg Court.

The major breakthrough was caused by *MSS*,[19] a landmark judgment of the ECtHR following a conspicuous line of cases on the interaction between detention

[15] Ibid, Art 28.

[16] As argued, this 'undermines the protective nature of making an asylum claim which normally would prevent the deportation of an asylum-seeker until his/her claim is determined so as to ensure that deportation does not amount to *refoulement*'. See Cathryn Costello and Minos Mouzourakis, 'EU Law and the Detainability of Asylum-Seekers' (2016) 35 *Refugee Survey Quarterly* 47, 66.

[17] See among many on this aspect M Reneman, 'Speedy Asylum Procedures in the EU: Striking a Fair Balance Between the Need to Process Asylum Cases Efficiently and the Asylum Applicant's EU Right to an Effective Remedy' (2014) 25(4) *International Journal of Refugee Law* 717–48.

[18] See for a recent overview on the CJEU's approach to Asylum, B Zalar, 'Comments on the Court of Justice of the EU's Developing Case Law on Asylum' (2013) 25(2) *International Journal of Refugee Law* 377–81.

[19] ECtHR, *MSS v Belgium and Greece*, Application No 30696/09, judgment of 21 January 2011. Among many commentaries, see V Moreno-Lax, 'Dismantling the Dublin System: M.S.S. v. Belgium and Greece' (2012) 14 *European Journal of Migration and Law* 1–31; P Mallia, 'Case of M.S.S. v. Belgium and Greece: A Catalyst in the Re-thinking of the Dublin II Regulation' (2011) 30(3) *Refugee Survey Quarterly* 107–28.

and asylum law,[20] and on detention conditions as well.[21] *MSS* concerned an Afghan national transferred under the Dublin II Regulation from Belgium to Greece, where he was placed in degrading detention conditions. The ECtHR condemned Greece and Belgium for their violation of Article 3 ECHR.[22] The ECtHR noted that Belgium was exercising the margin of discretion left by Article 3(2) of the Dublin Regulation, and it could not have presumed the compliance of Greek authorities with fundamental rights. The unanimity of international reports on poor detention conditions in Greece had determined a redistribution of the burden of proof concerning the demonstration of a possible violation of Article 3 ECHR. On applying the Dublin Regulation 'systematically',[23] Belgian authorities had failed to verify how the Greek authorities applied their legislation on asylum in practice.[24]

Those principles were internalised in EU law through the *NS* and *ME* judgment, concerning the transfer of two asylum-seekers from England and Ireland to Greece under the Dublin II Regulation.[25] The Court reaffirmed the principle that, where states exercise discretion left by EU law, they are implementing the latter and therefore are bound by the Charter under Article 51 CFREU. The principle of mutual trust founding the CEAS implies the presumption that asylum seekers are treated in compliance with the Charter, the Geneva Convention and the ECHR throughout the Union. However, only a rebuttable presumption is compatible with EU law. Where the sending state cannot be unaware that systemic deficiencies in the asylum procedure and in the reception conditions in the receiving state would expose the applicant to a serious risk of inhuman or degrading treatment, a transfer would be unlawful and make the sending state liable under Article 4 CFREU.[26]

Therefore, the transferring state must continue to examine the criteria set out in the Dublin Regulation, to establish whether other criteria enable another Member State – even the transferring state itself – to be identified as responsible

[20] M Bossuyt, 'The Court of Strasbourg Acting as an Asylum Court' (2012) 8(2) *European Constitutional Law Review* 203–45.

[21] See in particular ECtHR, *TI v UK*, Application No 43844/98, judgment of 7 March 2000; ECtHR, *KRS v UK*, Application No 32733/08, judgment of 2 December 2008.

[22] Belgium was condemned for direct and indirect *refoulement*: the former regarded the deportation of the applicant to Greece, where there was a serious risk of violation of Article 3 ECHR; the former concerned the fact that Belgium had transferred MSS to a country (Greece) which was very likely to expel the applicant to a third-country where there were high chances that he would experience violations of his fundamental rights.

[23] *MSS*, n 19 above, para 352.

[24] As stated, after *MSS*: 'It is safe to assume that in the face of such evidence it would belong to the sending State to submit concrete counterevidence that the risk would not materialise in the particular case': V Moreno-Lax, 'Dismantling the Dublin System', n 19 above, 29.

[25] Joined cases C-411/10, *NS v Secretary of State for the Home Department* and C-493/10, *ME and Others v Refugee Applications Commissioner and Minister for Justice, Equality and Law Reform*, [2011] ECR I-13905. See E Brouwer, 'Mutual Trust and the Dublin Regulation: Protection of Fundamental Rights in the EU and the Burden of Proof' (2013) 9 *Utrecht Law Review* 135–47; V Mitsilegas, 'The Limits of Mutual Trust', n 4 above, 355 onwards.

[26] *NS*, n 25 above, Court's judgment, paras 86–96.

for the examination of the asylum application. While praised for the contribution in terms of fundamental rights protection, the judgment undoubtedly set the bar high: overcoming the presumption of human rights compliance would require *systemic deficiencies* in both reception conditions and asylum procedures; a line of reasoning that was confirmed in the following cases at the CJEU.[27]

A further challenge to that test was brought once again by the ECtHR's judgment in *Tarakhel*,[28] concerning the transfer of an Afghan family from Switzerland to Italy. The applicants challenged their transfer, claiming that they would be subject to inhuman or degrading treatment. The ECtHR stated that systemic deficiencies are not the only grounds for refusing transfer, in a case where the sole *conditions* of reception (detention conditions especially) might result in violations of Article 3 ECHR.[29] The CJEU followed suit in *CK*,[30] a case regarding the transfer of a Syrian national from Slovenia to Croatia. While not concerned with detention conditions, the Court found that the general and absolute prohibition under Article 4 CFREU precluded an interpretation of the Dublin Regulation as prohibiting the transfer *only where systemic flaws are at stake*. Mutual trust – to which the common standards established by the Reception Conditions Directive contribute[31] – would not be imperilled by that finding,

> since, far from affecting the existence of a presumption that fundamental rights are respected in each Member State, it ensures that the *exceptional situations* referred to in the present judgment are duly taken into account by the Member States.[32]

The establishment of a level playing-field confirms that the trust-building nature of secondary law emerged in the context of judicial cooperation. In both cases, common standards reinforce trust, which in turn underpins mutual recognition and ensures its effective functioning. In asylum law as well, detention conditions are capable of limiting forced movement of people within the EU, where even non-systemic deficiencies can result in the violation of an absolute prohibition.

As in Part III, the question arises as to what to make of the vast limbo where detention conditions possibly violate Article 5: the wide, grey area lying between lawful conditions and inhuman or degrading treatment. Secondly, the discussion homes in on how the right to liberty can help address the issues of legal certainty and proportionality emerging from EU asylum law concerning grounds for and procedures of detention of applicants for international protection.

[27] Case C-394/12, *Shamso Abdullahi v Bundesasylamt*, judgment of 10 December 2012, EU:C:2013:813, para 62.

[28] ECtHR, *Tarakhel v Switzerland*, Application No 29217/12 judgment of 4 November 2014. For a comment see: http://eulawanalysis.blogspot.be/2014/11/tarakhel-v-switzerland-another-nail-in.html.

[29] Ibid, paras 111 onwards.

[30] Case C-578/16 PPU, *CK and Others v Republika Slovenija*, judgment of 16 February 2017, EU:C:2017:127.

[31] The reference is in particular to Arts 17 to 19.

[32] *CK*, n 30 above, para 95.

IV. Grounds and Limits of Detention of Asylum-Seekers

As stated above, CEAS rules on detention have both a static and dynamic dimension, with the latter being related to transfer procedures under the Dublin Regulation. The analysis highlights the high interrelation between these legal frameworks, with conditions in one state affecting the inter-state transfer of the applicant. The interplay concerns not only different parts of the CEAS, but also the effect of interaction of the CEAS and EU law on irregular migrants. The rules on grounds for detention and time-limits of deprivation of liberty give rise to concerns in terms of legal certainty and proportionality.

An example of static grounds for detention is that based on reasons of national security or public order laid down in the Reception Conditions Directive. The validity of such grounds was challenged before the CJEU in *JN*.[33] The case regarded a third-country national sentenced to imprisonment, and made subject to an expulsion order and a 10-year entry ban in The Netherlands. Afterwards, he lodged an application for international protection and was detained under Article 8(3)(e) of the Reception Conditions Directive. Mr N claimed that his detention was contrary to the second limb of Article 5(1)(f) ECHR, under which the detention of a foreign national may be justified only by the fact that action is being taken against him with a view to deportation.[34]

The Court found that the challenged ground for detention complies with Articles 6 and 52 CFREU. It is provided by law (the Reception Conditions Directive), and is per se in line with an objective of general interest. It also respects the essence of the right to liberty for two main reasons: it is flanked by procedural safeguards laid down in Articles 8 and 9 of the Directive; and it is in line with the wording of Article 6 CFREU, which refers to the right to liberty *and* security of the person.[35]

To be compatible with the principle of proportionality, detention can be ordered only following an individual assessment of the seriousness of the threat posed to national security or public order, which must correspond at least to the gravity of the interference with the liberty entailed by that measure. The grounds for detaining Mr N were related to offences he had committed, the expulsion and entry ban decisions, which had become final. The fact that Mr N made another application after the entry ban was not incompatible with detention under the Reception Conditions Directive. Article 5(1)(f) and the relevant case-law state that an asylum claim does not as such imply that the detention of a person who has

[33] Case C-601/15 PPU, *JN v Staatssecretaris van Veiligheid en Justitie*, judgment of 15 February 2016, EU:C:2016:84.

[34] See ECtHR, *Nabil and Others v Hungary*, Application No 62116/12, judgment of 22 September 2015, para 38, stating that the detention of an asylum seeker is contrary to Art 5(1)(f) of the ECHR when it is not imposed with a view to removal.

[35] *JN*, n 33 above, para 53.

made an asylum application is no longer 'with a view to deportation' that was ordered before the lodging of the application. Furthermore, the obligation to carry out the removal under the Return Directive would not be met if the removal were delayed because, following the rejection of the application, a return procedure had to start afresh.[36]

A dynamic instance of grounds for detention is that provided in the Dublin III Regulation. Article 28(2) permits the detention of applicants, in order to secure transfer procedures in accordance with that regulation, when there is a significant risk of the applicant absconding. Article 2(n) of the Dublin Regulation defines the term 'risk of absconding' as the existence of reasons in an individual case, which are based on objective criteria defined by law, to believe that the person concerned may abscond. In *Al Chodor*,[37] the CJEU was asked whether Article 2(n) and Article 28(2) require Member States to establish, in a national law, objective criteria underlying the reasons for believing that an applicant subject to a transfer procedure may abscond, and whether the absence of those criteria in a national law leads to the inapplicability of Article 28(2). Firstly, the Court found the definition of 'risk of absconding' to be a matter for national law. Secondly, the Court assessed whether 'law' under Article 2(n) could also include settled case-law confirming a consistent administrative practice – in the present case, the practice of the Czech Police Force.[38] The Court regarded the guarantees on detention added by the Dublin III Regulation as giving substance to Article 6 CFREU. First and foremost, the right to liberty protects against arbitrariness through the requirement that detention rests on a clear, predictable and accessible legal basis. Legal certainty marks the boundaries of the discretion enjoyed by national authorities when assessing the risk of absconding. The criteria underlying the reasons for believing that an applicant subject to a transfer procedure may abscond must be defined clearly by an act which is binding, foreseeable and of general application. In the absence of such a provision, detention – including that at stake in the instant case – must be considered unlawful, 'which leads to the inapplicability of Article 28(2) of the Dublin III Regulation'.[39]

Related to legal certainty is proportionality, another centrepiece of the right to liberty. The *Lanigan* and *Vilkas* cases discussed in Part III showed that time-limits in a system of forced transfer of persons within the EU are very relevant to the right to liberty. Article 28(2) authorises detention in case of serious risk of absconding. Article 28(3) of the Dublin III Regulation sets deadlines for submitting a request to take charge of the applicant and for carrying out the transfer when a person is detained, on the expiry of which s/he shall be released. The transfer shall take place within six weeks of: acceptance of the request by another Member State; the lapse

[36] Ibid, paras 74–81.

[37] Case C-528/15, *Policie ČR, Krajské ředitelství policie Ústeckého kraje, odbor cizinecké policie v Salah Al Chodor and Others*, judgment of 15 March 2017, EU:C:2017:213.

[38] Ibid, paras 27–30.

[39] Ibid, paras 40–47.

of the suspension of the appeal or review provided in Article 27(3). In that context, when does the six-week count start? How does detention relate to that calculation?

In *Khir Amayry*,[40] the Court was asked whether Article 28(3) precludes national legislation which provides that, where the detention of an applicant begins after the requested state has accepted taking charge, detention may be maintained for no longer than two months in principle, no longer than three months if there are serious reasons to exceed two months, and no longer than 12 months if it is probable that the transfer will take longer than three months due to a lack of cooperation by the person concerned or if it takes time to obtain the necessary documents. Firstly, the Court noticed that none of the deadlines established in Article 28 – and in the third paragraph especially – runs from the moment of detention, but from other trigger-events: acceptance of taking charge, or expiry of suspension of appeal or review. Secondly, the CJEU acknowledged that Article 28(3) does not clarify whether the six-week term applies to all situations, or only when the person is already detained when a trigger-event takes place.[41]

In the absence of clear wording and the maximum duration of detention pending transfer, the Court provided the following interpretation. The six-week period starts running from acceptance of taking charge or elapse of suspension only when the person is already in detention at the occurrence of those events. Stating otherwise would imply that the power to detain would be limited to a period shorter than six weeks regardless of the conduct of the person concerned. Article 29(2) states that the transfer deadline may be extended by up to 18 months if the person concerned absconds. Interpreting the six-week deadline as applicable even where the person is not already detained would encourage them to abscond for six weeks and to re-appear at the end of that term, when they could no longer be detained.

For situations where, instead, detention does start after acceptance, the deadlines of 28(3) apply, where appropriate, only from the date on which the suspension of the appeal or review lapses under Article 27(3).[42] In that context, the days spent in detention after acceptance should not be deducted from the six-week period that will start from the lapse of the suspension.

The interpretation is therefore to the effect that Article 28 does not preclude national legislation which provides that detention may be maintained for no longer than two months, provided that the duration of the detention: does not go beyond the period of time which is necessary for the purposes of that transfer procedure; and is not longer than six weeks from the date when the appeal or review ceases. It *does* preclude national legislation which allows the detention to be maintained for three or 12 months during which time the transfer could be reasonably carried out.[43]

[40] Case C-60/16, *Mohammad Khir Amayry v Migrationsverket*, judgment of 13 September 2017, EU:C:2017:675.

[41] Ibid, para 28.

[42] Ibid, paras 33–40.

[43] Ibid, para 49.

V. The Right to Liberty in EU Asylum Law. Adequate Level of Protection?

The administrative detention of asylum-seekers is a long-debated and controversial practice. It implies deprivation of liberty for reasons unrelated to the commission of criminal conduct, and affects persons who are (at least potentially) fleeing from situations of conflict, or at risk of being subject to inhuman or degrading treatment or torture. As early as in 1986, the UNHCR was voicing concerns as to the spread of detention of asylum-seekers.[44]

Over the years, reasons of public security – especially after 9/11 – have caused a significant increase in the use of immigration detention, even more so in cases where the asylum-seekers were victims of trafficking.[45] At 'the juncture of International human rights and international refugee law',[46] administrative detention of asylum-seekers sees the *favor libertatis* going hand in hand with the obligation to comply with a set of guarantees protecting the right to liberty.[47]

Concerning the CEAS specifically, the system of shared responsibility set up by the Dublin Regulation led to the adoption of harsh mandatory detention measures in the most exposed countries through the EU.[48] The breadth of provisions regarding immigration detention causes significant differences amongst states' legislation in terms of length, modalities and requirements of detention.[49]

Other than the principle that asylum-seekers should not be detained 'for the sole reason that he/she is an applicant for asylum' and the basic principles derived from human rights law, authors have argued that EU asylum law somehow crystallises Member States' practice on detention.[50]

The functioning of the CEAS entails a high degree of interaction between Member States. Compliance with fundamental rights is the natural backbone of such a system, where dynamic instruments such as the Dublin Regulation

[44] M Elewa Badar, 'Asylum Seekers and the European Union: Past, Present and Future' (2004) 8(2) *International Journal of Human Rights* 159–74.

[45] D Weissbrodt and S Meili, 'Human Rights and Protection of Non-Citizens: Whether Universality and Indivisibiliy of Rights?' (2010) 28(4) *Refugee Survey Quarterly* 34–58.

[46] C Smyth, 'Is the Right of the Child to Liberty Safeguarded in the Common European Asylum System?' (2013) 15 *European Journal of Migration and Law* 111–36.

[47] J van der Klaauw, 'Refugee Rights in Times of Mixed Migration: Evolving Status and Protection Issues' (2010) 28(4) *Refugee Survey Quarterly* 59–86.

[48] R Cholewinski and P Tara, 'Migration, Governance and Human Rights: Contemporary Dilemmas in the Era of Globalisation' (2010) 28(4) *Refugee Survey Quarterly* 1–33. For an insight into the practice of detaining asylum-seekers in Norway, see M Valenta and K Thorshaug, 'Failed Asylum-Seekers' Responses to Arrangements Promoting Return: Experience From Norway' (2012) 30(2) *Refugee Survey Quarterly* 1–23.

[49] For a comparative analysis of alternatives to detention, see P De Bruycker and others, *Alternatives to Immigration detention and asylum detention in the EU time for implementation*, 2015, accessibleat:http://odysseus-network.eu/wp-content/uploads/2015/02/FINAL-REPORT-Alternatives-to-detention-in-the-EU.pdf.

[50] K Hailbronner, 'Detention of Asylum Seekers' (2007) 9 *European Journal of Migration and Law* 159–72.

are flanked by trust-building measures like the Reception Conditions Directive, aiming to establish a legal level playing-field. The Dublin system has matured into a proper area of EU law. Protection of fundamental rights has been keeping pace with a system of migration management whose original priority was to assuage state concerns sparked by the abolition of internal frontiers.[51]

Consistent with the system of forced transfer of persons envisaged in judicial cooperation, the Dublin Regulation may not apply in case of serious risk of inhumane or degrading treatment in the specific case. While it is clear that systemic deficiencies are not required for such risk to arise, the question remains as to whether breaches of relative rights such as the right to liberty can limit transfer operations, and to what extent. Similarly to what was argued in Part III, the *LM* case-law might be applied to intra-EU transfers of asylum-seekers. Poor detention conditions, by violating the essence of the right to liberty and creating a situation of arbitrary detention, can activate the *exceptional circumstances* clause. In that case, the presumption of mutual trust should be halted and the transfer not to be operated. Article 6 CFREU is the focal point of detention of applicants for international protection, traditionally one of the most controversial issues of asylum policies at national and supranational levels.[52] Proportionality and legal certainty are involved in the EU right to liberty when deprivation of asylum-seekers' liberty is at stake.

The CEAS provides for a *numerus clausus* of grounds for detention in the Reception Conditions Directive and the Dublin Regulation. The issue lies in the interpretation and application of those grounds. The possibility to detain in order to determine those elements on which the application for international protection is based which could not be obtained in the absence of detention is a one-size-fits-all provision that challenges the statement that grounds for deprivation of liberty in the CEAS are actually exhaustive. Secondly, the recourse to the security argument should be carefully assessed. When asked about the application of public policy or public security reasons, the Court has not deeply engaged with the meaning of that provision. While the question referred by the national court was on the validity rather than on its specific content, the CJEU has stopped short of providing guidelines on the use of Article 8(3)(e). This concerns the role of criminal conduct for the purposes of determining the existence of public policy grounds. Furthermore, Article 6 CFREU was used to legitimate deprivation of liberty, but very cursorily and without considering the extent of that interpretation. What dimension of security – or what threshold – is capable of 'triggering' the second part of Article 6 CFREU? Or, in other words, to what extent can security be used to turn Article 6 from a shield into a sword against

[51] Cornelisse defined this as a process of constitutionalisation of detention of TCNs pending asylum claim and removal. Galina Cornelisse, 'Territory, Procedures and Rights: Border Procedures in European Asylum Law' (2016) 35 *Refugee Survey Quarterly* 74.

[52] Authors have analysed and discussed resistance to detention as a way for the migrants to reaffirm their existence in the society. Alessandro Spena, 'Resisting Immigration Detention' (2016) 18 *European Journal of Migration and Law* 201.

personal liberty? In its interpretation, the CJEU seems to regard the individual's security in Article 6 as an emanation of public security.[53]

National judges have, however, a powerful ally in the *Al Chador* finding that the law must establish clear criteria for the application of grounds for refusal in a provision of general application. The ruling has the potential to limit administrative discretion in the practice of asylum detention. What is more, it signals how problematic national approaches in this area can be, with applicants transferred to a Member State where the criteria for detention may be significantly different from those of the sending state. Such infra-EU heterogeneity on grounds for detention aligns the forced movement of persons in EU asylum law with that of judicial cooperation.

This is an issue that is becoming thornier due to the absence of a time-limit for detention.[54] The absence of rigid deadlines after which the person must be released – like in the Return Directive – is regrettable. Firstly, it would be more in compliance with the principle of proportionality to allow deduction of the days spent in detention after acceptance, from the six-week period starting after the lapse of the suspension. Secondly, the Court's finding that detention may not be maintained for three (or 12) months during which the transfer could be reasonably carried out is rather obscure. Can detention be maintained for that long where the transfer may not be carried out regardless of the applicant's conduct? Asylum detention features no moment where detention must cease no matter what. Thirdly, the question arises as to whether or not the clock of detention pending removal merely suspends its ticking while an asylum claim is being examined, and resumes from the moment it had stopped once the application is rejected. Interpreting the period of pre-return detention as starting again every time would allow the limits imposed by EU law to be bypassed.

The third set of remarks concerns the state of detention conditions of asylum-seekers throughout the EU, an issue definitely brought under the spotlight of EU law by the *NS* and subsequent case-law. EU provisions legitimate opacity surrounding detention centres, by laying down restrictive rules concerning access and providing Member States with a broad leeway for further limitations. However, it is once again submitted that detention conditions may fall under the established procedures requirement of the right to liberty. The existing framework concerning grounds for and procedures of detention lacks legal certainty and provides an insufficient level of safeguarding of the right to liberty. Specifically, and similarly to what was stated in the context of the FDs on transfer of prisoners, probation measures and ESO, two main arguments are submitted. Firstly, immigration detention

[53] For an assessment of the grounds for detention in the EU asylum system, see Evangelia Tsourdi, 'Asylum Detention in EU Law: Falling between Two Stools?' (2016) 35 *Refugee Survey Quarterly* 7, 19 onwards.

[54] It has been shown that both no limits or very short limits to asylum detention can have detrimental effects. See Mary Bosworth and Marion Vannier, 'Comparing Immigration Detention in Britain and France: A Matter of Time?' (2016) 18 *European Journal of Migration and Law* 157.

needs *proceduralisation* of detention conditions. This could improve reception conditions and individual rights. Secondly, EU asylum law currently leaves unprotected the dynamic dimension of asylum detention. The person's journey between different legal universes within the EU is not accompanied with guarantees facilitating his/her navigation through variance of rules and conditions. A code of transfer – or, more simply, enlargement of the current horizons of the Dublin Regulation – and proceduralisation of detention conditions in the way endorsed in Part III,[55] are two cornerstones of the re-conceptualisation of the right to liberty suitable for the Union legal order.

VI. Conclusions on Deprivation of Liberty in EU Asylum Law

The scenario on the application of mutual trust to asylum law brings to the fore how dramatic the relationship between integration and constitutionalisation can be. On the one hand, asylum law as part of the AFSJ, and before the very establishment of the Dublin system, was triggered by the need to offset the consequences caused by the creation of an area without internal frontiers. This is well known, as is the fact that the Dublin system has been conceived with the primary aim of controlling cases of asylum-shopping.[56] On the other hand, the method of integration is once again one of mutual recognition. As for judicial cooperation in criminal matters, such a mechanism is founded on mutual trust (eg the presumption of respect for fundamental rights) and is therefore characterised by a high degree of automaticity. The system of forced transfer within the EU requires an even higher standard of protection, both in its static and dynamic dimensions. Administrative detention is a cornerstone of the CEAS.

Conditions in one state that could result in inhuman or degrading treatment may limit the operation of EU law. The extent to which the right to liberty is protected, and possible violations thereof properly addressed, is more controversial. The grounds for refusal – while formally a closed list – create issues of legal certainty. Very broadly worded cases for deprivation of liberty in EU law can foster the emergence of obscure practices on asylum detention, as testified to in the *Al Chodor* ruling. Secondly, the reliance on public policy and public security reasons leaves great discretion to Member States, with the Court endorsing an interpretation of the right to liberty in a security-oriented fashion. Intra-EU movement of asylum-seekers must be read jointly with the variance amongst state laws and practices on grounds for and procedures of detention. Such diversity – though within the flexible perimeter of EU law – requires strong procedural safeguards,

[55] Chapter 8, Section III.C.

[56] Valsamis Mitsilegas, 'Solidarity and Trust in the Common European Asylum System' (2014) 2 *Comparative Migration Studies* 181, 185.

whereby the applicant can be apprised of the specifics of the state system. The first step towards a more level playing-field involves the establishment of a code of detainees' rights, which could promote the improvement of the functioning of detention centres. Uncertainty challenges proportionality in the context of the right to liberty with regard to time-limits as well. The absence of explicit deadlines for asylum detention, to which the CJEU's interpretation poses no significant limitations, might give rise to extended periods of deprivation of liberty. The interaction with the system of pre-removal detention established by the Return Directive only enhances the risk. The next chapter focuses on the deprivation of liberty of irregular TCNs, completing the picture concerning immigration detention and the right to liberty in EU law.

11

Irregular Migration

I. Introduction

Directive 2008/115/EC introduced common standards and procedures in Member States for returning illegally staying TCNs, and constitutes the centre of gravity of Union law on removals. Every other act – or 'subsidiary instrument' – of EU law dealing with a situation of irregular staying by TCNs in the Union territory tacitly presupposes the application of the Return Directive's rules on detention.[1] The present chapter focuses on Directive 2008/115/EC, by paying special attention to the provisions on grounds for and enforcement of detention. Thereafter, some 'subsidiary' instruments are briefly presented as examples of the potential reach of applicability of the Return Directive: Directive 2004/38/EC (or 'the Citizens' Directive'),[2] Directive 2003/109/EC (or 'the Long-resident Directive'),[3] Directive 2003/86/EC (or 'the Family Reunification Directive'),[4] and Regulation 2016/399 (or 'the Common Borders Code or Schengen Borders Code').[5]

The chapter then discusses the CJEU's interpretation of the Directive, with a focus on grounds and procedures of detention, and limits to the Member States' use of deprivation of liberty. Administrative detention in the context of irregular migration is closely connected to asylum law. The analysis reveals the problematic interaction between the Return Directive and the CEAS. It highlights issues of legal certainty and proportionality posed to the right to liberty by the common rules and procedures.

[1] Directive 2008/115/EC of the European Parliament and of the Council of 16 December 2008 on common standards and procedures in Member States for returning illegally staying third-country nationals, [2008] OJ L348/98, 24.12.2008. See, for an illuminating overview, D Wilsher, 'Article 6 – Right to Liberty and Security' in S Peers and others (eds), *The EU Charter of Fundamental Rights. A Commentary* (Oxford, Hart Publishing, 2014) 121–52.

[2] Directive 2004/38/EC of the European Parliament and the Council of 29 April 2004 on the right of citizens of the Union and their family members to move and reside freely within the territory of the Member States, [2004] OJ L158/77, 30.4.2004.

[3] Council Directive 2003/109/EC of 25 November 2003 concerning the status of third-country nationals who are long-term residents, [2004] OJ L16/44, 23.1.2004.

[4] Council Directive 2003/86/EC of 22 September 2003 on family reunification, [2003] OJ L251/12, 3.10.2003.

[5] Regulation (EU) 2016/399 on a Union Code on the rules governing the movement of persons across borders (Schengen Borders Code), [2016] OJ L77/1, 23.3.2016.

II. Secondary Law

A. The Return Directive

Directive 2008/115/EC is the first piece of legislation in immigration adopted under a co-decision procedure. The approval of the Directive proved significantly lengthy and cumbersome,[6] and the final text has been criticised for crystallising Member States' (bad) practices in EU law.[7]

The Directive applies to TCNs staying illegally on the territory of a Member State. Nevertheless, Member States may decide not to apply the Directive to TCNs who: are subject to a refusal of entry in accordance with Article 13 of the Schengen Borders Code; are apprehended or intercepted by the competent authorities in connection with the irregular crossing by land, sea or air of the external border of a Member State and who have not subsequently obtained an authorisation or a right to stay in that Member State; are subject to return as a criminal law sanction or as a consequence of a criminal law sanction, according to national law; or are the subject of extradition procedures.[8]

On being a measure of last resort, deprivation of liberty is subject to the principles of proportionality and necessity: detention must be used only when other less coercive measures would not be sufficient to achieve the aims of the Directive, which is to prepare the return of an irregular migrant or to carry out the removal process. The migrants should be located in specialist detention facilities, and they should be treated in a humane and dignified manner with respect for their fundamental rights.[9] Detention for the purposes of removal is regulated by Chapter IV of the Directive. Member States can detain a TCN with a view to completing return procedures, and in particular when there is a risk of absconding or when the person avoids or hampers the preparation for his/her return or the removal process.[10]

Detention must be motivated in fact and in law; speedy judicial review (initially and when detention is underway) shall be ensured; deprivation of liberty

[6] See, most of all, D Acosta, 'The Good, The Bad and The Ugly in EU Migration Law: is the European Parliament becoming Bad and Ugly?' (2009) 11 *European Journal of Migration and Law* 19–39; M Schieffer, 'Directive 2008/115/EC' in K Hailbronner (ed), *EU Immigration and Asylum Law. A commentary* (München, Beck, 2010) 1489 onwards.

[7] See for instance A Baldaccini, 'The Return and Removal of Irregular Migrants under EU Law: An Analysis of the Return Directive' (2009) 11 *European Journal of Migration and Law* 1–17; D Wilsher, *Immigration Detention. Law, History, Politics* (Cambridge, Cambridge University Press, 2012) 171 onwards; ECRE, *Information Note on the Directive 2008/115/EC of the European Parliament and of the Council of 16 December 2008 on common standards and procedures in Member States for returning illegally staying third-country nationals*, July 2009; for a different view on the part of the UN Special Rapporteur, see M Kamto, *Expulsion of aliens* (International Law Commission Report, 2011).

[8] Directive 2008/115/EC, n 1 above, Art 2(2).

[9] Ibid, recitals 16–17.

[10] Ibid, Art 15(1).

must cease when the removal or the return are no longer achievable.[11] Each Member State may set a period of detention of up to six months, which can be extended to 18 months 'where regardless of [Member States'] national efforts the removal operation is likely to last longer owing to: a lack of cooperation by the third-country national [or] delays in obtaining the necessary documentation from third countries'.[12]

As far as detention conditions are concerned, the Directive states the obligation to provide detainees with information explaining the rules applied in the facility as well as their rights and obligations. However, the Directive stipulates that visits to the centres from relevant and competent organisations or bodies may be subject to authorisation.[13]

B. Subsidiary Instruments

The potential of the Return Directive is better understood when put in the broader context of the Union's measures for expulsion of TCNs.[14] The Long-term Residents Directive sets out the conditions to grant TCNs long-term resident status.[15] Deprivation of liberty under the Return Directive might come into play in three scenarios: a refusal to confer the status in question on grounds of public policy and public security;[16] an expulsion decision, adopted by the Member State concerned when the long-term resident constitutes an actual and sufficiently serious threat to public policy or public security;[17] a refusal to renew, or the withdrawal of, residence, as well as an order for the person concerned and for his/her family members to leave the territory, on grounds of public policy or public security, or where the third-country national is not lawfully residing in the Member State concerned.[18]

Likewise, the Family Reunification Directive contemplates the possibility for the Member State to reject the application for entry and residence of family members on grounds of public policy, public security or public health; furthermore, the Member State may withdraw, or refuse the renewal of, a residence

[11] Ibid, Art 15(2), (3), and (4).

[12] Ibid, Art 15(5).

[13] Ibid, Art 16(4).

[14] See, for an illuminating overview, D Wilsher, 'Article 6 – Right to Liberty and Security' in S Peers, T Hervey, J Kenner and A Ward (eds), *The EU Charter of Fundamental Rights. A Commentary* (Oxford, Hart Publishing, 2014) 121–52.

[15] For an analysis see S Peers, 'Implementing Equality? The Directive on Long-Term Resident Third-Country Nationals' (2004) 29 *European Law Review* 437–60.

[16] Directive 2003/109/EC, n 3 above, Art 6 and 17.

[17] Ibid, Art 12.

[18] Ibid, Art 22. See in particular paragraph (3), where the Member State concerned is authorised to adopt a decision to remove the third-country national from the territory of the Union on serious grounds of public policy and public security.

permit.[19] A third-country national is very likely to be illegally staying, once an application is refused or withdrawn. Furthermore, the Directive mentions 'relevant decisions' to be made by the Member State. The Citizenship Directive also provides for expulsions of TCNs on grounds of public policy or public security.

Lastly, the Schengen Border Code regulates entry into the Union by TCNs. The Regulation sets up a system of border surveillance to prevent unauthorised border crossing, and to take measures against anyone who has crossed the border illegally (including the apprehension of such individuals crossing).[20] The use of coercive measures is also envisaged where border guards are required to prevent the entry into the Member State concerned by non-EU citizens who are not in compliance with the conditions established in the Regulation. The examples above result in situations of illegal staying by TCNs, with consequent application of the rules on pre-removal detention laid down in the Return Directive.

III. The Right to Liberty of Irregular Migrants and the CJEU's Interpretation

The Return Directive does not establish an exhaustive legal framework concerning pre-removal detention, but leaves a considerable margin of discretion to Member States. The leeway has caused significant interpretative dilemmas, brought to the attention of the CJEU over the years. The following section analyses the possible impact of the Court's interpretation on the principle of proportionality and the right to liberty. The discussion focuses on: grounds for and time-limits of detention, procedural rights and detention conditions. The combined analysis of the legislative and judicial approach of EU law to immigration detention reveals its unsuitability for the challenges posed by the enhanced integration in this area of law.

A. Time-Limits of Immigration Detention

Time-limits of detention under the Return Directive were at stake in the *Kadzoev* case,[21] concerning an undocumented Chechen who could not be removed owing to a lack of valid identity documents. He was placed in detention in 2006. In 2009,

[19] Directive 2003/86/EC, n 4 above.

[20] Regulation (EC) No 2016/399, Art 13.

[21] Case C-357/09 PPU, *Proceedings concerning Said Shamilovich Kadzoev (Huchbarov)*, [2009] ECR I-11189. For commentaries, see G Cornelisse, 'Case note' (2011) 48(3) *Common Market Law Review* 925–45; E Mincheva, 'Case Report on *Kadzoev*, 30 September 2009' (2010) 12 *European Journal of Migration and Law* 361–71.

the Bulgarian Supreme Administrative Court (SAC) asked for a preliminary ruling at a time when the Directive had been passed, but the date for transposing it had not yet expired. Between 2006 and 2009, and while in pre-removal detention, Mr Kadzoev had submitted several different asylum applications.

Unlike the AG,[22] who opted for an interpretation more focused on the right to liberty, the CJEU's answers revolved around effectiveness of the Directive. The functional argument underpinned the finding that detention occurred before the Directive's entry into force, or pending judicial review, and must be included in the 18-month time-limit established by the Directive.[23] Otherwise, the objective of setting a rigid maximum term for deprivation of liberty would be jeopardised. However, time spent in detention pending examination of an asylum application may not be counted in the 18 months, as long as that detention was in compliance with conditions and procedures established in national and EU asylum law. The two types of deprivation of liberty pursue different aims, and fall under different legal regimes.[24] Anyway, the Court stated that under no circumstance should the detention pending removal exceed 18 months.[25]

In *Arlsan*, the rule was clarified that the Return Directive does not apply to TCNs who decide to seek asylum while being in pre-removal detention. This is so

> during the period from the making of the application to the adoption of the decision at first instance on that application or, as the case may be, until the outcome of any action brought against the decision is known.[26]

An applicant for international protection may not be considered as 'illegally staying', and Directive 2005/85/EC ('the Asylum Procedures Directive') entitles asylum-seekers to remain in the state while their application is being examined.[27] However, a TCN who has applied for international protection may be kept in detention under the Directive 2008/115

> on the basis of a provision of national law, where it appears, after an assessment on a case-by-case basis of all the relevant circumstances, that the application was made solely to delay or jeopardise the enforcement of the return decision and that it is objectively necessary to maintain detention to prevent the person concerned from permanently evading his return.[28]

[22] *Kadzoev*, AG's Opinion, EU:C:2009:691, para 52.

[23] *Kadzoev*, Court's judgment, EU:C:2009:741, paras 37–39; 54–57.

[24] Ibid, paras 45–48. The CJEU stated that the national court should have verified whether or not, in the instant case, detention had been subject to a different legal regime. It should be noted that the AG held that the discussed differences were absent and, as a consequence, the period at issue was to be counted in the 18 months.

[25] Ibid, paras 63–71.

[26] Case C-534/11 of 30 May 2013, *Mehmet Arslan v Policie ČR, Krajské ředitelství policie Ústeckého kraje, odbor cizinecké policie*, EU:C:2013:343, para 49.

[27] Council Directive 2005/85/EC of 1 December 2005 on Minimum Standards on Procedures in Member States for Granting and Withdrawing Refugee Status, [2005] OJ L326/13, 13,12.2005, Art 7(1).

[28] *Arslan*, n 26 above, para 62.

B. Criminal and Administrative Detention

The CJEU has repeatedly held that the Return Directive does not prevent states from criminalising illegal staying or entry by TCNs. However, it has rigorously reviewed specific measures in light of their possible impact on the return policy. In the seminal *El Dridi* judgment, the Court found that a custodial penalty punishing the non-compliance with a return decision allowing for a period of voluntary departure is incompatible with the Directive, as it would risk 'jeopardising the attainment of the objective pursued by the Directive, namely, the establishment of an effective policy of removal and repatriation of illegally staying third-country nationals'.[29] The same holds true for home detention in the form of a criminal penalty for the illegal stay, should the national law provide no guarantees that deprivation of liberty would come to an end as soon as the removal was enforceable.[30] A threat to the effectiveness of the return policy – and therefore incompatible with EU law – occurs upon the application of custodial penalties to the TCN found to be illegally staying, instead of initiating expulsion procedures and consequent pre-removal detention.[31] However, EU law does not preclude the imposition by a Member State of a custodial penalty on an illegally staying TCN who, after having been returned to his country of origin in the context of an earlier return procedure, unlawfully re-enters the territory of that Member State in breach of an entry ban.[32]

The CJEU strongly anchors its interpretation to the effectiveness of the Directive, and to the pursuit of a common return policy especially. The purposive approach of the Court in *El Dridi* shines even brighter, when compared to the reasoning of the AGs. The latter usually focused on the need to limit individual liberty only in order to prepare the return, and on condition that other less coercive measures cannot be effectively applied.[33] The former paid attention to the states' duties and the need to ensure that the return policy is effectively pursued. As argued, the two perspectives end up with the same result.[34]

[29] Case C-61/11 PPU, *Hassen El Dridi, alias Soufi Karim*, 28 April 2011, [2011] ECR I-3015, para 59. See, in particular, R Raffaelli, 'Criminalizing Irregular Immigration and the Return Directive: An Analysis of the El Dridi Case' (2011) 13 *European Journal of Migration and Law* 467–89; A di Martino and R Raffaelli, 'La libertà di Bertoldo: "Direttiva rimpatri" e diritto penale italiano' (2011) *Diritto penale contemporaneo*.

[30] Case C-430/11, *Criminal proceedings against Mr Sagor*, 6 December 2012, EU:C:2012:777, para 45.

[31] Case C-329/11, *Alexandre Achughbabian v Préfet du Val-de-Marne*, [2011] ECR I-12695, paras 29–45. See R Raffaelli, 'Case note. The Achughbabian case. Impact of the Return Directive in national criminal legislation' (2012) *Diritto Penale Contemporaneo*. See also with regard to *Kadzoev* and *El Dridi*, N Hatzis, 'Detention of Irregular Migrants and the European Public Order' (2013) 38(2) *European Law Review* 259–76.

[32] Case C-290/14, *Criminal proceedings against Skerdjan Celaj*, 1 October 2015, EU:C:2015:640, para 33.

[33] AG's Opinion, Case C-61/11 PPU, *Hassen El Dridi, alias Soufi Karim*, 1 April 2011, EU:C:2011:205, para 28.

[34] Raffaelli, *Case note*, n 31 above, 7.

Following the CJEU's interpretation, indeed, criminal detention may take place (respectively) neither during, nor before the return procedure has commenced. The finding on the punishment of entry-ban violation, however, reveals that effectiveness is heavily prioritised over the protection of personal liberty. The persons concerned have benefited from the Court limiting the use of custodial penalties by a Member State. This has happened nearly incidentally, and in the context of an interpretation centred on the implementation of the EU expulsion policy.

C. Grounds for Detention

The Return Directive provides no exhaustive grounds for detention, but indicates that Member States may detain TCNs pending removal particularly when there is a risk of absconding, or when the person obstructs the completion of return. The previous chapter showed that the way in which these grounds are interpreted and applied at state level may be controversial. The CJEU addressed a question raised on the meaning of these grounds in *Mahdi*.[35] Mr Madhi refused the option for voluntary departure and the Sudanese authorities refused to issue the travel documents required, based on Mr Mahdi's statement that he was not willing to return to Sudan. As the initial period of six months was going to expire, the director of the immigration detention centre asked that Mr Mahdi be kept in detention, in light of his lack of cooperation and the administrative difficulties in acquiring the necessary documentation. Three main issues were at stake: the depth of judicial review on the extension of detention; the assessment of the risk of absconding and lack of cooperation as grounds for extending detention beyond the first six months. Firstly, the CJEU found that a decision on detention must be in the form of a written measure that includes the reasons in fact and in law. Secondly, that decision must be based on an individual assessment. The judicial authority has the power to take into account all the circumstances, even those not reported by the administration, and to deal with the person concerned through less coercive measures.

On the one hand, the Directive precludes – as was provided in the national law – an assessment of the risk of absconding based solely on the fact that the TCN has no valid identity documents.[36] On the other, the fact that the TCN has not obtained an identity document which would have made the removal possible may be regarded as a 'lack of cooperation' only if an examination of his conduct during the period of detention shows that he has not cooperated in the implementation

[35] Case C-146/14 PPU, *Bashir Mohamed Ali Mahdi*, 5 June 2014, EU:C:2014:1320. For a comment, see at: http://eulawanalysis.blogspot.co.uk/2014/06/marie-laure-basilien-gainche.html.

[36] *Mahdi*, Court's judgment, para 69.

of the removal operation and that it is likely that that operation will last longer than anticipated because of that conduct, a matter which is to be determined by the referring court.[37]

The grounds defined in Article 15 may be considered direct grounds for detention. However, the Directive provides for indirect grounds for detention as well. While Directive 2008/115/EC states that the grant of a term for voluntary departure is a rule,[38] Article 7(4) provides that if the person concerned poses a risk to public policy, public security or national security, Member States may refrain from granting a period for voluntary departure, or may grant a period shorter than seven days. If that period is denied for such serious reasons, the person will most probably be detained pending removal.

The *Z Zh* case revolved around the interpretation of the public policy exception.[39] The preliminary ruling concerned two TCNs illegally staying in the Netherlands, and the possibility for a Member State to deny them a period for voluntary departure on grounds of public policy.

Mr Zh was arrested at Schiphol Airport, while in transit to Canada, on the grounds that he was travelling with false documents and for this reason he was sentenced to imprisonment. He was then placed in pre-removal detention, as the national authorities believed he could not be granted a term for voluntary departure because of the offence committed. Mr O was detained as suspected of domestic abuse and issued an expulsion measure without a term for voluntary departure on public policy grounds.

The Court stated that the 'public policy' exception must be interpreted strictly and following an individual assessment. The public policy exception may not be applied on the mere (suspicion of) commission of a criminal offence. However, Article 7(4) does not require the conviction to have become final and absolute, where other circumstances related to the situation of the person concerned justify detention for reasons of public policy.[40] Such circumstances include the nature and seriousness of that act, the time elapsed since it was committed, the fact that the person was in the process of leaving the territory of the state or the absence of documentation substantiating the accusation against the TCN.[41] Where return procedures comply with those conditions, as well as general principles and fundamental rights, Article 7(4) may be applied without conducting a fresh examination of the matters which have already been examined in order to establish the existence of the risk to public policy.[42]

[37] Ibid, para 85.

[38] See recital 10 of the Return Directive, n 1 above.

[39] Case C-554/13, *ZZh v Staatssecretaris voor Veiligheid en Justitie and Staatssecretaris voor Veiligheid en Justitie v IO*, 11 June 2015, EU:C:2015:377.

[40] *ZZh*, paras 44–54.

[41] Ibid, paras 57–65.

[42] Ibid, paras 69–75.

D. Procedural Rights and Detention Conditions

The Return Directive – in particular Article 15(2) and (6) – sets out specific procedural guarantees concerning the first decision on detention pending removal, but not with regard to its extension beyond six months.[43] The Court found that the right to be heard is a relative one, and may be restricted in compliance with the principle of proportionality. In the absence of EU rules, it is for the national law to regulate the exercise of that right and the consequences of its infringement.[44] The Court in *MG and NR* referred to the Directive's objectives as the establishment of 'an effective removal and repatriation policy, based on common standards, for persons to be returned in a human manner and with the full respect of their fundamental rights and dignity'. However, the CJEU found that

> where the extension of a detention measure has been decided in an administrative procedure in breach of the right to be heard, the national court responsible for assessing the lawfulness of that extension decision may order the lifting of the detention measure only if it considers … that the infringement at issue actually deprived the party … of the possibility of arguing his defence better, to the extent that the outcome of that administrative procedure could have been different.[45]

Detention conditions are a notoriously thorny issue in the context of administrative deprivation of liberty of TCNs. To this end, Article 16(1) provides that migrants in pre-removal detention cannot be accommodated in prison, unless situations occur where an exceptionally large number of third-country nationals to be returned places an unforeseen heavy burden on the capacity of the detention facilities of a Member State or on its administrative or judicial staff.[46] In that context, a federal state may not derogate from the mentioned rule because one of its constituent States has no specialised detention facilities, but must ensure that accommodation in specialist facilities in its other federated States is provided.[47] Furthermore, Article 16(1) cannot be derogated from even where the person concerned consents to that.[48]

[43] Case C-383/13, *MG and NR v Staatssecretaris van Veiligheid en Justitie*, 10 September 2013, EU:C:2013:533. On the latter case see P De Bruycker and S Mananashvili, '*Audi alteram partem* in immigration detention procedures, between the ECJ, the ECtHR and Member States: G & R' (2015) 52 *Common Market Law Review* 569–90.

[44] *MG and NR*, Court's judgment, paras 31–32.

[45] Ibid, para 45.

[46] Directive 2008/115, n 1 above, Art 18(1).

[47] Joined Cases C-473/13 and C-514/13, *Adala Bero v Regierungspräsidium Kassel* and *Ettayebi Bouzalmate v Kreisverwaltung Kleve*, 17 July 2014, EU:C:2014:2095, para 32.

[48] Case C-474/13 *Thi Ly Pham v Stadt Schweinfurt, Amt für Meldewesen und Statistik*, EU:C:2014:2096, 17 July 2014, para 23.

IV. The Right to Liberty in EU Law and Immigration Detention

The absence of internal frontiers and fundamental rights protection are two distinct – though interrelated – pillars of the Union project. Legal integration serves the purpose of securing free movement – as exemplified by the European Arrest Warrant Framework Decision – and of strengthening the foundations on which free movement-through-integration is built. This is clear in the case of the presumption of mutual trust and trust-building measures such as the procedural rights Directives. Detention of TCNs irregularly staying in the Union is a key tool to enable the implementation of a common return policy. This broader objective is, in turn, part and parcel of a migration management strategy meant to keep a borderless area sustainable. Its barycentric role is confirmed by the preliminary rulings issued by the CJEU on the Return Directive, the vast majority of them focused on the use of administrative deprivation of liberty.[49]

In this context, legal integration has led to constraints on states' use of coercive measures, with the Court aiming to balance national interests and fundamental rights issues. The CJEU's case-law intersects national discretion, with the Directive's provisions remaining somehow vague or totally silent. The following sections discuss the ambiguous approach of EU law to the detention of irregular migrants and fundamental rights protection, and the right to liberty in particular. On the one hand, the focus is on the broader Union's understanding of permissible restrictions and 'tolerable' violations of TCN's rights. On the other, the analysis highlights the current content of the right to liberty in EU law and the need for a Union-specific habeas corpus.

A. Limitations and Violations of Fundamental Rights in Immigration Detention

The full operation of EU law on deprivation of liberty, and mutual recognition especially, relies heavily on the rebuttable presumption that fundamental rights are complied with by Member States. To this end, two main situations should be firmly kept separate. On the one hand, restrictions to rights and freedoms are subject to the test laid down in Article 52(1) CFREU: they must be provided by law, respect the essence of the right, pursue an objective of general interest and be proportionate. Article 51(2) is not a stand-alone provision, but operates in conjunction with the specific Charter Article subject to limitation. The partner-right here is the right to liberty enshrined in Article 6 CFREU.

[49] For an interesting analsysis, see V Mitsilegas, 'Immigration Detention, Risk and Human Rights in the Law of the European Union. The lessons from the Return Directive' in V Mitsilegas, M Joao Guia and R Koulish (eds), *Immigration Detention, Risk and Human Rights* (Cham, Springer, 2016) 25.

On the other hand, breaches of fundamental rights fall outside the scope of Article 52(1) – a breach cannot be provided for by law by definition. The assessment may concern past (*Radu* scenario)[50] or prospective (*NS* situation)[51] violations. The former scenario may determine the unlawfulness of the decision issued following the breach, whereas the latter materialises in a risk assessment possibly leading to the non-implementation of a specific piece of legislation. As previous Parts of the story showed, the question of what breaches can rebut the presumption of mutual trust – and so the application of EU law – is a key one.

EU law on immigration detention is relevant to both levels of analysis. Proportionality aims to balance the extent to which two or more interests limit each other. The interests at stake here being effectiveness of the Directive and the right to liberty, three sets of limits come into play: limits in time to the use of detention; limits to the use of custodial penalties; and limits to individual rights in relation to detention pending removal. In all scenarios, the effectiveness of the Directive leads to the interpretation of what these limits are. After 18 months in pre-removal detention the person must be released, and stating otherwise would jeopardise one of the objectives of the Directive. Member States cannot resort to criminal law detention, as long as this hampers the completion of return procedures. Limits to – namely, breaches of – the right to be heard do not make detention unlawful, to the extent that the outcome of the procedure would not have been different in case of compliance with the right.

Is the problem of an effectiveness-driven interpretation of rules concerning immigration detention an actual problem? Or, as argued, is what matters that the AG's and Court's approaches – the former being fundamental rights-based – end up with the same result? After all, the CJEU repeatedly stated that the objective of the Directive is the (1) implementation of a common return policy (2) in a humane and dignified manner. The problem is that these two poles are not inseparable, and protection of the right to liberty is guaranteed as long as it pulls in the same direction of effective removal procedures. In limiting the Member States' use of criminal law, the horizon of the interpretation is exclusively the efficiency of expulsion procedures. This is confirmed in *Celaj*, where imprisonment to punish the violation of a re-entry ban was declared compatible with the Return Directive. There exist provisions in the Return Directive meant to protect personal liberty, such as the 18-month limit. However, the interpretation is not always as straightforward as it may seem. The previous chapter highlighted how the time-limit might be significantly extended, where asylum-detention and removal-detention interplay.

[50] Case C-396/11, *Proceedings relating to the execution of European arrest warrants issued against Ciprian Vasile Radu*, 29 January 2013, EU:C:2013:39.

[51] Case C-411/10, *NS v Secretary of State for the Home Department* and C-493/10, *ME and Others v Refugee Applications Commissioner and Minister for Justice, Equality and Law Reform*, 21 December 2011, EU:C:2011:865.

Secondly, what happens in even less clear-cut cases, where Member States are left with a considerable margin of discretion? An answer may be given in *MG and NR*. If conditions for the exercise of the right to be heard and the consequences ensuing from its violations are not laid down in EU law, national law must do so in compliance with the principle of equivalence and effectiveness. However, the recognition of that right must not undermine the effectiveness of the Directive, as would happen if every breach could determine the release of the person concerned. For that reason, the national judge must have power to assess whether the decision would have been different had no breach occurred. The Court seems not to treat restrictions and breaches of rights differently, which is legally questionable. Furthermore, the question arises as to whether there is a minimum threshold of *difference* required to declare the unlawfulness of detention. Should the procedures be re-opened only where detention would not have been prolonged at all, or also in the scenario where, for example, the extension would have been granted for a significantly shorter amount of time?

The foregoing legal questions show that personal liberty is caught between the maintenance of a borderless area and fundamental rights protection. The following sub-section stresses that legal integration in this area requires a reconsideration of the right to liberty suitable for the legal developments in this area.

B. Grounds and Procedures for Immigration Detention

The analysis of immigration detention confirms the idea that deprivation of liberty in EU law operates on two main levels. The first, broader area of analysis, is that involving the balance between the construction and preservation of an area of free movement and fundamental rights protection. The second, more specific, debate concerns the understanding of strongholds of personal liberty, conceived and developed in the context of nation-states, and that are under pressure following the growing involvement of a supranational polity in the deprivation of liberty.

The right to liberty requires that detention occurs only in cases and according to procedures established by law in a clear, foreseeable and accessible way. The interaction between the discretion left by the Return Directive, one the one hand, and laws and practices at state level, on the other, raises issues with regards to both grounds and procedures of detention. By means of the words *in particular*, Article 15 leaves Member States free to detain TCNs on grounds other than risk of absconding and obstruction of their removal. This can result in situations like the one envisaged by the Italian law on foreigners, which at Article 14 used to authorise detention *when the expulsion is not immediately enforceable, due to transitional situations which hamper the preparation of the return* (emphasis added).[52]

[52] Decreto Legislativo 25 luglio 1998, n. 286.

Though such a requirement was dropped by Law as of 30 October 2014, n. 163[53] – and not because of pressure from EU institutions, since that ground was added following the *El Dridi* judgment – it gives an idea of potential one-size-fits-all grounds for detention introduced at state level. Legal uncertainty arises also from definition of the grounds for detention established in the Directive, including the indirect ground represented by the public policy exception.

From the analysis in Chapters ten and eleven, two main conclusions can be drawn. Firstly, binding provisions of general application must establish objective criteria underlying the use of a ground for detention. Secondly, an individual assessment must support the finding that those criteria are met in the specific circumstances of the case; or, in other words, there is very reduced room for presumption and automaticity. These are powerful tools in the hands of national judges when dealing with an area – administrative detention – that relies by definition on practices of the administration and law enforcement agencies. This is even more so in the present scenario, where the establishment of common rules on returns is not flanked by a level playing-field on deprivation of liberty.

Legal uncertainty affects procedures of detention, and detention conditions especially. The CJEU's findings concerning the right to be heard show that national procedural autonomy is constrained by the pursuit of effective return procedures.

A worse scenario emerges from the issue of conditions in the detention centres. Studies on detention conditions in immigration centres are transversal and involve monitoring activities,[54] efforts of classifications[55] and accommodation

[53] For a comment see L Masera, 'Ridotto da 18 a 3 mesi il periodo massimo di trattenimento in un CIE: la libertà dei migranti irregolari non è più una bagattella?', *Diritto Penale Contemporaneo*, 10 November 2014, available at http://www.penalecontemporaneo.it/materia/-/-/-/3412-ridotto_da_18_a_3_mesi_il_periodo_massimo_di_trattenimento_in_un_cie__la_libert___dei_migranti_irregolari_non____pi___una_bagattella/

[54] See the monitoring activity of the Council of Europe's Committee on the prevention of torture (CPT) in this respect. See, among many, CPT/Inf (2007) 18 of 18 April 2007, which reports on detention conditions in Germany; CPT/Inf (2006) 1 of 20 December 2006 which criticises two centres in Greece; and CPT/Inf (2005) 13 of 21 July 2005 which criticises detention preceding deportation in Austria. See also, for latest reports, http://www.globaldetentionproject.org/publications/detention-profiles.html. As for immigration detention in Greece, see L Cheliotis, 'Behind the veil of Xilophenia: the politics of immigration detention in Greece' (2013) 10(6) *European Journal of Criminology* 725–45; on immigration detention in Malta, see D De Bono, '"Less than human": the detention of irregular migrants in Malta' (2013) 55(2) *Malta, Race and Class* 60–81. See also the empirical study on the Dutch system of immigration detention conducted by A Leekers and D Broeders, 'A Case of Mixed Motives?: Formal and Informal Functions of Administrative Immigration Detention' (2010) 50(5) *The British Journal of Criminology* 830–50,

[55] E Guild, 'A Typology of Different Types of Centers in Europe' (2005) Report for the European Parliament, Directorate-General Internal Policies of the Union, IP/C/LIBE/FWC/2005-22; UNHCR, *Reception Standards for Asylum seekers in the European Union*, 32 (last visited 25 may 2012). A commendable attempt at categorisation of immigration centres is carried out in M Flynn, 'Who must be detained? Proportionality as a tool for critiquing immigration detention policy' (2012) 31(3) *Refugee Survey Quarterly* 40, 55 onwards, wherein the author distinguishes the centres along basic criteria, firstly: criminal, administrative and ad hoc, with each one of them divided into specific subcategories.

in prison.[56] The CJEU has rightly denied the possibility to accommodate TCNs in prison outside the exception provided in the Return Directive, and recognised the immaterial value of TCNs' consent to waive their rights due to their extreme weakness and psychological deprivation, as well as rare access to interpretation and legal aid.[57] However, and in spite of having committed no criminal offences, Member States recognise that migrants placed in prisons would enjoy 'more favourable treatment', for those facilities would 'offer a wider and more extensive range of activities, leisure and care than that provided in specialised detention facilities and better supervision too in terms of safety'.[58]

Article 16(5) Return Directive requires that migrants be informed of the rules applied in the facilities *and* their rights and obligations. While the Directive establishes the link between individual rights and the functioning of the centres, subjecting visits to such facilities to authorisation contributes to the idea of immigration centres as a black hole of the rule of law. Situations in Member States reinforce the argument.[59]

In line with the argument put forward in Part III, it is submitted that detention conditions should be part of the right to liberty, and not only as a matter of proportionality.[60] The arbitrariness test elaborated by the ECtHR includes detention conditions, so reinforcing the idea that violations of Article 5(1) ECHR may arise during the phase of enforcement of detention.[61] The established procedures requirement enshrined in the right to liberty is met so long as the relevant rules are endowed with the quality of the law, and they spell out how the deprivation of liberty concretely takes place.[62] The source of law must be adequate, with, for example, an administrative decree (or an unpublished circular not being in

This parameter intersects the other, according to which there exist five sorts of facilities, divided by level of control: high-security, secure, semi-secure, non-secure, mixed regime. The less freedom of movement detainees have, the higher the level of security.

[56] The Council of Europe's Committee on the Prevention of Torture pointed out that conditions in immigration centres may be worse than those of prison establishments (CPT/Inf (2006) 11 – Poland, para 59; CPT/Inf (2006) 41 – Greece). At the same time, several countries continue to use prisons to accommodate migrants (European Committee for the Prevention of Torture, Inhuman and degrading Treatment or Punishment. Visit report: Ireland (2006) CPT/Inf (2007) 40).

[57] Ibid, paras 201–202.

[58] Ibid, para 153.

[59] In Italy, for example, every aspect concerning individual rights and the functioning of the centres is referred to the administration and the only existing rules are contained in an executive act implementing the Italian law on foreigners – d.P.R. 394/1999 (decree of the President of the Republic). For an overview on the migrant centres in Italy, see A di Martino, F Biondi Dal Monte, I Boiano and R Raffaelli, *The Criminalization of Irregular Migration: Law and Practice in Italy* (Pisa, Pisa University Press, 2013) 95 onwards, at: http://www.wiss-lab.dirpolis.sssup.it/files/2013/05/Libro-dirpolis-1.pdf.

[60] See, from this perspective, G Cornelisse, *Immigration Detention and Human Rights: Rethinking Territorial Sovereignty* (Leiden, Martinus Nijhoff Publisher, 2010) 259 onwards.

[61] See eg ECtHR, *Mubilanzila Mayeka and Kaniki Mitunga v Belgium*, Application No 13178/03, judgment of 12 October 2006, paras 102–103.

[62] A di Martino, 'La disciplina dei CIE è incostituzionale' (2012) *Diritto Penale Contemporaneo*. The author engages in an assessment against the yardstick of Article 13 of the Italian Constitution, which resembles Article 6 CFREU and Article 5 ECHR.

compliance with the legal basis requirement).[63] The content of the procedures must be laid down in a clear and accessible way, so as to reduce the scope of discretion and guarantee the correct exercise of individual rights.

The EU and Member State laws on immigration detention leave a serious shortage of safeguards for the right to liberty of TCNs. The concerns voiced by the European Commission have materialised in the codifying endeavour on immigration detention rules currently put in place by the CoE.[64] Consistent with the findings presented in the analysis of mutual recognition, the case is hereby made for the adoption of an EU law instrument carrying out proceduralisation of detention conditions of TCNs pending removal or examination of an asylum claim.

V. Conclusions on Immigration Detention in EU Law

The analysis of EU law on pre-removal detention completes the picture on administrative deprivation of liberty of TCNs within the Union. Detention is key to migration management and the CEAS. While the Return Directive aims to establish a level playing-field on expulsions from the EU, there are still a number of concerning issues on the table. Though the general understanding is that the Directive and the CJEU's interpretation have improved TCNs' protection, the standard ensured to the right to liberty leaves much to be desired. In the effectiveness-based approach to the Directive, the completion of return procedures outweighs rights protection. The case-law on the use of custodial penalties confirms the idea that any benefits to personal liberty might be somehow 'accidental'.

The findings in *MG and NR* go in the same direction. Firstly, granting procedural rights to TCNs must not jeopardise the effectiveness of the Directive. Secondly, breaches of rights make detention unlawful only where they affect the outcome of the procedure. The CJEU seems to conflate legitimate rights restriction and rights violations in one test. Furthermore, it adopts a rather sharp approach to consequences for the rights of TCNs deprived of liberty. This clashes with the interests at stake, where the absence of nuance and depth in the Court's reading applies to the extension of detention up to 18 months.

[63] ECtHR, *Amuur v France*, Application no 19776/92, judgment of 25 June 1996, paras 50–54.

[64] See the Communication from the Commission to the Council and the European Parliament on EU Return Policy, Brussels 28.3.2014, COM(2014) 199 final. See also the declaration by the European National Preventive Mechanism against torture, available at: http://www.coe.int/t/democracy/migration/Source/migration/Strasbourg%20Declaration.pdf; and the standards established by the Council of Europe Committee on the Prevention of Torture ('CPT standards' document CPT/Inf/E (2002) 1 – Rev. 2013, available at: www.cpt.coe.int/en/docsstandards.htm, and the first draft of immigration detention rule at: https://rm.coe.int/cj-dam-2017-8-legal-instruments-refered-to-in-the-1st-draft-codifying-/16807252ce.

The introduction of a time-limit for immigration detention, after which the person must be released, is a great achievement. The devil, however, lies in the detail, and circumstances might jeopardise the attainment of that objective. In the absence of clear criteria, the interaction between asylum and pre-removal detention might stretch the 18-month deadline. This has to do with the method of calculation where the two types of detention are interposed with each other. Secondly, it concerns the criteria for distinguishing between them: how can national courts decide whether detention was pending an asylum application or pending removal? In *Kadzoev*, the Court referred to the application of the relevant EU asylum law as a possible criterion. Further specification might be needed, in order to understand when one legal regime has been applied, rather than the other.

The two centrepieces of the right to liberty are under pressure as well. On the one hand, the open wording of the Directive on grounds for detention requires a continuous endeavour toward legal certainty. The analysis of asylum law confirms that, even when they formally operate within the boundaries of EU law, Member States might abuse that discretion and cause violations of the right to liberty. Furthermore, concerns can be voiced on national grounds for detention other than those explicitly mentioned in the Return Directive, framed as a *one-size-fits-all* detention requirement. On the other hand, the complete lack of transparency and accessibility to the functioning of the detention centres may be emphasised. The great leeway left to national authorities is bound to impede any mprovement. For this reason, this chapter argues in favour of proceduralisation of detention conditions in a similar way to what was proposed in judicial cooperation.

Concluding Remarks on Asylum and Immigration Detention in EU Law

Administrative detention of TCNs is a phenomenon of increasing relevance in EU law. Over the years, it has come to the fore in legislation and judgments as one of the most controversial aspects of migration management in Europe. In the Union, it is placed in the broader context of the creation of an area of free movement. This holds true for the two arenas where detention takes place: pending asylum or pending return procedures. The establishment of a level playing-field aims to increase mutual trust, which in turn underpins further legal integration in the area. This is especially so in the case of the CEAS, which revolves around a system of mutual recognition of allocation of responsibility and consequent transfer of asylum-seekers between Member States.

Deprivation of liberty has a static and a dynamic dimension: rules on grounds for and procedures of detention are closely linked to those on forced movement of TCNs within or outside the EU. Detention conditions certified as degrading may result in limiting the operation of secondary EU law. The *NS* and subsequent case-law are important because they reveal the importance of detention conditions to the functioning of the system. Furthermore, they set the conditions for rebutting the presumption of mutual trust without requiring systemic deficiencies. However, and as emerged from the analysis of judicial cooperation, this relates to an absolute prohibition like Article 4 CFREU.

What happens in the case of past or prospective violations of a relative fundamental right? For prospective violations, the *LM* case-law can be translated into asylum and immigration law. This *exceptional circumstances* clause might be activated, as argued in Part III, when poor detention conditions violating the essence of the right to liberty are involved. As for past violations, the CJEU might have given an answer in *MG and NR*, where it stated that a breach of the right to be heard connected to a decision on detention would make the latter unlawful only if compliance with the right would have led to a different outcome. The Court opted for a not very nuanced approach – especially in a case where detention could be extended up to 18 months – with recognition of rights to TCNs being limited in the name of the effectiveness of return procedures. The impression is that in most cases effectiveness would override concerns over fundamental rights protection.

The right to liberty in immigration detention is faced with tough challenges. These challenges concern not only, as just recalled, procedural rights, but its foundations: clear, accessible and foreseeable grounds for and procedures of detention. On the one hand, the CEAS establishes a closed number of grounds but provide no time-limit for deprivation of liberty pending application. The practice reveals, however, that those exhaustive cases for detention can be stretched at national and EU law level. While the principle stated by the Court in *Al Chodor* has the potential to limit considerably the discretion of states in their administrative practices, the *JN* case shows not much engagement with the relationship between criminal conduct and the public policy ground. Furthermore, it uses Article 6 CFREU to legitimate detention on security grounds. The very flexible finding in *Khir Amayry*, and the absence of a deduction obligation concerning the period spent in detention before the elapse of the suspension, create further concerns in terms of certainty and proportionality.

The analysis of the Return Directive confirms issues of discretion as for grounds for detention. The problems here arise from the way cases provided in the Directive are applied at national level. The open wording of Article 15 – allowing states to provide for further cases for detention – risks a further increase in discretion and uncertainty. The establishment of an ultimate term of 18 months, after which detention must cease no matter what, is certainly a great achievement. However, this progress might be jeopardised by the interaction between detention pending asylum, on the one hand, and pending removal, on the other. The Court stated in *Kadzoev* that the former type of deprivation of liberty cannot be considered for the calculation of the 18-month period, provided that rules of the CEAS apply. The criterion might not be of sufficient help, and the need emerges for a proper test or guidelines on how to distinguish between those two sorts of deprivation of liberty. Where detention pending removal is interrupted by asylum detention and then starts again after, for example, the rejection of the claim, it seems only logical that the 18-month period should resume and not start again.

Conditions of detention, rights of TCNs and functioning of specialised facilities are intertwined aspects particularly relevant to the right to liberty. Detention centres throughout the EU have experienced serious problems of transparency and respect for the most basic fundamental rights. Detention conditions are also solidly part of the arbitrariness test of the ECtHR on Article 5(1)(f), relied on by the CJEU as well. Poor conditions not resulting in inhuman or degrading treatment can create all the same situations of arbitrariness and unlawfulness. In a similar way to what was argued in the chapter on judicial cooperation, the way forward might be the provision of a detailed set of procedural rights of TCNs in detention. Such proceduralisation of detention conditions would improve both individual rights and the system of detention centres broadly.

PART V

Deprivation of Liberty and EU Citizenship

12

Integration and Reintegration in the EU Civic Status of Detainees

I. Introduction

The present chapter concludes the story on the EU and deprivation of liberty told in this book. Previous Parts highlighted the trajectory of the Union's involvement in detention, having its main character in free movement as laboratory, trigger and horizon. That path started in the context of the internal market as a way of limiting Member States' use of custodial penalties for the benefits of free movement. It then expanded to include criminal, immigration and asylum law, under the broader argument that further legal integration was necessary to make the abolition of internal frontiers sustainable. A body of law emerged where deprivation of liberty and forced movement of persons within or outside the Union territory have been relied on in the name of the preservation of the sustainability of free movement. Both criminal and immigration detention see static and dynamic measures work in symbiosis. On the one hand, approximation of substantive criminal law aims to prevent forum-shopping and facilitate judicial cooperation, so increasing effectiveness of EU law. On the other, similarly to what happens with the EAW, the interstate transfer of asylum-seekers pursuant to the Dublin system is possible when (detention) conditions in the receiving state respect the absolute prohibition under Article 4 CFREU.

Such a development resulted in the establishment of an evolutionary legal framework that places traditional strongholds of personal liberty under pressure. The peculiarities of the Union legal order create new challenges to the principle of legality and the right to liberty, and call for a reconceptualisation of those safeguards.

Beginning with the genesis of deprivation of liberty in EU law and continuing with its growth outside the internal market, this story ends with an analysis of the impact of detention on individuals as rights-holders. While the analysis so far has focused on the *reasons for* and *implementation of* deprivation of liberty in EU law, this chapter follows – and complements – that discussion logically and chronologically.

Detention per se triggers different rights limitations. These can present nuances and express multiple rationales. This last Part, however, is not concerned with *any* restrictions ensuing from detention in EU law, but focuses on the consequences that the Union legal order explicitly attaches to deprivation of liberty as a 'response' thereto. In this context, detention embodies a wrongdoing, to which EU law can react in different ways.

The question addressed here concerns the role for current and former detainees of EU citizenship. The attention is particularly on residence security, understood as the right to enter and stay, which is 'at the core of what the essential legal essence of the citizenship status is now about'.[1] Both EU nationals and TCNs are involved, since, pursuant to Article 45 CFREU, freedom of movement and residence may be granted, in accordance with the Treaties, to nationals of third countries legally resident in the territory of a Member State.[2] Instruments of secondary EU law give substance to such a right, whereby TCNs can enjoy derived rights because of their 'tie' to an EU national.[3]

The concluding chapter addresses the *consequences* of deprivation of liberty for the legal status of the person concerned. The freedom of movement and residence across the EU – at the core of, though not exhaustively defining, what Union citizenship is about – allows persons to establish themselves in states other than those of their nationality. There they may find employment, start a family and – less fortunately at times – be imprisoned for (suspicion of) having committed wrongdoings. To understand how detention affects citizenship entails an assessment of the Union law response to what detention represents in terms of blameworthiness. In particular, it requires an assessment of the EU's approach to integration and reintegration, and the impact of detention on those two factors.

The two aspects are closely interrelated. Integration is a centrepiece of EU citizenship, and underlies a number of measures and rulings in judicial cooperation. Reintegration has across-the-board relevance as well. On the one hand, the concept is a fundamental objective in instruments of forced movement of persons, such as the Framework Decision on the transfer of prisoners. On the other, it emerges as an important factor to consider in the Court's interpretation of the Citizenship Directive. The analysis below shows that reintegration can be relevant when assessing the compliance of expulsion measures with EU law. Together, integration and reintegration are key to protecting the enjoyment of residence security. For example, giving persons the chance to serve a custodial sentence in the state

[1] D Kochenov and B Pirker, 'Deporting the Citizens Within the European Union: A Counter-Intuitive Trend in Case C-348/09, PI v. Oberbürgermeisterin der Stadt Remscheid' (2013) 19(2) *Columbia Journal of European Law* 369, 374 onwards.

[2] For a commentary, see D Ashiagbor, 'Article 15. Freedom to choose an occupation and right to engage in work' in S Peers, T Hervey, J Kenner and A Ward, *The EU Charter of Fundamental Rights: A Commentary* (Oxford, Hart Publishing, 2014) 423.

[3] See in particular Articles 2 and 3 Directive 2004/38/EC of the European Parliament and of the Council of 29 April 2004 on the right of citizens of the Union and their family members to move and reside freely within the territory of the Member States amending Regulation (EEC) No 1612/68 and repealing Directives 64/221/EEC, 68/360/EEC, 72/194/EEC, 73/148/EEC, 75/34/EEC, 75/35/EEC, 90/364/EEC, 90/365/EEC and 93/96/EEC.

where they live presupposes a degree of integration there. However, imprisonment can negatively affect that integration assessment and subsequently jeopardise the possibility to pursue rehabilitation in that state. The relationship is therefore a circular one. Reintegration here is a post-detention question, and the focus is on the possible impact of restrictive measures on the subject's reintegration following the deprivation of liberty.

Detention is a crucial factor in the balance between legal integration towards an area of free movement and impact on individual rights. The establishment of Union citizenship implies further involvement of EU law in assessing how detention can curb that status. In that context, the question arises as to what impact detention has on residence security.

The chapter answers the question as follows. Firstly, it outlines the relevant EU citizenship law and the CJEU's interpretation of the impact of detention on integration. The analysis shows that the Court has recently shifted from a rights-expanding approach to an understanding of citizenship to support the objectives of EU criminal policy. On the one hand, integration is no longer an objective of EU citizenship but a reward for obedience to the law. On the other, public security moves from being a strictly interpreted exception to residence security, to a one-size-fits-all category used to contribute to the Union's security agenda. Secondly, the chapter presents the Union's approach to reintegration as emerging from the FDs on the EAW, transfer of prisoners and probation measures. Section III emphasises the supra-individual stance on reintegration hinted at by the Court in section II, and the significantly reduced space for individual involvement in the process of rehabilitation.

Both scenarios, however, reveal room for protection of residence security of detainees when forced movement outside the Union is at stake. The joint reading of the two scenarios brings to the fore the weak civic status of detainees in EU law, though opening potentially interesting developments and questions for the future.

II. Integration and EU Citizenship

The legal approach usually regards citizenship as a combination of two elements.[4] On the one hand is citizenship as a status, linking the state to its citizens. On the other is citizenship as bearer of a complex set of rights enjoyed by citizens.[5] As we know, the very core of EU citizenship is the right, for Union nationals, to move and

[4] D Kochenov, 'Ius Tractum of Many Faces: European Citizenship and the Difficult Relationship Between Status and Rights' (2009) 15(2) *Columbia Journal of European Law* 169.

[5] However (ibid), the author found that the relationship between status and rights may be flexible, and another distinction is possible to be drawn between '"formal" citizenship, resting on the status, and "informal" citizenship, emphasising the importance of the possibility of enjoying citizenship rights as opposed to the importance of possessing the formal legal status of a citizen'.

reside freely within the EU regardless of their nationality,[6] and without requiring links to the performance of an economic activity.[7]

Directive 2004/38/EC gives substance to Articles 18, 20 and 21 TFEU, mainly through the right to enter and stay permanently in the territory of another Member State.[8] This system of residence security rests on two main pillars: the right to residence and the protection against expulsion. In the bigger scheme of the Directive, these centerpieces emerge as means of, rather than (just) a reward for, integration. The Directive – providing the conditions for free movement and residence across the EU by the Union's citizens and their family members – aims to promote social cohesion and give Union citizens the chance for integration throughout the EU.

To this end, EU citizens and their family members are granted the unconditional right to reside in the host Member State for a period of up to three months. Should the stay be longer, the right is made subject to specific requirements.[9] The right to permanent residence, provided for in Article 16, is conferred upon Union citizens after they have legally resided for a continuous period (which is not affected by temporary absences) of five years in the host Member State. Once acquired, the right of permanent residence shall only be lost through absence from the host Member State for a period exceeding two consecutive years.

As for protection against expulsion, recital 23 sees such a measure as capable of seriously harming persons who have become genuinely integrated into the host Member State; the degree of integration and the length of residence are to be considered, when carrying out the proportionality test on the expulsion decision.[10]

The Directive laid down general principles concerning expulsion from the host state. Such a measure shall follow an individual assessment of the person's conduct as a genuine, present and sufficiently serious threat to one of the fundamental

[6] Case C-224/98, *Marie-Nathalie D'Hoop v Office national de l'emploi*, [2002] ECR I-6191, para 28; Case C-184/99, *Rudy Grzelczyk v Centre public d'aide sociale d'Ottignies-Louvain-la-Neuve*, [2001] ECR I-6193, para 31; Case C-138/02, *Brian Francis Collins v Secretary of State for Work and Pensions*, [2004] ECR I-2703, para 61 onwards.

[7] The link is currently codified in Articles 18, 20 and 21 of the TFEU, and was established in instruments then replaced by the Citizenship Directive such as Council Directive 90/364/EEC of 28 June 1990, [1990] OJ L180/26 and Council Directive 90/365/EEC of 28 June 1990, [1990] OJ L180/28. See Case C-76/05, *Herbert Schwarz, Marga Gootjes-Schwarz v Finanzamt Bergisch Gladbach*, [2007] ECR I-6849, [2007] ECR I-6849, para 89; *Grzelczyk*, n 6 above, paras 36–37; Case C-413/99, *Baumbast and R v Secretary of State for the Home Department*, [2002] ECR I-7091, para 81. See also J Shaw, 'Citizenship: Contrasting Dynamics at the Interface of Integration and Constitutionalism', (2010) *EUI Working Papers RSCAS 2010/60*, 9 onwards.

[8] As Kochenov argued, 'Residence security is at the core of what the essential legal essence of the citizenship status is now about', which also explains why (even the mere possibility of) being deported and expelled 'play[s] an essential role in outlining with clarity the scope of those who are citizens of a polity, as opposed to merely residents'. D Kochenov and B Pirker, 'Deporting the Citizens within the European Union: A Counter-Intuitive Trend in Case C-348/09, PI v Oberburgermeisterin Der Stadt Remscheid' (2012) 19(2) *Journal of European Law* 369. For an analysis of EU citizenship and the territory, see L Azoulai, 'The (Mis)Construction of the European Individual: Two Essays on Union Citizenship Law', *EUI Department of Law Research Paper*, no 2014/14 (2014).

[9] Directive 2004/38/EC, n 3 above, Articles 6(1) and 7(1).

[10] Ibid, recital 23.

interests of society.[11] The Citizenship Directive contemplates three levels of protection against the expulsion of the Union's citizens from host Member States: the 'basic' level, on grounds of public policy and public security; an intermediate level, on the basis of which persons who have acquired permanent residence in the host state may be expelled for *serious* grounds of public policy or public security; and enhanced protection, whereby persons that have lived in the host state for longer than 10 years can be subject to expulsion only on grounds of *imperative grounds of public security*.[12]

As a result, the Directive gives substance to EU citizenship, by setting the goal of effective integration of the Union's citizens into every Member State. Such an aim is mainly pursued through two complementary tools. On the one hand, the right to reside is defended by the guarantee not to be expelled from the host Member State; on the other, protection against expulsion is achieved after the person concerned has spent a determined period of residence therein.

Detention and citizenship are highly interdependent. On the one hand, there is the issue as to whether rights are regarded as a vehicle of, or a reward for, integration. On the other, if integration is a prerequisite for acquiring and maintaining rights, the consequences a polity attaches to detention can dramatically change the position of the citizen. The Court has traditionally been adamant that curtailing EU citizenship rights for deterrence purposes is incompatible with EU law, and that the impact of wrongdoings on citizenship rights must reflect the blameworthiness of the individual.

However, the Court's approach to the area has more recently moved away from the traditional logic crystallised in the Citizenship Directive outlined above. Such a U-turn emerges from the analysis of the following cases: *Tsakouridis*,[13] *PI*,[14] *Onuekwere*,[15] *MG*,[16] *CS*[17] and *Rendón Marín*.[18] These rulings concern different situations: *Tsakouridis* and *PI* are concerned with expulsion from one Member State to another; *Onuekwere* and *MG* raise the question whether time spent in prison can be considered for the purpose of acquiring the right to permanent residence or protection against expulsion from the host Member State; *Rendón Marín* and *CS* deal with the expulsion due to criminal convictions, from the

[11] Ibid, Art 27(2).

[12] Ibid, Art 28.

[13] Case C-145/09, *Land Baden-Württemberg v Panagiotis Tsakouridis*, judgment of 23 November 2010, [2010] I-11979.

[14] Case C-348/09, *PI v Oberburgmeisterin der Stadt Remscheid*, judgment of 22 May 2012, EU:C:2012:300.

[15] Case C-378/12, *Nnamdi Onuekwere v Secretary of State for the Home Department*, judgment of 16 January 2014, EU:C:2014:13.

[16] Case C-400/12, *Secretary of State for the Home Department v MG*, judgment of 16 January 2014, [2014].

[17] Case C-304/14, *Secretary of State for the Home Department v CS*, judgment of 13 September 2016, EU:C:2016:674.

[18] Case C-165/14 *Alfredo Rendón Marín v Administración del Estado*, judgment of 13 September 2016, EU:C:2016:675.

Union altogether, of third-country nationals having full custody of minors who are EU citizens.

Such variance notwithstanding, they are part of a bigger picture on the impact of detention – and what it represents – on the persons concerned. That picture is drawn along two main lines. On the one hand, the effectiveness of the Directive must be preserved. Since the system rewards genuine integration, granting residence rights to detainees would divest the Directive of its objectives. Deprivation of liberty follows violation of the host state's laws, which in turn shows disregard for that state's values.[19] On the other hand, the findings are based on a debatable concept of public security, constructed by categorisation of dangerous groups of individuals: terrorists, drug traffickers and child abusers. Where a person is placed in one of the categories of individuals identified, s/he turns into a *threat* to *public security* who is to be removed from the territory.

Two levels of discussion are to be kept separate: the broader issue of the impact of criminal behaviour on citizenship rights, and the specific case of expulsion based on *public policy* and *public security* and the interpretation thereof. The commission of a crime might well lead to denial/restriction/withdrawal of rights, without necessarily resulting in expulsion measures. For example, the commission of criminal conduct during the five-year period under Article 16 of the Citizenship Directive might stand in the way of acquiring the right to permanent residence in the host state. Though this may not necessarily result automatically in expulsion from the state, it is nonetheless capable of affecting residence security for the person concerned.[20]

Historically, the CJEU has not been prone to passively accept restrictions to free movement posed by Member States merely as a consequence of criminal behaviour. Rather, it has looked at the substance of the conduct and the proportionality between that conduct and the resulting limitation. EU law subjects the adoption of coercive measures to the condition that an actual and present *threat*[21] to public policy (understood as a fundamental interest of the society) must be present[22] or – the stricter test of – public security grounds (internal and external security of the state).[23] The existence of previous criminal convictions is relevant insofar as the latter are symptoms of the *threat* mentioned above.[24] Furthermore, the requirement for individual assessment continues even once the coercive measure

[19] Case C-378/12, *Nnamdi Onuekwere Secretary of State for the Home Department*, AG's Opinion, 3 October 2013, para 47.

[20] The analysis below shows that, according to national law of certain Member States, sentencing to a given threshold of imprisonment results automatically in either the loss of the right to residence, or liability to expulsion.

[21] Case 36/75, *Roland Rutili v Minister for the Interior*, judgment of 28 October 1975, para 19.

[22] Case C-30/77, *Régina v Pierre Bouchereau*, judgment of 27 October 1977 [1977] ECR 1999, para 35.

[23] Case C-367/89, *Criminal proceedings against Aimé Richardt and Les Accessoires Scientifiques SNC*, judgment of 4 October 1991, [1991] ECR I-4621, para 22.

[24] *Bouchereau*, n 22 above, para 28.

has been adopted.[25] These constraints reveal the wariness in the field of EU citizenship towards any kinds of automaticity and abstraction:[26] coercive measures must be anchored to a case-by-case assessment. The Court has been vigilant over Member States' use of criminal law to restrict citizenship rights. The more recent paradigm shift in the Court's understanding sees disobedience to the law as a lack of integration, which leads to the denial of residence security and little space left for reintegration.

A. Change of Paradigm. Imprisonment and Permanent Residence

The first example of the Court's change of understanding concerned a case of already acquired permanent residence and custodial penalties imposed for drug dealing. Mr Tsakouridis was born in Germany in 1978, where he became entitled to unlimited residence in 2001. He was arrested in Greece in 2006 and transferred to Germany, where he was sentenced to six years and six months' imprisonment. According to German law, the conviction for certain offences would deprive the person of the right of entry and residence in Germany: the reason why he was served an expulsion order on 'imperative grounds of public security'. The Citizenship Directive allows expulsion: on serious grounds of public policy and public security, if the person has the right to permanent residence; and on imperative grounds of public security, if the person has resided in the host state for the 10 years preceding the expulsion.

The Court had to answer the question as to what absences from the host Member State during the 10-year period could prevent that person from enjoying the enhanced protection laid down in that provision of the Directive. This is a crucial question, as it leads to the decision as to what level of protection to afford the person – 'serious' or 'imperative' grounds, the latter clearly being a much higher threshold to be met. Once decided on that point of law, the Court had to answer on the interpretation of the concept of 'imperative grounds of public security'; and, more specifically, whether that concept covered Mr Tsakouridis' behaviour.

On the former issue, it must be considered whether the absence from the host state implied a transfer to another state of the person's centre of family or occupational interests. An overall assessment must be carried out based on a number of factors, such as the duration of each period of absence from the host state, the cumulative duration and the frequency of those absences, and the reasons why

[25] Joined Cases C-482/01 and C-493/01 *Georgios Orphanopoulos and Others v Land Baden-Württemberg* and *Raffaele Oliveri v Land Baden-Württemberg*, judgment of 29 April 2004, [2004] ECR I-5295, para 82.

[26] *Criminal proceedings against Donatella Calfa*, judgment of 19 January 1999, [1999] ECR I-11, paras 27–29.

the person concerned left the host Member State. In that context, the Court stated that the fact that Mr Tsakouridis had returned to Germany (the host state) only because he had to serve a custodial penalty, and that the time spent in prison 'may be taken into account as part of the overall assessment required for determining whether the integrating links previously forged with the host Member State have been broken'.[27]

Having – subtly but clearly – introduced integration as a condition of accessing enhanced protection against the expulsion, the CJEU moved on to interpret the concept of public security. The Court recalled its 'standard' definition of that concept, which covers the internal and external security[28] of the state and which may be affected by the functioning of the institutions and essential public services and the survival of the population, as well as the risk of a serious disturbance to foreign relations or to peaceful coexistence of nations, or a risk to military interests.[29] The fight against drug trafficking, it said, does not necessarily fall outside that established understanding, especially considering the devastating social and economic effects of drug trafficking. The Court referred to Framework Decision 2004/757/JHA, stating that drug trafficking poses a threat to the security of Member States.[30]

On the one hand, the Court started expanding and watering down the boundaries of public security. When developing its reasoning, the CJEU followed the Advocate General and blurred the distinction between public policy and public security, and the different levels of protection laid down in the Directive more broadly.[31] On the other, citizenship law was somehow used as a means to an end for tackling crime and supporting EU criminal law.

From the 'overall assessment' mentioned by the Court, nothing would lead one to conclude that the person had transferred to Greece the centre of his personal interest. The focus therefore became the crime committed by Mr Tsakouridis, which the CJEU had just considered as potentially falling under the concept of public security: namely, dealing in narcotics as part of an organised group. A balance must be struck between the threat (considering the time of the expulsion decision,[32] the possible penalties and sentences, the involvement in the criminal activity, and the risk of reoffending)[33] and the risk of compromising the social rehabilitation of the Union citizen in the Member State in which he has

[27] *Tsakouridis*, n 13 above, para 34.

[28] Case C-273/97 *Angela Maria Sirdar v The Army Board*, [1999] ECR I-7403, para 17; Case C-285/98 *Tanja Kreil v Bundesrepublik Deutschland*, judgment of 11 January 2000, [2000] ECR I-69, para 17.

[29] Case 72/83 *Campus Oil Limited and Others v Minister for Industry and Energy*, judgment of 10 July 1984, [1984] ECR 2727, paras 34 and 35; Case C-70/94 *Werner* [1995] ECR I-3189, para 27; Case C-423/98, *Albore*, [2000] ECR I-5965, para 22.

[30] FD 2004/757/JHA, recital 1.

[31] Case C-145/09, *Land Baden-Württemberg v Panagiotis Tsakouridis*, AG's Opinion, 8 June 2010, EU:C:2010:322, para 59.

[32] See, inter alia, Joined Cases C-482/01 and C-493/01 *Orphanopoulos and Oliveri* [2004] ECR I-5257, n 25 above, paras 77 to 79.

[33] Case 30/77 *Bouchereau*, n 22 above, [1977] ECR 1999, para 29.

become genuinely integrated, which is not only in his interest but also in that of the EU in general.[34]

When balancing these two interests, the national court must take into account the nature and seriousness of the offence committed, the duration of residence of the person concerned in the host Member State, the period which has passed since the offence was committed and the conduct of the person concerned during that period, and the solidity of their social, cultural and family ties with the host Member State.[35] A sentence of imprisonment can lead to an expulsion decision only if considered in the context of that broader complex of factors. That being the guidance on factors to be considered for the balance, the Court formally left the final choice to the national court: should the court consider that Mr Tsakouridis enjoyed the enhanced protection of Article 28(3), the fight against dealing in narcotics as part of an organised group *is capable of* being covered by the concept of 'imperative grounds of public security'; and should the referring court conclude that the protection of Article 28(2) is involved, the fight dealing in narcotics as part of an organised group *is* covered by 'serious grounds of public policy or public security'.

The judgment lays the groundwork for a shift of paradigm in many respects. Firstly, integration is regarded – though incidentally and without detailed discussion – as a requirement to access citizenship rights. Secondly, reintegration stands out as ambiguous in nature. On the one hand, rehabilitation emerges as a factor potentially contributing to residence security. When deciding on whether to use the expulsion measure, the national court must consider (also) the possible impact thereof on reintegration. On the other hand, the link between reintegration and the EU's interests more broadly hints at a supra-individual dimension of that function of penalty. The question arises whether the pursuit of reintegration in the name of a collective interest may pave the way to restrictions of rights of the person concerned. The following analysis shows that this is the case.

Thirdly, the alignment between citizenship rights and objectives of EU criminal law and policy contributes to broadening the concept of public security. The existence of a specific EU instrument (FD 2004/757/JHA) testifies to the importance of a given criminal phenomenon; which, in turn, legitimates the adoption of restrictive measures on public security grounds. A provision of citizenship law covers an 'active' goal such as the fight against drug trafficking.

The departure from the traditional, restrictive understanding of public security goes hand in hand with restricted room for substantial balance between different interests. The Court seems to be leaving to the national judge the choice on what level of protection to afford (paragraph (2) or (3) of Article 28). In reality, it is saying that protection is afforded on proof of integration, on which link hangs a form of conduct that *is* covered by serious grounds of public security. Ultimately, that balance involves a crime that the Court explicitly defines – with no nuances

[34] *Tsakouridis*, n 13 above, para 50, citing point 95 of AG's Opinion, n 31 above.
[35] *Tsakouridis*, n 13 above, para 53.

whatsoever – as a threat to public security. While debatable from different points of view, the judgment is only the first step towards a re-conceptualisation of the Court's approach to detention and citizenship.

B. A Fundamental Interest of Society?

PI further shifts the paradigm in the CJEU's approach. Mr PI[36] was born in Italy and had lived in Germany since 1987, where he was granted a residence permit. In 2006, he was sentenced to seven years and six months' imprisonment for sexual assault, sexual coercion and rape of a minor. In 2008, he lost the right to enter and reside in Germany, and was served an expulsion measure.

On that ground, the Court was asked whether the 'imperative grounds of public security' cover only threats posed to the internal and external security of the state in terms of the continued existence of the state with its institutions and important public services, the survival of the population, foreign relations and the peaceful co-existence of nations. The Court was therefore called on again to express itself on the interpretation of public security in the context of enhanced protection against expulsion. *Tsakouridis* had highlighted how that concept might have a significant impact on the residence security of the person concerned.

The Court's reasoning revolved entirely around EU criminal law. Firstly, Article 83(1) TFEU considers the sexual exploitation of children to be one of the areas of particularly serious crime in which the EU may enact substantive criminal law.[37] Secondly, the particularly high penalties and imprisonment terms imposed by Directive 2011/93/EU for sexual exploitation of children reflect the objective established by primary law and testify to the seriousness of those offences.[38] On those grounds, the Court concluded that

> it is open to the Member States to regard criminal offences such as those referred to in the second subparagraph of Article 83(1) TFEU as constituting a particularly serious threat to one of the fundamental interests of society, which might pose a direct threat to the calm and physical security of the population and thus be covered by the concept of 'imperative grounds of 'public security', capable of justifying an expulsion measure under Article 28(3) of Directive 2004/38, as long as the manner in which such offences were committed discloses particularly serious characteristics, which is a matter for the referring court to determine on the basis of an individual examination of the specific case before it.

[36] L Azoulai and S Coutts, 'Restricting Union Citizens' Residence Rights on Grounds of Public Security. Where Union Citizenship and the AFSJ Meet: P.I.' (2013) 50(2) *Common Market Law Review* 553–70; Kochenov and Pirker, 'Deporting the Citizens within the European Union', n 1 above.

[37] *PI* judgment, n 14 above, para 25.

[38] Ibid, paras 26–27. The Courts referred to the Directive 2011/93/EU of the European Parliament and of the Council of 13 December 2011 on combating the sexual abuse and sexual exploitation of the children and child pornography, and replacing Council Framework Decision 2004/68/JHA, [2011] OJ L335/1, 17.12.2011.

The Court mitigated its conclusions by finding that this examination includes the individual's propensity to act in the same way in the future, the integration into that state and the extent of his/her links with the country of origin, and any material change in the circumstances since the expulsion order was issued.[39]

The judgment built on the findings in *Tsakouridis*. EU criminal law has become the only authoritative argument to justify a reformed understanding of public security, which in turn significantly jeopardises the tenability of residence security as envisaged by citizenship law. The reference to secondary EU law – introduced in *Tsakouridis* – is here flanked by a controversial use of Article 83(1). As noted, that provision 'serves as a legal basis circumscribing the competence of the European Union to adopt legislation on criminal offences and sanctions, and not as a legal basis for interpreting exceptions to EU free movement and citizenship rights'.[40] The end result of this transplant is that

> in terms of EU citizenship, it serves to dilute the protection offered by EU law; in terms of EU criminal law, by elevating the enumeration of the conduct listed in Article 83(1) to a ground justifying exceptions to rights granted under EU law, it affirms an uncritical securitised vision of EU criminal law and transforms Article 83(1) TFEU into symbolic criminal law.[41]

The judgment therefore makes citizenship and criminal law speak the same language. Imperative grounds of public security are no longer genuine, present and sufficiently serious threats in one of the exceptional circumstances referred to by the Court in its traditional understanding. That concept is no longer a restrictively interpreted exception to the rule (residence security), but a tool whereby citizenship pulls in the direction of EU criminal policy and rights are curbed in order to comply with the objectives established in that area.

This further departure from a traditional understanding is visible in the reduced space that the reasoning devotes to the individual assessment, which is something expressly prescribed by the Directive. In comparison to *Tsakouridis*, the engagement with the personal circumstances in *PI* – let alone the proportionality test – is significantly weaker. The use of reintegration is a showcase for such development. Not only

> The revitalization of punishment-plus-banishment is difficult to square with the objective of rehabilitation, rooted in human dignity and committed to by the States yet it feeds a misplaced expectation that States can always exclude 'bad' Union citizens – as if the intended strengthening of protection through the Directive had never happened.[42]

[39] *PI*, Court's judgment, n 14 above, paras 28–34.

[40] V Mitsilegas, *EU Criminal Law after Lisbon* (Oxford, Hart Publishing, 2016) 232–33.

[41] Ibid.

[42] N Nic Shuibhne, 'Limits Rising, Duties Ascending: The Changing Legal Shape of Union Citizenship' (2015) 52(4) *Common Market Law Review* 889, 923–24.

Though included in the factors to be considered when deciding on the application of Article 28(3), the actual meaning of reintegration is considerably downplayed when placed in the broader picture drawn by the CJEU in *PI*. Similarly to *Tsakouridis*, reintegration must be considered jointly with integration in a case where the CJEU itself is acknowledging that the conduct at stake may be considered an imperative ground of public security. On the other hand, the tendency to re-offend plays clearly at the expense of reintegration. That tendency should be a reason for pursing rehabilitation, whereas here it becomes a criterion for denying citizenship rights. Reintegration gives way to the interests of the security of states, that are granted the opportunity to remove non-nationals considered to be a source of disturbance, regardless of their having exercised citizenship rights.[43]

C. Integration and Prison Time

Under EU citizenship law, (1) permanent residence and (2) enhanced protection against expulsion (allowing expulsion only on imperative grounds of public security) can be acquired after (1) five, and (2) ten years of residence in the host state, respectively. What happens where part of that time is spent in detention?

Onuekwere concerned a third-country national who applied for permanent residence in the UK, having been repeatedly jailed during the five-year period provided for in the Citizenship Directive. *MG* concerned a Portuguese national who had been living in the UK for over 10 years, before being imprisoned following conviction, and served an expulsion order on serious grounds of public security.

On the one hand, the question arose as to whether time in prison can be taken into account as 'qualifying' time in a Member State to access permanent residence (*Onuewkere*) or enhanced protection (*MG*). On the other hand, the Court was asked whether detention erases the precedent 'good' period of residence, so requiring the integration clock to start ticking again.

Firstly, the Court regarded integration as a precondition of the acquisition of the right to permanent residence and enhanced protection, based on territorial, temporal and qualitative elements.[44] A prison sentence ensues from a violation, by the person concerned, of Member States' criminal law, which in turn enshrines the societal values of that state.[45] Thus, a conviction is a denial of genuine integration, and granting citizenship rights in spite of that circumstance would run counter to the aim of the Directive. If these rights require integration, the latter in turn is achieved through continuity of legal residence.[46] However, the intrinsic

[43] Ibid.
[44] *Onuekwere*, n 15 above, para 24.
[45] Ibid, para 26.
[46] Ibid, para 30.

incompatibility between detention and integration means that prison time interrupts the continuity of residence,[47] so precluding the access to citizenship rights.

For someone that commits a crime and goes to prison, the integration clock stops ticking, and starts again when the person is set free.[48] In *MG*, the CJEU tentatively mitigated its harsh conclusions by stating that

> the fact that the person concerned has resided in the host Member State during the 10 years prior to imprisonment may be taken into consideration as part of the overall assessment for determining whether the enhanced protection will be granted.[49]

After reinforcing the understanding of integration in EU citizenship as a requirement rather than objective, the CJEU generalises the equation of criminal behaviour with disregard for societal values. Taking prison time into account would run counter to the objectives of the Directive. When asked about the possibility of leaving some room to the national judge[50] – to assess whether the concrete circumstances of the case might express a lack of integration – the AG denied such a possibility, with which the Court implicitly agreed: offences and penalties vary significantly throughout the Union, and 'it is for the European Union legislature to define the criteria on the basis of which and the thresholds within which it should be considered that a period of residence in prison does not interrupt residence'.[51] Not only are incredibly serious restrictions of citizenship rights justified, if in line with primary and secondary EU criminal law, but it is also for EU law to harmonise the conditions on which crime – and in particular prison time – can curb those rights.

In balancing rehabilitation and retributive functions of custodial penalties, the AG in *Onuekwere* found that clearly 'the sentence also serves the essential purpose of retribution', and

> rehabilitative function cannot result in a situation where a period spent atoning for the crime committed confers on the convicted person a right the acquisition of which requires recognition and acceptance of social values which he specifically disregarded by committing his criminal act.[52]

The judgments expressly elevate integration to the role of a precondition to citizenship rights, and erase the reference to personal circumstances through the equation of crime with lack of integration. They consolidate the instrumental role of citizenship for the goals of EU criminal law, and entrust the Union legislature to establish the rules of the game in this regard.

[47] Ibid, para 32.
[48] *MG* judgment, n 16 above, paras 28–33.
[49] Ibid, paras 34–37.
[50] This approach was advocated by Germany and the Commission.
[51] *Onuekwere*, AG's Opinion, n 19 above, para 72.
[52] Ibid, paras 54–55.

In that context, reintegration is between a rock and a hard place. The Court's reasoning makes rehabilitation nearly disappear from the citizenship vocabulary, and renders reintegration very difficult to pursue in practice. The process of rehabilitation follows the imposition of a sentence, which in turn however denies integration. In what cases then is a person entitled to reintegration in a state other than that of his/her nationality?

D. National Presumption and Expulsion from the Union

Loss of residence security may result in EU nationals being forced to return to their country of nationality. The scenario surfaced in *Rendón Marín* and *CS*, two TCNs having full custody of minor Union citizens. In *Rendón Marín*, the coercive measure would ensue from the person concerned illegally staying in Spain, as he was refused the right to reside therein. This refusal was based on Spanish law, which automatically excludes the right to residence to those who have a criminal record. As for *CS*, the UK law provides that third-country nationals convicted of a criminal offence of a certain gravity (in this case, punishable by one year imprisonment) are automatically liable to deportation. The children – as family members dependent on the TCN – would be subject to expulsion as well.

The TCNs fell within the scope of EU law as bearers of rights derived from EU nationals. Article 20 TFEU, enshrining Union citizens' right to free movement and residence within the EU, prohibits measures depriving those citizens of the genuine enjoyment of the substance of the rights conferred by Union citizenship.[53] That would be the case in a scenario where denying the right of residence to the TCNs would oblige the citizens (in this case the children) to leave the territory of the EU altogether.

Member States remain free to rely on public policy and public security exceptions, which, however, must be applied in compliance with EU law. This means respecting the principles laid down in Articles 27 and 28, applied to TCNs in this specific situation on the basis of Article 3(1) of the Citizenship Directive.[54] To this end, expulsion could not result solely from the criminal record of the person concerned. The personal conduct of the individual concerned must represent a genuine and present threat.[55] The CJEU distinguishes more clearly between public

[53] Case C-34/09, *Gerardo Ruiz Zambrano v Office national de l'emploi (ONEm)*, judgment of 8 March 2011, EU:C:2011:124.

[54] The provision states that the Directive shall apply also to, inter alia, the dependent direct relatives in the ascending line.

[55] The Court has pointed out that the condition relating to the existence of a present threat must, in principle, be fulfilled at the time when the measure at issue is adopted. See, inter alia, Case C-30/77 *Bouchereau*, n 22 above, [1977] ECR 1999, para 28), and that justifications on grounds of a general preventive nature and ordered for the purpose of deterring other foreign nationals cannot be accepted. See to that effect, Case C-33/07, *Jipa* [2008] ECR I-5157, paras 23 and 24; and Case C-441/02, *Commission v Germany* [2006] ECR I-3449, para 93.

policy and public security,[56] although it does not elaborate on which level of protection the persons concerned would be entitled to. Furthermore, the CJEU recalled its previous case-law and reaffirmed that the fight against drug trafficking or against terrorism *is* covered by the concept of public security.[57]

The assessment in terms of public policy or public security (based on the personal conduct of the individual concerned, the length and legality of his residence on the territory of the Member State concerned, the nature and gravity of the offence committed, and the extent to which the TCN concerned is currently a danger to society)[58] must be balanced against the child's best interests[59] and the right to private and family life, enshrined by Articles 24(2) and 7 CFREU respectively.[60]

The Court's rulings in *Rendón Marín* and *CS* seem to mitigate the harsh stance taken in the previous decisions analysed above. This could be explained, amongst other factors, by the specific circumstances of the cases. Unlike other judgments, the refusal of the right to residence and protection against expulsion as a consequence of criminal convictions could have led the persons concerned – and the Union citizens of whom the TCNs were fully in charge – to be deported outside the EU.

On closer inspection, however, the judgment shows a significant degree of continuity with the previous chapters of the saga. This can be seen specifically in the way the CJEU reconstructs the concept of public security. While declaring the need to interpret it narrowly, the Court confirms its previous case-law. By endorsing an understanding of public security built around the identification of dangerous categories of individual – the drug trafficker,[61] the rapist, the terrorist[62] – the CJEU brings EU citizenship and EU criminal law even closer together. At first sight, the Court's approach might express an attempt at establishing commonality of values within the EU through criminal law. On closer inspection, and in light of the case-law discussed so far, quite the opposite seems true. With the fight against drug trafficking, for example, being covered by Article 28 Directive 2004/38, public security – and, broadly, citizenship rights restrictions

[56] Case C-165/14 *Alfredo Rendón Marín v Administración del Estado*, n 18 above, para 83. In particular, 'the concept of "public policy" presupposes the existence, in addition to the disturbance of the social order which any infringement of the law involves, of a genuine, present and sufficiently serious threat affecting one of the fundamental interests of society', whereas public security includes the internal security of a Member State and its external security, including a threat to the functioning of institutions and essential public services and the survival of the population, as well as the risk of a serious disturbance to foreign relations or to peaceful coexistence of nations, or a risk to military interests.

[57] Case C-304/14, *Secretary of State for the Home Department v CS*, n 17 above, para 39.

[58] Case C-165/14, *Alfredo Rendón Marín v Administración del Estado*, n 18 above, para 86.

[59] The CJEU made reference in particular to his age, his situation in the Member State concerned and the extent to which he is dependent on the parent. See ECtHR, *Jeunesse v The Netherlands*, Application No 12738/10, judgment of 3 October 2014, para 118.

[60] Case C-165/14, *Alfredo Rendón Marín v Administración del Estado*, n 18 above, para 81.

[61] *Tsakouridis*, n 13 above, paras 45 and 46.

[62] Case C-100/01, *Ministre de l'Intérieur v Aitor Oteiza Olazabal*, judgment of 26 November 2002, [2002] ECR I-10981, paras 12 and 35.

based also on that concept – is used to actively contribute to the priorities of the EU agenda in criminal law. Where these priorities have not yet been established, it is for the Union legislature to decide on how detention can restrict citizenship rights. Values might then be more a means to an end for legitimating the use of EU criminal law. By reaffirming an understanding of public security as it has emerged from previous judgments, the Court further turns EU citizenship law upside down, by relying on abstract anthropological models of offenders and restricting the space for individual assessment as required by EU citizenship law.

E. Detention, Wrongdoings and Citizenship Rights

EU citizenship law – and Directive 2004/38/EC in particular – explicitly aims to promote the integration of citizens throughout the Union. Residence security as the core of that system – the right to enter and stay in the territory of another state – has one fundamental centrepiece in the obligation to found potentially detrimental measures on a strict and individual assessment, based on the existence of an actual and present threat. Such a test is required by both *public policy* and *public security* exceptions. These concepts, in the traditional approach of the CJEU and the Citizenship Directive, are clearly kept separate, with public security requiring a much higher threshold to be met. This is especially the case when it comes to persons who have legally resided in the host state for many years prior to the measure in question.

The cases discussed above represent a stretch in the interpretation of the impact of detention on citizenship rights. As conditions and limits are reversed as instances of obligations or responsibility,[63] personal integration into the host society – resting on quantitative, territorial and qualitative elements – emerges as the overriding duty and the decisive criterion for allocating rights. The Court then 'shift[s] away from equal rights as a means for integration, towards an output-oriented assessment that links citizens' rights to the degree of integration'.[64]

This approach rests on a drastic change in the interpretation of the EU citizenship objectives, and an expanding interpretation of public security. If rights are considered rewards for integration, detention stands in the way. The construction of public security through the identification of categories of threats waters down the different levels of protection laid down by the Directive. Detention, and what it represents, attracts a strong stigma that reduces the possibility for individual assessment. This process of abstraction is explicitly upheld by the AG in *Onuekwere*, where the possibility for a proportionality test at national

[63] N Nic Shuibhne, 'Limits Rising, Duties Ascending', n 42 above, 900 onwards.

[64] D Thym, 'The elusive limits of solidarity: Residence rights of and social benefits for economically inactive Union citizens' (2015) 52(1) *Common Market Law Review* 17–50, 39.

level is sacrificed on the altar of the autonomy of the EU legislature. It would be hard to argue that the legislation already includes a sufficiently detailed set of circumstances as to recreate a sort of proportionality test. Since *Tsakouridis*, the CJEU has explicitly acknowledged that the impact of detention and crime on citizenship rights is an aspect of EU law which is silent. This explains why, inter alia, the Court's traditional and more legally sound understanding of public security – translated into the Citizenship Directive – was based on an individual and case-by-case assessment.

One of the arguments used by the Court is that the Directive requires *legal* residence for achieving the rights at stake, which would exclude detention periods. With the strongly residence-based framework of EU citizenship law in mind, if we accept an equation between detention and illegality of residence – and the further consequences stemming from that presumption – what might be questioned is the prohibition of grounding restrictive measures merely on criminal record.

This acts as a bridge between the present discussion and the next section. The consequences of such an understanding might be even broader. Firstly, the Court's findings seem to be based on the assumption that you cannot pursue reintegration without integration first – denied per se by any criminal conduct. Admittedly, reintegration is tentatively referred to as *one of* the factors to be included in the overall assessment for the national judge when deciding on the expulsion measure. In *Tsakouridis*, a connection was established between the EU's interests and reintegration. In *PI*, the propensity to re-offend (a logical trigger of rehabilitation measures) was acknowledged as a criterion for deciding whether to remove the source of disturbance from the state. This not only reveals the belief that wrongdoers are mostly a problem of their state of nationality – which somehow contradicts the very spirit of EU citizenship and the creation of the Union as a borderless area. It is the bellwether of an understanding of reintegration that – consistent with what emerges from other areas of Union law discussed below – is mainly oriented to the protection of the public rather than individual rehabilitation.

Furthermore, a strong link emerges from these cases and EU criminal law. The 'serious areas of crime' approach is present in the Union law and policy, where institutional documents and law refer to the need for fighting specifically identified major crime threats. This interaction is embodied by the Court's use of Article 83(1) TFEU in *PI* and *Tsakouridis*. The legal basis for the Union's exercise of competences in substantive criminal law – and in secondary law instruments adopted pursuant to that provision – is an authoritative argument to legitimate the adoption of rights restriction. Or, from a different angle, citizenship rules on rights restrictions are used to legitimate EU criminal law – and EU competences more in general. Such a dynamic finds mature completion in *Onuekwere*. There the AG – with the CJEU silently agreeing – denied the national judge the possibility to apply a proportionality test, and to decide to take into account prison time for the purposes of permanent residence: it is for the Union legislature to determine the relationship between crime and citizenship.

Admittedly, *Rendón Marín* and *CS* should be distinguished from *Tsakouridis*, *PI*, *Onuekwere*[65] and *MG* in that they: constitute examples of *static* cases – like *Ruiz Zambrano*, there is no cross-border element at play;[66] and would imply expulsion from the Union altogether of EU citizens for acts they have not committed. However, those judgments state the need for a restrictive interpretation of *public policy* and *public security*, and simultaneously confirm (especially in *CS*) the broader understanding of those concepts established through the judgments discussed above. Those judgments reveal, however, the potential for use of the Charter to limit the impact of crime and detention on citizenship rights.

The use of a Union territory-based argument, however, should not be mistaken for an allusion to values commonality in Europe. The Court is simply establishing a higher threshold for an undeniably more harmful situation: the expulsion from the EU of minor Union citizens who are atoning for someone else's misbehaviour. The CJEU, when referring to values, mostly refers to the values of the host Member State. The overriding concern hereby addressed is the state's power to get rid of the deviant, independently of his/her status of EU citizen. Citizenship, indeed, rests on the existence of an underpinning community, where the polity reaction is meant to deal 'collectively with the wrong' and to preserve – rather than deny – the offender's civic standing.[67]

Section III focuses on measures of EU law pursuing reintegration of the person concerned. The analysis complements section II, and confirms the idea of a state-centred approach to reintegration where the persons concerned are sidelined for reasons of public security.

III. Deprivation of Liberty and Reintegration in EU Law

A. Specific Deterrence and Mutual Recognition in Criminal Matters

Freedom of movement and residence in states across the EU is the epitome of Union citizenship. That fundamental status rests on the right to enter and stay, and pursues integration through recognition – inter alia – of the right to residence and protection against expulsion. If social cohesion beyond the formal relationship of

[65] Albeit *Onuekwere* concerned the right to residence, the analysis of the case-law showed how intertwined that right and the protection against expulsion can be.

[66] To be thorough, in *Rendón Marín*, n 18 above, there was a potential cross-border element as his daughter was living in Spain while having Polish nationality.

[67] RA Duff, 'A Criminal Law for Citizens' (2010) 14(3) *Theoretical Criminology* 293–309. See also RA Duff, 'Law, Language and Community: Some Preconditions of Criminal Liability' (1998) 18(2) *Oxford Journal of Legal Studies* 189–206.

nationality is to be achieved, re-conceptualisation is important for principles traditionally applied – nearly – exclusively in the context of the countries–nationals relationship. It is against that background that the present discussion takes place. The question is, once again, whether the creation of an EU law of deprivation of liberty (be it in immigration, asylum, criminal matters or citizenship) is tenable without a rethink of strongholds of personal liberty.

The previous analysis revealed the close connection between integration and reintegration, and the impact this link can have on citizenship rights of those subject to a custodial penalty. The post-*Tsakouridis* case-law brought to the fore the role of integration as: a pre-condition for acquisition of residence security, with the latter acting as a reward for citizens' obedience of states' laws; denied per se by detention and criminal behaviour. That stance is relevant to the rehabilitative function of (custodial) penalties, acknowledged by Member States and referred to by the AG as a general principle of EU law. If crime denies integration, the question arises as to what room there actually is for EU-reintegration, understood as reintegration into the state where the citizens have established themselves.

Secondly, the very understanding of reintegration in EU law – if any – must be investigated. The reference in *Tsakouridis* to reintegration in the interest of the person *and* the EU itself reflects the debate on the possible approaches to the subject. Broadly, rehabilitation is an expression of consequentialist theories of punishment and is meant 'to reintegrate the offender into society after a period of punishment, and to design the content of the punishment so as to achieve this'.[68] It can be pursued from a supra-individual perspective and be directed towards ensuring that the criminal no longer poses a threat to society; it can focus on the person, and aim towards their constructive return to society.[69] Scholars have shown wariness of the former perspective, objecting that 'mere utility for society cannot be the only reason to attempt rehabilitation', and that 'morally, rehabilitation is required to be undertaken in the best interest of the offender to be at least given a chance to become a positive, productive member of the community'.[70]

Since rehabilitation presupposes the existence of an underlying community into which to reintegrate, the question arises whether an EU-wide approach can be envisaged. The homogeneity of the EU as a community of values is not as strong as that of Member States. However, the very concept of EU citizenship seems barely compatible with an understanding of 'collective dealing with the wrong' as mere cooperation between authorities to coercively move the offender from one state to another; or, in other words, to allow the host state to get rid of the source of disturbance. Quite the contrary, it is for the state to take charge of the person, and

[68] B Hudson, *Understanding Justice: An introduction to ideas, perspectives and controversies in modern penal theory*, 2nd edn (Buckingham, Open University Press, 2003) 26.

[69] MS Moore, *Law and Psychiatry: Rethinking the Relationship* (Cambridge, Cambridge University Press, 1984) 234.

[70] MC Materni, 'Criminal Punishment and the Pursuit of Justice' (2013) 2 *British Journal of American Legal Studies* 263, 292.

reaffirm his/her existence as part of that community that goes through (re)inclusion of the person in the society where s/he lives.

The traditional understanding of EU citizenship is not one where the wrongdoer is – almost – automatically refused or withdrawn rights, and physically removed from the territory of the *host* Member State. However, when the Court states – as it does in one of the cases discussed below – that detention and crime deny integration *tout court*, it is depersonalising the citizen. If detention precludes integration, in certain cases it erases the integration link already established. On this view, the detrimental effect on reintegration caused by expulsion, denial or withdrawal of rights is not relevant: in the absence of integration, there is no reintegration to pursue. The *host* states are places where non-nationals (but still EU citizens) are living oxymora: they are perpetually temporary visitors.[71]

The analysis of the case-law on the Citizenship Directive highlighted the CJEU's stance on reintegration that can be indirectly inferred from its understanding of reintegration. This section completes the picture and focuses on those pieces of EU law that expressly engage with rehabilitation. These are three instruments of mutual recognition in criminal matters: the EAW Framework Decision, and specifically Article 4(6) thereof; the Framework Decision on transfer of prisoners; and the Framework Decision on probation measures. While the EAW FD is mainly an instrument of forced movement, Article 4(6) is an optional ground for refusing execution of the EAW with a view to pursuing the reintegration of the person concerned in the host state. Therefore, it works as a limit to forced movement for the benefit of a person's residence security in a state other than that of his/her nationality. Symmetrically, the other two FDs aim to enhance chances of reintegration through transfer of the person from the state of conviction to where they have deeper personal connections even beyond the mere nationality link. Therefore, and in spite of being instruments of coercive transfer, these measures are in theory aimed at reinforcing residence security. They constitute a foundation in creating an EU-wide understanding of reintegration, where citizens can serve their penalty where they have their real social, family and economic links. Facilitating reintegration can pave the way to strengthening the connection with the state where detainees have 'hung their hats', which is something that section II brought to the fore as a decisive factor in enjoying their fully-fledged status of EU citizens.

Is, therefore, the creation of a borderless area flanked by (the possibility of) reintegration without frontiers? On closer inspection, this seems not really to be the case. In the following sub-section, the analysis revolves around three CJEU rulings

[71] The original draft of the Directive as proposed by the Commission would have prevented the expulsion of permanent residents. See S Maslowski, 'The Expulsion of European Union Citizens from the Host Member State: Legal Grounds and Practice' (2015) 4(2) *Central and Eastern European Migration Review* 61–85, 69.

on Article 4(6): *Kozlowski*,[72] *Wolzenburg*[73] and *Lopes Da Silva*.[74] While the Court here upholds reintegration into the host state, it mitigates its stance through granting the Member State a 'certain margin of discretion' and requires of the person a minimum level of integration therein. Thereafter, the analysis moves on to the FDs on probation measures and transfer of prisoners. The instruments reveal the EU legislature's approach to reintegration as focused on states' interests and public safety. The joint reading of the scenarios on integration and reintegration further highlights the problematic Union standpoint on detainees and citizenship rights.

B. Reintegration and Judicial Cooperation

Kozlowski,[75] *Wolzenburg* and *Lopes Da Silva* concerned the interpretation of Article 4(6) EAW FD. Such a provision allows the national judge to refuse the execution of an EAW, where 'the requested person is staying in, or is a national or a resident of the executing Member State and that State undertakes to execute the sentence or detention order in accordance with its domestic law'.[76] *Kozlowski* concerned a Polish national convicted to a custodial sentence in Germany. The Polish authorities issued an EAW against him for another conviction. The core of the reference related to the function to be attached to Article 4(6) EAW FD and the meaning of the terms 'resident' and 'staying'. The AG highlighted the relevant function of this rule, that is to say facilitating the reintegration of the convicted person at the end of his sentence. Generally speaking, both the EU[77] and Council of Europe[78] acknowledge that prison sentences are intended to have a corrective

[72] Case C-66/08, *Szymon Kozlowski*, judgment of 17 July 2008, [2008] ECR I-6041.

[73] Case C-123/08, *Dominic Wolzenburg*, judgment of 6 October 2009, [2009] ECR I-9621.

[74] Case C-42/11, *Proceedings concerning the execution of a European arrest warrant issued against João Pedro Lopes Da Silva Jorge*, judgment of 5 September 2012.

[75] For comments see E Herlin-Karnell, 'European Arrest Warrant Cases and the Principles of Non-Discrimination and EU Citizenship' (2010) 73(5) *The Modern Law Review* 824; Mitsilegas, 'The Limits of Mutual Trust in Europe's Area of Freedom, Security and Justice' (2012) 31(1) *Yearbook of European Law* 319, 338 onwards; TP Marguery, 'EU Citizenship and European Arrest Warrant: The Same Rights for All?' (2011) 27(73) *Merkourios* 84–91; Janssen, *The Principle of Mutual Recognition in EU Law* (Oxford, Oxford University Press, 2013), 207 onwards.

[76] L Marin, '"A Spectre Is Haunting Europe": European Citizenship in the Area of Freedom, Security and Justice – Some Reflections on the Principles of Non Discrimination (on the Basis of Nationality), Mutual Recognition and Mutual Trust Originating from the European Arrest Warrant' (2011) 17(4) *European Public Law* 705–28.

[77] European Parliament Resolution on respect for human rights in the European Union (1997) ([1999] OJ C98, 279), where it is stated that custodial sentences must have a corrective and reintegrative function (para 78). At Member State level, see for example, Article 2 of the German Law on the execution of sentences of imprisonment (*Strafvollzugsgesetz*). With regard to Spain and Italy Constitutions, see Article 25(2) and Article 27(3) respectively.

[78] See Recommendation No R (87) 3 of the Committee of Ministers to Member States on the European Prison Rules, adopted on 12 February 1987 and replaced by Recommendation Rec(2006)2,

and a social rehabilitation function, and that their main objective is the human and social reintegration of the prisoner. In the relevant documents, the Member States hold that an imprisonment regime should not cause the detainee to feel excluded from the community. This is possible when detention conditions help the person concerned to preserve his family life, as well as to (re)acquire employment at the end of the sentence.

The Court agreed with the AG, as to the rehabilitative function of Article 4(6). It found that the meaning of 'resident' and 'staying' are autonomous concepts of EU law, and so have to be interpreted uniformly. The CJEU found that the former covers those situations in which the requested person has established an actual place of residence (intended as the main centre of interest) in the executing Member State. On the other side, the same person is 'staying' when, following a stable period of presence in that Member State, they have acquired connections with it which are of a similar degree to those resulting from residence. In order to establish whether this is the case, the national court must take into consideration factors such as the length, nature and conditions of presence and the family and economic connections which that person has with the executing Member State.

An involution in the approach to reintegration can be seen in *Wolzenburg*. The case concerned a German national who moved to The Netherlands and was employed therein. The German authorities issued an EAW against Mr Wolzenburg. The referring court asked for a preliminary ruling relating to the compatibility with the EAW FD of the Dutch law implementing it. The Dutch law distinguished between Dutch and other nationals. As for the first category, the refusal of the execution was automatic. However, should the warrant involve a non-Dutch national, the domestic judge would verify whether or not the person concerned was in possession of a residence permit of an indefinite duration, achievable by virtue of Article 16 of the Citizenship Directive (namely after five years' residence therein). Therefore, at stake there was in particular the compatibility of such a distinction with Article 4(6), the principle of non-discrimination.

The Court regarded such a difference of treatment as falling within the margin of discretion granted to Member States by Article 4(6). The Member State of execution is therefore entitled to pursue the reintegration objective only with those persons who have demonstrated a certain degree of integration into the society of that Member State. This allows refusal to surrender a Member State's nationals, as well as the requirement of a five-year period of residence in that state for other EU citizens. The Court stated that Article 4(6) precludes a Member State from making the application of that ground for refusal subject to the possession of a permanent residence permit. However, it found that the principle of non-discrimination does not preclude refusal to execute an EAW against its own nationals, while requiring other EU citizens to have lawfully resided therein for a

adopted on 11 January 2006. See also the Convention of the Council of Europe on the Transfer of Sentenced Persons of 21 March 1983.

continuous period of five years. Therefore, Member States have a margin of discretion as to who – as a non-national – is entitled to reintegrate there. The pursuit of reintegration may presuppose a degree of integration, expressed for example by a period of residence of five-years – which is also the threshold provided in the Citizenship Directive for the acquisition of permanent residence.

In *Lopes Da Silva*,[79] the CJEU was asked as to the compatibility of the French law implementing the EAW FD with the principle of non-discrimination. In particular, the national legal regime automatically excluded non-French nationals from the scope of Article 4(6). The Court recognised the function underlying Article 4(6), and found that Member States must exercise their discretion consistently with the duty to respect fundamental rights laid down in the FD.[80] Furthermore, Member States cannot exclude a non-national from the scope of Article 4(6), without allowing an individual assessment.

This case-law is particularly important in that it introduced the reintegration element into the EAW FD. However, the judgments allude to an approach to reintegration less person-centred, and more as a tool in the hands of Member States to fight crime. Firstly, non-nationals are afforded the opportunity to pursue *reintegration* in the host state *so long as* they show a certain level of *integration* in that society. On coupling the *Wolzenburg* and *Onuekwere* findings, the question arises as to what is the margin for reintegration in the host state, if a crime per se denies any integration there? Secondly, the AG stressed that reintegration is key to *society interests* and the *fight against crime*. Such an argument seems to be embedded in a supra-individual dimension of reintegration that the Court has already manifested in *Tsakouridis*. The Court in *Kozlowski* and *Lopes Da Silva* upheld an interpretation of Article 4(6) EAW FD that enhances the position of non-nationals to reintegrate into the state they have moved to, which in turn can strengthen their connection with the latter and increase their residence security. Allowing for the requirement of a certain degree of integration to pursue reintegration, as the Court did in *Wolzenburg*, is not unreasonable per se. It becomes worrying, however, if read in conjunction with the presumption that integration is denied by any criminal behaviour. Reintegration logically ensues from the commission of an offence, which per se is incompatible with integration.

The FDs on probation measures and transfer of prisoners are showcases for the use of reintegration with this supra-individual mind-set. The FD on the transfer of prisoners[81] creates a mechanism of mutual recognition of judgments involving deprivation of liberty between Member States. When the judgment is recognised

[79] Case C-42/11, *Proceedings concerning the execution of a European arrest warrant issued against João Pedro Lopes Da Silva Jorge*, judgment of 5 September 2012, para 49.

[80] *Lopes Da Silva*, Court's judgment, ibid, para 34.

[81] Council Framework Decision 2008/909/JHA of 27 November 2008 on the application of the principle of mutual recognition to judgments in criminal matters imposing custodial sentences or measures involving deprivation of liberty for the purposes of their enforcement, [2008] OJ L327/27, 5 December 2008.

by the executing Member State, the prisoner is consequently transferred thereto. The purpose of the FD is to increase the prisoners' chances of reintegration. However, in the preamble it is stated that the requirement of consent of the person concerned should no longer be dominant.[82] The FD foresees the transfer of prisoners to another Member State without requiring their consent when: the executing state is where the sentenced person lives; the sentenced person will be deported once s/he is released from the enforcement of the sentence on the basis of an expulsion or deportation consequential to the judgment. Furthermore, the prisoner is provided with no guarantees in any phases of the recognition/transfer procedure, save a generic 'opportunity' to express his/her opinion.[83]

The side-lining of the prisoner is rather telling of the EU law approach to reintegration. Consistent with the stance emerging from the case-law on the Citizenship Directive, rehabilitation is not in the hands of the person concerned. The removal of the need for consent to the transfer is very problematic not only in itself, but also for the grounds underlying it: the person will be transferred to the state where s/he would have been sent on the basis of an expulsion measure.[84] Section II clearly showed that the CJEU has legitimated extremely controversial expulsions from Member States where Union citizens had resided for most of their lives. The combined operation of the EU law approach to integration and reintegration seriously jeopardises residence security for detainees and weakens their citizenship status significantly.

The FD on probation measures[85] provides for the application of mutual recognition to judgments and probation decisions with a view to the supervision of probation measures and alternative sanctions. The aims of the FD are to enhance the prospects of the sentenced person being reintegrated into society *and* to improve monitoring of compliance with probation measures and alternative sanctions. To this end, the FD provides that the recognition is carried out where: the sentenced person has returned or wants to return to the Member State in which he/she is 'lawfully and ordinarily residing'; or the individual has opted for another Member State, with the latter having allowed for the execution.[86] Though the FD may be triggered also by the person concerned, EU law even in this case provides the individual with no procedural rights during the entire phase of recognition and transfer. Furthermore, the FD provides for a one-size-fits-all ground (where exceptional circumstances occur) for postponing the transfer until further notice,

[82] Ibid, recital 5, Art 4.

[83] Ibid, Art 6.

[84] For a critical assessment of the approach to social rehabilitation in the FD, see Adriano Martufi, 'Assessing the resilience of "social rehabilitation" as a rationale for transfer: A commentary on the aims of Framework Decision 2008/909/JHA' (2018) 9 *New Journal of European Criminal Law* 43.

[85] Council Framework Decision 2008/947/JHA of 27 November 2008 on the application of the principle of mutual recognition to judgments and probation decisions with a view to the supervision of probation measures and alternative sanctions, [2008] OJ L337/102, 16 December 2008.

[86] Ibid, Art 5.

and for delaying *sine die* the release of the persons concerned and their process of reintegration.

These two FDs seem to confirm the idea of the EU law approach to reintegration that is largely in the hands of Member States. Apart from setting aside the involvement of the person concerned in any phase of the procedure, they allow Member States to suspend the transfer on very broadly-worded grounds, so postponing until further notice the pursuit of reintegration at states' complete discretion.

C. No Salvation Outside the Union? Extradition and Citizenship

What if judicial cooperation forces a Union citizen outside the EU territory? The CJEU was asked this question in the *Petruhhin* case.[87] The facts concerned an Estonian national arrested in Latvia, with the latter Member State requested to extradite him for prosecution purposes by the Russian Federation. The referring court asked whether Articles 18 TFEU and 21 TFEU must be interpreted as meaning that, for the purposes of applying an extradition agreement concluded between a Member State (Latvia) and a third state (Russian Federation), nationals of another Member State (Estonia) must benefit from the rule which prohibits the extradition by the first Member State of its own nationals. The Court firstly acknowledged that, in the absence of an international agreement between the EU and the third country concerned, the rules on extradition fall within the competence of the Member States. Nonetheless, in situations covered by EU law, the national rules concerned must have due regard to the latter.[88] This was the case of Mr Petruhhin who, by moving from Estonia to Latvia, fell within the scope of application of Article 18 TFEU.[89]

The Latvian rules on extradition afford protection against extradition only to Latvian nationals. The difference of treatment resulting in the extradition of a Union citizen who has moved to another Member State amounts to a restriction of freedom of movement under Article 21 TFEU.[90] This restriction can be justified only where it is based on objective considerations and is proportionate to the legitimate objective of the national provisions.[91] According to Article 3(2) TEU,

[87] Case C-182/15, *Aleksei Petruhhin v Latvijas Republikas Ģenerālprokuratūra*, judgment of 6 September 2016, EU:C:2016:630.

[88] C-135/08, *Janko Rottmann v Freistaat Bayern*, judgment of 2 March 2010, [2010] ECR I-1449, para 41.

[89] Case 186/87, *Ian William Cowan v Tresor public*, [1989] ECR 195, judgment of 2 February 1989, paras 17–19.

[90] Case C-182/15, *Aleksei Petruhhin*, n 87 above, paras 32–33.

[91] See, in particular, C-391/09, *Malgožata Runevič-Vardyn and Łukasz Paweł Wardyn v Vilniaus miesto savivaldybės administracija and Others*, judgment of 12 May 2011, EU:C:2011:291, para 88.

the EU offers its citizens an area of freedom, security and justice without internal frontiers, in which the free movement of persons is ensured in conjunction with appropriate measures with respect to external border controls and the prevention and combating of crime. The fight against impunity pursued through extradition procedures should be achieved, where possible, without depriving the person of the rights provided for in Article 21 TFEU. On the basis of the principle of sincere cooperation and the existence of instruments of intra-EU surrender such as the EAW FD, the Court found that the host state (Latvia) must exchange information with the Member State of the nationality of the person concerned (Estonia), and prioritise the possible issue of an EAW over extradition.[92]

While in the *Pisciotti* case the Court has subsequently admitted the possibility for Member States to refuse extradition only of their own nationals and to surrender other EU citizens, it has also stated a caveat along the same lines as the *Petruhhin* principle: differences of treatment are possible

> provided that the requested Member State has already put the competent authorities of the Member State of which the citizen is a national in a position to seek the surrender of that citizen pursuant to a European arrest warrant and the latter Member State has not taken any action in that regard.[93]

The Court in *Petruhhin* was also asked whether, where the requested Member State intends to extradite a national of another Member State at the request of a third state, the requested state must verify that the extradition will not prejudice the rights referred to in Article 19 CFREU, and, in such a case, which criteria must be taken into account for the purposes of that verification.[94] As stated, an extradition case such as that in the main proceedings falls within the scope of EU law and, as a consequence, of the Charter. Article 19 CFREU prohibits extradition to a state where there is a serious risk that the person will be subject to inhuman or degrading treatment. The Court made it clear that the mere accession, by the requesting state, to international treaties is not sufficient to ensure adequate protection, where reliable sources have reported practices resorted to or tolerated by the authorities of that state which are manifestly contrary to the principles of the ECHR. To that end, the competent authority of the requested Member State must 'rely on information that is objective, reliable, specific and properly updated'. That information may be obtained from, inter alia, judgments of the international courts (eg the ECtHR) and of the courts of the requesting third state, as well as 'decisions, reports and other documents produced by bodies of the Council of Europe or under the aegis of the United Nations'.[95]

[92] Case C-182/15, *Aleksei Petruhhin*, n 87 above, paras 47–50.

[93] Case C-191/16 *Romano Pisciotti v Bundesrepublik Deutschland*, judgment of 10 April 2018, EU:C:2018:222, para 56.

[94] The Court confirmed its findings on this point in another, subsequent case: Case C-473/15, *Peter Schotthöfer & Florian Steiner GbR v Eugen Adelsmayr*, judgment of 6 September 2017.

[95] See, to that effect, Joined Cases C-404/15 and C-659/15 PPU, *Pál Aranyosi and Robert Căldăraru v Generalstaatsanwaltschaft Bremen*, judgment of 5 April 2016, para 89.

The *Petruhhin* judgment is remarkable, though controversial in various respects.[96] It challenges the rules of international cooperation in criminal matters to protect the exercise of free movement, with scholars predicting that the combination of the principles of free movement and non-discrimination will soon affect many practices in national criminal justice systems based on nationality.[97] The Court has interpreted the restriction of free movement broadly as 'disadvantage simply because they have exercised their freedom to move within the Union'.[98] Unlike *Ruiz Zambrano*, *Rendón Marín* and *CS*, no minor EU citizens and derived rights-bearers were involved, whereas the cross-border element emerged more clearly. However, and similarly to those cases, in *Petruhhin* the Court is metaphorically reinforcing the external borders of the EU and protecting its citizens by making it harder for them to leave coercively. Two non-cumulative elements of exceptionality must be highlighted. Firstly, we see forced movement outside the Union as jeopardising the substance of EU citizenship also for independent and adult Union nationals. It is safe to assume that, were minors involved, the threshold would be much higher. Secondly, the risk of an extremely serious violation of fundamental rights such as that enshrined in Article 19 CFREU acts as a further limit to surrender.

Either of these factors – at the core of EU citizenship and individual rights in the third country – can activate the EU border-wall, or, to better say, the need to prioritise the intra-EU system of surrender above extradition. Similarly to what was discussed in *NS* and *Căldăraru*, the question arises as to what threshold is required to halt extradition in grey areas: where, in other words, there has been no EAW issued by the Member State of nationality (*Pisciotti* rule allowing for extradition) and there is a risk of breaches of fundamental rights not as serious as inhuman or degrading treatment. Scholars have suggested a much lower threshold than the one relied on for intra-EU transfer, and argued for the restriction of free movement ensuing from extradition to be balanced against individual rights such as reintegration into society and effectiveness of defence rights.[99]

D. Detention and Reintegration: In What Name?

Integration, reintegration and residence security are inextricably linked elements shaping the EU approach to detention and citizenship rights. Reintegration

[96] Martin Böse, 'Mutual recognition, extradition to third countries and Union citizenship: *Petruhhin*' (2017) 54(6) *Common Market Law Review* 1781; Miguel João Costa, 'The Emerging EU Extradition Law. Petruhhin and Beyond' (2017) 8(2) *New Journal of European Criminal Law* 192; André Klip, 'Europeans First!: Petruhhin, an Unexpected Revolution in Extradition Law' (2017) 25(3) *European Journal of Crime, Criminal Law and Criminal Justice* 195.

[97] Klip, 'Europeans First!: Petruhhin, an Unexpected Revolution in Extradition Law', n 96 above, 8.

[98] Böse, 'Mutual recognition, extradition to third countries and Union citizenship: *Petruhhin*', n 96 above, 1786.

[99] Ibid, 1792. On the importance of reintegration for limiting extradition of Union citizens, see Costa, 'The Emerging EU Extradition Law. Petruhhin and Beyond', n 96 above, 202 onwards.

presupposes integration, and both are key to achieving residence security in the host Member State. Reintegration in EU law – pursued through judicial cooperation – emerges more as an instrument in the hands of Member States and having a supra-individual dimension. Reintegration should be facilitated by Article 4(6) EAW FD, as well as by the FDs discussed above. In *Kozlowski*, the Court admitted that those who are not formally resident in the host Member State should also be able to reintegrate into the host state. *Wolzenburg* allowed a certain margin of discretion to Member States in pursuing reintegration of the offenders in their territory, while *Lopes Da Silva* ruled out the lawfulness of an automatic exclusion of non-nationals from the scope of Article 4(6). However, equating crime to non-integration (*Onuewkere*) and allowing states to require a degree of integration to allow for reintegration of non-nationals (*Wolzenburg*) seems difficult to reconcile with an understanding of reintegration without borders.

The FDs on transfer of prisoners and probation measures give legislative substance to the supra-individual approach to reintegration hinted at by the Court in *Tsakouridis*. In particular, this collective interest points to concerns of public security. The coercive transfer epitomises an approach to reintegration that disregards the person concerned. As stated in the FD on the transfer of prisoners, the requirement of consent of the person concerned should no longer be dominant: in a system of mutual recognition, automaticity of judicial cooperation overrides the involvement of the person concerned.

To this end, the consensual element featured in the probation measures FD can be seen as an exception to the rule constituting the coercive transfer and the great discretion left to Member States. Their power to suspend *sine die* the transfer procedure goes hand in hand with the absence of individual guarantees and the stress on the protection of the public. Other instruments of mutual recognition involving deprivation of liberty – though not aimed at reintegration – confirm such a security-oriented approach. The FD on the mutual recognition of pre-trial measures alternative to detention[100] sets the monitoring of defendants' movements for the protection of the public as its first objective, and also the enhancement of the right to liberty and the presumption of innocence of the persons concerned.[101] The FD does not confer any rights on the person to the use, during criminal proceedings, of a non-custodial measure as an alternative to custody. The Court's approach to expulsion of EU citizens living in the host Member State for longer than 10 years (*Tsakouridis*, *PI*, *MG*) and the reasons behind shrinking the prisoner's position (no consent required in case of expulsion measures) jointly contribute to a legal framework where the citizenship status of detainees is degraded.

[100] Council Framework Decision 2009/829/JHA of 23 October 2009 on the application, between Member States of the European Union, of the principle of mutual recognition to decisions on supervision measures as an alternative to provisional detention, [2009] OJ L294/20.

[101] Ibid, recitals 3 and 4.

Rendón Marín and *CS*, on the one hand, and *Petruhhin*, on the other, might be seen as an attempt, by the Court, at increasing the level of protection of the Union's citizens – be it through the use of Treaty provisions on citizenship or the Charter. These cases, however, concerned rather exceptional circumstances. They dealt with a case where the genuine substance of EU citizenship or the risk of inhuman treatment was at stake. Similarly to what emerged in the discussion on mutual recognition, the question arises as to what the role can be for breaches of relative rights in limiting forced transfer within and outside the Union.

The EU law approach is in line with coercive conceptions of rehabilitation where the focus is no longer the offender, but the protection of the law-abiding citizen.[102] This trend has raised major concerns in those who see

> how anchoring the justification of criminal punishment to the defense of society (a defense, moreover, which shows the colors of necessity, and, as the saying goes, necessity knows no law) can open the door to limitless preventive punishment exacted in the name of protecting society.[103]

As observed, justifying reintegration in the public interest is prone to result in abuses and clearly makes offenders' rights weaker:

> The offender becomes less and less an active participant and more and more an object to be assessed through technologies applied by professionals and compulsorily engaged in structured programmes and offender management processes as required elements of legal orders imposed … irrespective of consent.[104]

The reading of integration and reintegration creates a short-circuit where there is little space for rehabilitation of detainees in a Union-wide sense. These factors, as shown, have a huge impact on residence security, and therefore on citizenship status. Detention and crime show no integration, which in turn deprives the person of reintegration in the state to which s/he moved. Where reintegration is – allegedly – pursued, this occurs in conjunction with objectives of public safety and with scant involvement of the person concerned. The short-circuit is worsened by the self-expanding use of public security. The space for state discretion at the expense of the individual increases with the presence of expulsion measures and the emphasis on public security. If those factors are given an incredibly broad interpretation as highlighted above, the actual reach of rehabilitation for detainees in an area without internal frontiers is nullified.

[102] P McCulloch and F McNeill, 'Consumer Society, Commodification and Offender Management' (2007) 7(3) *Criminology and Criminal Justice* 223–42; G Robinson and F McNeill, 'Purposes Matter: Examining the "Ends" of Probation' in G Mair (ed), *What Matters in Probation Work* (Cullompton, Willan, 2004) 277.

[103] Materni, 'Criminal Punishment and the Pursuit of Justice' n 70 above, 296.

[104] F McNeill, 'When Punishment is Rehabilitation' in G Bruinsma and D Weisburd (eds), *The Springer Encyclopedia of Criminology and Criminal Justice* (Berlin, Springer, 2014).

IV. Conclusions on Deprivation of Liberty and EU Citizenship

Residence security – the right to enter and stay in the territory of another Member State – is at the core of Union citizenship, the cornerstone in the creation of a borderless area beyond the economic freedoms. Primary and secondary law aim to promote integration of citizens in states where they 'hang their hat' in a place other than that of nationality. The Citizenship Directive – reflecting the foundational case-law of the Court – preserves that objective by: anchoring the adoption of coercive measures to an individual assessment and a strict proportionality test that refuses any generalisation; and distinguishing between different levels of protection and exceptions to residence security based on public policy *and* public security.

Freedom of movement inevitably creates more possibilities for criminal behaviour and detention ensuing from the latter beyond the territory of nationality. This in turn raises questions on what to do with Union citizens that are convicted and detained in the state they have moved to and lived, possibly for many years. Shall they be treated as mere sources of disturbance and removed from the host territory? Or else, in line with the creation of Union citizenship and a borderless area, shall they be given the opportunity to reintegrate into the state they are living and preserve their residence security? The question is even more pressing, when considering that Directive 2004/38 is silent on the impact of crime and detention on citizenship rights.

The EU law of integration and reintegration of detainees that has emerged over recent years shows the significant impact that deprivation of liberty may have on Union citizenship. Previous Parts of the book showed that the growing body of Union measures on deprivation of liberty places pressures on traditional guarantees such as the principle of legality and the right to liberty. Hitherto, the response of the EU has not lived up to the challenges. In *Tsakouridis* and *PI*, the Court sees integration as a precondition for citizenship rights. It merges the different levels of protection against expulsion laid down in the Directive, and the key distinction between public policy and public security, in the one-size-fits-all test of 'general interest of society'. In doing so, it turns the exceptions to protection against expulsion and residence security into tools to pursue the objectives of EU criminal policy (fights against drug trafficking, sexual exploitation of children, and terrorism). Symmetrically, it uses the legal basis for EU legislative competences and secondary law as a legal argument for the adoption of seriously harming measures. *Onuekwere* and *MG* complete the departure from citizenship law, by placing rights as a reward for obedience to the law and establishing an equation between detention and non-integration. The tentative, double-headed references to personal circumstances and reintegration in *Tsakouridis* and *PI* (rehabilitation being in the offender's and the EU's interest) disappear in subsequent cases. The judgments exclude an individual assessment of whether detention might actually be compatible with integration in the specific circumstances of the case.

The potential drawbacks of such an approach might be worse if read jointly with that on reintegration. Though pursued through judicial cooperation, the EU law on reintegration might have the potential to preserve residence security and Union citizenship rights, either by opposing a forced transfer (Article 4(6) EAW FD) or promoting movement of detainees to the place where they have substantive connections. *Kozlowski* and *Da Silva* acknowledge the need that a fully-fledged area without internal frontiers should entitle EU citizens to reintegrate into a place that is not necessarily that of their nationality but where they have established themselves. This does not exclude Member States from requiring a certain degree of integration, before allowing rehabilitation in their territory (*Wolzenburg*). If, however, crime and detention deny *tout court* integration, is there any effective room for reintegration – which follows, per se, a wrongdoing – beyond the state of nationality?

The extremely cautious approach to integration and reintegration without borders is flanked by a supra-individual approach to rehabilitation. The FDs on transfer of prisoners and probation measures refer expressly to the interest of public safety and the fact that the need for consent of the person should no longer be dominant. This translates, firstly, into broadly-worded grounds (exceptional or unforeseen circumstances) allowing the Member States to postpone *sine die* the transfer (and so trigger a reintegration process) at their convenience. Secondly, it results in detainees being the object of mutual recognition in the hands of states, with their consent being done away with if they have been subject to expulsion measures. That provision, combined with the very generous CJEU stance on expulsion powers, further shrinks the civic status of detainees.

There is, however, a haven for residence security. Similarly to the *NS* and the *Căldăraru* exceptions in asylum and criminal law, these are the exceptional circumstances under EU citizenship. Like in those areas of law, the forced movement is limited when it can cause exceptional harm. The transfer is, however, outside the Union territory, which creates a space where public security and the fight against crime (enshrined in Article 3 TEU) must be balanced against – and may be overridden by – other provisions of primary law: Article 21 TFEU, Article 7, 19, 24 CFREU. A decisive ally in halting extra-EU forced movement through extradition is the possibility to use instead the intra-EU EAW system; an argument which further legitimates the autonomy of EU law and its system of judicial cooperation in criminal matters. The protection of Union citizenship offered by this case-law leaves a number of questions unanswered. Firstly, can we envisage a comparable paradigm to limit intra-EU transfer and protect the residence security of detainees? The current interpretation of the law does not leave much space for that. It cannot be overlooked that the Court in *Rendón Marín* and *CS* has ultimately confirmed the interpretation of public security construed through categorisation of dangerous individuals put forward in its previous, controversial case-law. Secondly, those very controversial expulsion measures – upheld by the Court – activate the removal of consent under the FD on transfer of prisoners. Reintegration, as it is now pursued through judicial cooperation, is governed by mutual trust.

Only exceptional circumstances can limit its operation. A related question then arises: what is the role for breaches of relative rights, be they involved in an intra or extra-EU system? If the state that could have avoided extradition has not resorted to the EAW, can extradition be stopped by the prospect of those violations possibly occurring in the third country? If so, in which cases?

Though 'incomplete', this case-law opens questions and possible space for improving residence security and the citizenship status of detainees.

Epilogue

The completion of the internal market and the abolition of internal frontiers triggered the enlargement of the EU's action. Such an evolution did not change the distinctive DNA of the Union legal order, which remains the creation and preservation of a borderless area. The expansion of the horizons of the Union's project has resulted in increasing involvement of the EU in one of most intimate pockets of state sovereignty: deprivation of liberty. At first, that meant limiting the Member States' use of custodial penalties, if they jeopardised the exercise of free movement.

As time went by, free movement has progressively turned from a shield into a sword against personal liberty. The abolition of internal frontiers was used by the EU to adopt measures meant to offset possible drawbacks of free movement, and to pursue further legal integration in uncharted territories like criminal, immigration and asylum law. Detention has been a key factor in these additional areas of action. Recent decades have therefore witnessed the emergence of a proper EU law of deprivation of liberty. Though such a body of law involves realms as different as substantive criminal law, judicial cooperation, immigration and asylum, and citizenship, the story told in this book has highlighted the presence of consistent patterns and regular characters.

Firstly, the equilibrium of the borderless area has been pursued along the lines of forced movement within or outside the EU to protect (the safe exercise of) free movement. This is apparent in the AFSJ law and policy of deprivation of liberty, where coercive measures build on the rebuttable presumption that fundamental rights are respected throughout the EU. To this end, static and dynamic measures work in symbiosis. Approximation of levels of penalty facilitates judicial cooperation, which takes the shape of transfer of suspected and convicted persons across the EU. Preventing irregular secondary movement requires a system for allocation of responsibility for the examination of asylum claims, as well as the establishment of a common return policy. The former results in forced movement to the Member State responsible; the latter in removal from the Union. In both cases, detention pending examination of the asylum claim and transfer is key to securing the implementation of relevant EU law. This may hold true for citizenship as well, where detention and wrongdoings are used as leverage to remove the dangerous individual from the territory of the host state.

Across the board, this law rests on the two founding pillars of effectiveness and security. Effective implementation of EU law requires criminalisation and judicial cooperation, the use of pre-removal detention and the refusal to grant citizenship rights to detainees. Security legitimates the imposition of high imprisonment rates, detention of asylum-seekers and expulsion of Union nationals from Member States where they have been living for most of their lives. Behind those intermediate – and at times debatable – arguments, however, there is always the ultimate *raison d'état* constituted by the preservation of the Union as a borderless area.

Secondly, and relatedly, such de-individualisation and de-personalisation of free movement has worked at the expense of personal liberty. The ever closer – and bigger – Union has been concerned with measures to control and compensate for the side-effects of free movement. The EU has lost sight of the balance that that development would have required in terms of fundamental rights protection. The EU features a conspicuous set of general principles and fundamental rights now enshrined in the Charter and having the value of primary law. However, the coming into being and growth of EU law of deprivation of liberty has not been flanked by the re-conceptualisation of strongholds of personal liberty to make the latter suitable for the peculiarities of the Union as a polity.

In terms of the principles of legality and proportionality of penalties, the scarce transparency and accountability of comitology procedures might cause issues of legal certainty where acts adopted on that basis are called on to determine the boundaries of criminalisation. The pursuit of EU policy through criminal law has revamped the debate on directly applicable Union rules, which the CJEU has assuaged for the moment. The very criterion conceived to approximate levels of penalty (the minimum-maximum) not only proves to have an immaterial harmonising effect, but it also causes a 'race to the top' in imprisonment terms at national level, and has detrimental effects on the coherence of criminal justice systems if used in isolation.

The system of forced transfer of persons within the EU requires the configuration of a European habeas corpus, where clear, foreseeable and accessible cases and procedures for deprivation of liberty are guaranteed. This implies, on the one hand, that detention conditions are part of the established procedural requirement so resulting in a finding of violation of the right to liberty when they are not respected as provided in the law. Secondly, the persons involved in an inter-state transfer must be informed of their rights and duties in the sending and receiving state, so as to be aware on which grounds and according to which procedures they may be detained. Thirdly, clearer rules and better protection of the right to liberty are required in case of hiccups in the system (expiry of deadlines for execution of an EAW or transfer of asylum-seekers), especially where the person concerned is not responsible for those disruptions. The evolution of the CJEU approach on the subject has revealed that there is room for rebutting the presumption of mutual trust and so limiting the operation of the system where the violation of an absolute prohibition, such as that of inhuman or degrading treatment, is at stake. The unanswered questions here – which will possibly be dealt with in the near future – concern violations of relative rights: to what extent can they halt an inter-state transfer of persons? What is the threshold required for the breach to be significant: to stop the forced movement in case of prospective violations, or to make the decision on whether the transfer is unlawful, in case of past infringements?

A comprehensive protection of detainees and personal liberty operates through the status of persons as citizens and their right to enter and stay in the territory across the EU. On the one hand, the presumption of non-integration in the host state by Union nationals that have committed a crime and are detained, and the understanding of rights as a reward for 'integration' (read 'obedience to the law'), deny the need for an individual and case-by-case assessment embedded in the foundational case-law and legislation of EU citizenship. This is even more so where public security – provided in the Citizenship Directive as an exception to residence security – becomes a much larger umbrella used to actively contribute to the objectives of EU criminal policy. On the other hand, reintegration with a supra-individual dimension in mind leaves very little to say for a Union understanding of rehabilitation without frontiers. Reintegration as a tool in the hands of states and the persons that are the object of judicial cooperation has limited chance to be effective. If Member States require the non-national to have a certain degree of integration in the host state, but the commission of a crime itself denies integration (as stated by the Court in its more recent case-law), reintegration outside the state of nationality is simply and logically not possible. States can pursue reintegration without the consent of the person and transfer them from one state to the other, if they have been subject to expulsion from the sending country. If the expulsion is from the Member State where that person has lived for decades (as upheld in the judgments discussed in the last chapter) and on debatable grounds, residence security and the civic status of detainees is considerably impoverished. What is the connecting feature of all these persons subject to different kinds of transfer, within or outside the EU? They are foreigners. EU citizens living in a state other than that of their nationality are forcefully moved within the EU. Third-country nationals know the same fate until their asylum claim is rejected. Afterwards, extra-EU transfer under the Return Directive will take place; which, in turn, opens – inter alia – the question of what to do with those TCNs who live in limbo between the impossibility of being expelled and the absence of a valid title to stay in the territory after being denied the status of refugee.

The recent evolution has, however, seen the emergence of a reformed – to some extent – protection against forced movement of EU citizens outside the Union territory, with the Court balancing the objectives of fighting crime against fundamental rights. In cases of minor Union citizens, who would be obliged to follow their sole TCN carer out of the EU on the basis of an expulsion measure, the right to family life and the best interest of the child must be taken into account – and possibly override the public security reasons on which the expulsion is based. Time will tell what spaces such principles could open for further protection of TCNs' residence security within the EU.

When extradition to third countries is involved, the resistance to leaving the EU – and so to rules of international cooperation in criminal matters – has been supported by the existence of intra-EU systems to avoid impunity, such as the EAW FD. In doing so, the Court reaffirms the autonomy of the Union legal order with regard to international law, and strengthens the role for the EU outer boundaries as a protective sphere of its own nationals. This stance builds on the foundations of the genuine enjoyment of the substance of EU citizenship, non-discrimination and the right to free movement and residence. Such a newly individualised and less impersonal dimension of free movement and the Union status of citizens broadly, open interesting spaces of discussion. Once again, there is the question of whether breaches of relative rights may halt extradition of Union citizens when the 'responsible' state has not issued an EAW to avoid the transfer to the requesting state. The use of the principle of non-discrimination against other EU nationals might have significant repercussions if used against the criminal justice systems within the Union.

INDEX

www.ingramcontent.com/pod-product-compliance
Ingram Content Group UK Ltd.
Pitfield, Milton Keynes, MK11 3LW, UK
UKHW021908150926
475560UK00003B/257

9 781509 908080